"THIS VOLUME ...
SHOULD BE READ BY EVERY AMERICAN."
—JULIUS W. GATES
Sergeant Major of the Army (Ret.)

"His experiences are *real* army. . . . The book is down to earth, informative, historical, and occasionally humorous."
— RICHARD A. KIDD
Sergeant Major of the Army

"Bill Bainbridge has written a memoir that is both a chronicle of his times and a tribute to that unique military institution, the Corps of Non-Commissioned Officers. . . . Should strongly appeal to service and non-prior-service individuals as a practical guide to the core aspects that constitute leadership."
— MARTIN R. HOFFMANN
Secretary of the Army, 1975–77

"TOP SERGEANT is, in my view, a literary event. A unique and exceptionally well done book-length autobiography of one of our armed forces' stellar noncommissioned leaders."
— COL. KARL R. MORTON (Ret.)
Former Commandant
U.S. Army Sergeants Major Academy

TOP
SERGEANT

THE LIFE AND TIMES OF
SERGEANT MAJOR OF THE ARMY
WILLIAM G. BAINBRIDGE

SMA WILLIAM G. BAINBRIDGE
(U.S. ARMY, RET.) AND DAN CRAGG

FOREWORD BY GENERAL BERNARD W. ROGERS
(U.S. ARMY, RET.)

IVY BOOKS • NEW YORK

Ivy Books
Published by Ballantine Books
Copyright © 1995 by William G. Bainbridge

http://www.randomhouse.com

Library of Congress Catalog Card Number: 95-95317

ISBN 0-8041-0758-0

Manufactured in the United States of America

First Fawcett Columbine Hardcover Edition: July 1995
First Ivy Books Edition: July 1996

10 9 8 7 6 5 4 3 2 1

To Hazel, my life's only love, my constant companion, and my steadfast supporter; and my daughters, Kathryn and Mary, who have loved me always and who have never been out of my thoughts.

CONTENTS

FOREWORD

As they contemplated the stunning success of our armed forces during the Gulf War, a number of American leaders from various walks of life were heard to ask: "Where do they get such people?"—referring to the officers and noncommissioned officers of our forces. Well, that's what this book is all about—whence come people such as Bill Bainbridge, who rose to the highest noncommissioned position, Sergeant Major of the Army (SMA).

Like so many others who serve their country, Bill came from humble beginnings, from the farmland of Illinois. As is generally the case, that environment provided him with a set of values and a strength of character that were to be the hallmark of his service to others while he wore the Army uniform.

It was my good fortune to inherit Bill Bainbridge from my predecessor as Chief of Staff of the Army, Fred Weyand. Fred had chosen Bill to be the SMA. When I succeeded Fred, I asked that the SMA stay on. I figured that if he was good enough for a fine soldier like Fred Weyand, then he would be good enough for me. Keeping Bill on was one of my smart decisions as Chief.

As you will learn from reading this book—and as I learned from our three-plus years of service together—Bill is an intelligent and wise man who will "tell it to you like it is," completely unvarnished. Further, when he noted something that did not make sense from a soldier's standpoint, he set about correcting it with dogged tenacity, bringing to my attention only those few matters that he could not resolve himself. He could also anticipate actions that the Army should take, as well as what the reaction among the troops would be to decisions that would affect them.

To my way of thinking, perceptive anticipation, aggressive initiative, and total candor are three qualities in a person that are invaluable. Couple them with the highest level of integrity and a rich sense of humor, and one comes close to describing Bill Bainbridge.

Bill was more than just an adviser to me on matters affecting the troops. He would ensure that the thinking behind decisions and the climate at the top got down through the noncommissioned officer chain so the troops would have a better understanding of what was going on in the Pentagon. He also had a marvelous ability, employed tactfully but firmly, to take the air out of some pompous officer who thought he could speak for the troops on various matters. There was no one who could address such issues with the knowledge and authority of Sergeant Major Bainbridge.

Bill Bainbridge and I did not always agree on everything, but, in the end, events usually proved him to have been right.

This book is written in a manner that moves the reader from page to page with ease and interest. Filled with anecdotes, it sets out this soldier's story in the true Bainbridge style: forthright, amusing, firm, and confident, and with some of the earthy language to be found in a service that is dedicated to protecting the freedom and values of our nation. Its pages will strike many familiar chords with those who were soldiers during the period of SMA Bainbridge's service. And it helps to answer the question I posed at the outset. Read and enjoy it, as I have.

> Bernard W. Rogers
> General, U.S. Army (Retired)
> McLean, Virginia, October 1991

PROLOGUE

I was wearing a strange assortment of headgear when we were surrendered to the Germans in the Schnee Eifel in the late afternoon of December 19, 1944. I'd lost my steel helmet in a firefight the day before, and all I had left was my wool "go to hell cap"—a soft woolen cap with a short, stiff visor—and the hood off a protective suit the Army had issued in case of a gas attack. I have no idea how I happened to find a hood. I must have looked a sight, bedraggled and ragged after three days of continuous combat, but by golly, my ears were warm.

That's one thing about the Bulge—I was always cold. The snow that made life so miserable later on hadn't started yet, and the water in the roadside ditches was still unfrozen, I recall, but the weather was overcast, cold, and rainy—"raw" is the best word I can use to describe how it felt. It was ten times worse at the Bulge than it ever was back home, because after holding up under everything the Germans could throw at us for three and a half days, we were *surrendering*.

The officer who surrendered us was a major. I can't remember his name anymore, because he wasn't assigned to our outfit, but he was the ranking officer present. He surrendered us about four o'clock in the afternoon. I don't blame the major, because there was really nothing else he could do. My outfit, Company A, 1st Battalion, 423rd Infantry Regiment of the 106th Division, was way down below company strength by then. True, we were moving back at the time—withdrawing, not retreating—and the Germans had us surrounded, but up until then we'd held our own, even managed to capture an 88mm gun emplacement the night before. I was leading third squad, and of my twelve men I'd only lost one killed and another wounded.

We stripped our weapons and threw the parts away so they'd be

1

of no use to the Germans. It seems ironic—the Army had told us what to do with our weapons in the event of capture, but nobody'd told us what to do with *ourselves*.

The German soldiers who took us that afternoon were good frontline troops, possibly the best Germany had that late in the war. The soldier who searched me the next day discovered two D bars in the front pockets of my field jacket. Those were hard, concentrated chocolate bars issued to us in our field rations. *"Schokolade?"* he asked. I answered yes, and without comment he replaced them in my pockets. That simple act of kindness by a man who could have used the chocolate bars himself is something I have never forgotten. Those bars are what kept me and my assistant squad leader, Jim Poole, going over the next few days.

So there we stood, huddled in small groups, the night coming on fast, prisoners of war. That moment, in the woods just after we'd been surrendered, was the most depressing, hopeless experience I've ever had, and the days and weeks that lay ahead would prove to be the worst period of my entire life. A little while before I'd been an invincible nineteen-year-old sergeant squad leader. Now I was a prisoner of the Germans.

I thought we had failed. I know now that we had not—we'd stopped the Germans for three days, disrupted their timetable just long enough so the Allied armies had a chance to counterattack. But at the time I thought, My God, what have I done to my soldiers and my country? I thought, What in the hell am I doing here?

≡ 1 ≡

REVEILLE IN GALESBURG

I came into this life on April 17, 1925, in St. Mary's Hospital, Galesburg, Knox County, Illinois. My father was a fireman on the Chicago, Burlington & Quincy, the old CB&Q, now the Burlington Northern, and my mother was a housewife. Her maiden name was Beatrice Wells, and my father was James Lyle Bainbridge.

There have been some famous Bainbridges in the history of this country, with towns and ships named after them, but as far as I know, I'm not directly descended from anybody in that crowd. My grandfather was James Bainbridge. My paternal grandmother was a Trout. She came from Henderson, Illinois, a small town just north of Galesburg. It boasted a grain elevator and a railroad crossing, and they lived right next to the tracks.

My grandpa was a coal miner, as were a good many of the family. My dad was born in a little place called Soaperville, Illinois, just a little crossroads town that wasn't even on the map. Today it has just disappeared. My father had four brothers and two sisters who lived; there were others who did not survive childhood.

My mother was born in Iowa. My grandmother on my mother's side was a Hunt. She was a feisty thing about four foot two, and Granddad was about six foot two. However, Grandma was the boss. My mother had only one brother, who was older than she.

I believe my side of the family emigrated from England in my great-grandfather's day, possibly in the 1840s. I don't know what they did for a living back in England, but I suppose they came to this country for the opportunities it offered, as did so many immigrants of that time. There are today several Bainbridge families throughout the country, in New York, Pennsylvania, and the Midwest and out in California. I suspect we're all related somewhere along the line.

3

In the service I ran into maybe three or four other Bainbridges. One came through basic training when I was operations sergeant for the 3rd Battalion, 4th Training Regiment, at Fort Leonard Wood, Missouri; one was a chaplain with captain's rank whom I ran across when I was stationed in Germany; and another was in the 3rd Infantry Division Band—I pinned his sergeant's chevrons on him when I was Sergeant Major of the Army.

Of my direct ancestors, at least two have served our country in wartime. One, Manuel Trout from Grandmother Bainbridge's side of the family, her brother, I believe, was a private in Company B of the 102nd Illinois Infantry. He mustered into the unit at Knoxville, Illinois, on September 2, 1862, at the age of twenty-six, and was discharged June 6, 1865, at Washington, D.C. His was one of the first units to reach the top of Lookout Mountain, Tennessee, during that famous Civil War battle. The 102nd Illinois was with Sherman's army in Georgia, and Manuel was wounded at the Battle of Peach Tree Creek on July 20, 1864. And my father was in the Army during World War I. But there is no military "tradition" in my family, and I knew nothing about Dad's or my great-uncle's service when I was growing up. In fact, the idea of military service was perhaps the remotest possibility in my mind at any time when I was growing up.

My dad and mom were married in Galesburg about 1920. I was the second-born. I have an older brother, James, who was born December 6, 1922, in the same place, in Knox County. He died June 10, 1994, at the age of 72.

We lived there and in and around Galesburg until I joined the Army. Galesburg has a population of around 35,000 today. It is situated 165 miles southwest of Chicago, in the west-central part of the state, fifty miles west of Peoria, the heart of Illinois. I lived in and around that area—Knox County, Henry County, Warren County—all the time I was growing up. My father, who was injured in a railroad accident about the time I was born, took up farming, so I spent most of my childhood on farms.

During my early years we lived on a farm that was just south of Elmwood, Illinois, in Peoria County. Up through the eighth grade I was educated in one-room schoolhouses. The biggest school I attended during those years was the Trenton Corners elementary school, which had a basement and inside toilets—chemical toilets, which smelled just like the ones outside. The other schools were just one room with an outdoor toilet. My early schooling was a "character builder," because as a first grader I walked to school, two and a half miles each way, with strict instructions from my dad to come home on time to get my chores done. When I was a little guy my jobs were to gather eggs and to get in the kindling so that in the morning when my folks came down there would be dry kindling to start a fire. I was in big trouble if that job wasn't done. In those days we didn't have central heating.

My father died when I was five, and my mother remarried when I was seven. The man she married, Leon Simkins, has been my father ever since. They had two children: my sister Pat and my brother Danny. Both of them live in Illinois. Dad passed on in 1992 at the age of 83. Even after Mom remarried, we lived on a farm. During the off-seasons my stepfather worked on the highway. We had a 1927 Chevrolet. I can remember once he brought home his entire paycheck for two weeks, $40, in groceries—a hundred-pound sack of flour, fifty pounds of sugar, twenty-five pounds of coffee beans—our provisions for most of the winter. Mom made her own bread, because we didn't have a bakery, and besides, the town was six or seven miles from the farm over muddy roads. If you had a gravel road in those days you were lucky.

On the bad days we used to ride a horse named Babe to school. One day my brother and I decided that we could get to school quicker than the horse could take us, so we turned her loose after we got out of sight of the house and walked to school. The horse got home about three o'clock in the afternoon—that's how slow she was, because she ate her way back home. My dad was really upset that we'd let her wander all day long, so we never turned her loose again. Slow as she was, we continued to ride her to school.

We moved several times during those years. Each successive move was for a larger farm or a better deal on the rent or share of the crop, because we were sharecroppers. The landlord got a portion of the crop and provided some of the seed. We did general farming—corn, oats, alfalfa, and clover. We also raised hogs. We used to call them "mortgage lifters," because two litters per year per sow provided us with meat for our own consumption and for market. We raised our own feed for the livestock and ourselves.

We had beef occasionally. Once we had an old Jersey cow; I don't know how old she was at the time, but we couldn't breed her anymore, so we ate her. That was the toughest meat I have ever eaten. It took us two years to finish her. My mother did what was known as "cold packing," a method of home canning where she'd cook the meat in the jars and seal it. Well, eating that beef was like chewing on rubber, and the longer you chewed it the bigger it seemed to get. At least we had something to eat, and it made damn good gravy.

We never had a lot of money when I was growing up, but we always had a lot of TLC and plenty to eat. I learned that money is a great thing, but you can get by on a heck of a lot less of it than most people think. In those days you had to get by on a tight budget, because nobody had any money.

About 1937 or 1938, we moved to my grandfather's farm about a mile and a quarter south of Dahinda, Illinois, a little town in the central part of the state on the Spoon River. That farm was my family's first experience in real home-owning. We bought the place from my grandfather, so he could move to Iowa and take up farming there. Also, Dahinda is where I first met Hazel, who later became my wife. She was a lowly fourth grader and I was a sophisticated fifth grader. Not much has changed since then, except that Hazel went on to graduate and in many ways I'm still the "sophisticated" fifth grader. She lived in Dahinda, and I used to ride horseback into town to visit her, and not just on Sundays.

Even as a twelve- and thirteen-year-old I did a lot of farming. I took care of the gardening and worked in the fields during school vacations. I did plowing and operated the tractor, but I spent a lot of time walking behind a horse pulling the cultivator. We had a team of horses, Pet and Babe—Babe was the one we used to ride to school, you'll remember. Dad would give me the team because I didn't have a watch and they knew when it was time to go to lunch, so they'd go whether I wanted to or not. I worked in the fields right up to the time I went into the Army.

The one-room schoolhouse at Trenton Corners—the one that had a basement and inside toilets—was a couple of miles south of Dahinda, where Hazel went to school. I became "janitor" there for fifty cents a week, cleaning up after school was out and banking the fire in the furnace during cold weather. In the mornings I'd carry in the water and stoke the furnace to make sure the place would be warm when the teacher and the rest of the students came in. It was a small school, probably twelve to fifteen students, first through eighth grade, ranging in age up to fifteen or so. One of the kids I graduated with, Merlin Cadwell, was eighteen. One thing about Merlin, though—he didn't have to go to high school, he went right on to work. All eight grades were taught in that schoolhouse by the same teacher. And if there weren't enough pupils to fill each grade, the school just didn't have that grade that year. I believe the year I graduated, Trenton Corners didn't have a sixth-grade class.

I had no problems in grade school. In fact, while at Trenton Corners I discovered one of life's greatest pleasures: *National Geographic* magazine. The school had maybe two hundred back issues, and when my studies were done, I'd go into the back of the schoolhouse and read them. By the time I graduated I'd been through all of them. I found out all about such things as Pompeii, and I can still remember those graphic pictures. I still love that magazine.

My high school was at Williamsfield in what was then known as a "community high school." There were maybe 250 students in the school. Williamsfield was a town of about 500, and the kids who lived there went to the high school, of course, but there were also four bus routes that extended throughout the county and brought in another 150 kids from the surrounding farmlands. My stepfather and brother both graduated from that high school, although my stepfather actually grew up in and around Williams Field, Illinois.

Most of the time I was in high school I worked a 160-acre farm. The last two years I was in high school I did it all by myself. My brother was working and my dad had a milk route.

I was also active in sports and was vice president of the senior class and probably one of the biggest cutups in the whole school. I have always liked to make people laugh. I was in all the school plays and operettas. One play I remember was *Don't Take My Penny*, and I played the role of a dapper young salesman named Greg. I even continued to do that after I went into the Army, working with the local PTAs, when they raised money for their schools and so on. All through high school, whatever there was to get into, I got into it.

Since we were such a small school, we didn't have football. We started out in the fall with fast-pitch softball, which we'd been playing all summer. We had basketball in the winter and track and field in the spring. During my senior year we had seventeen boys on the track team. We went to the Knox County track meet that year, competing against Galesburg, Knoxville, and Abingdon, three of the biggest towns in that district. Knoxville had about 3,500 people, Abingdon about the same, and we, with the surrounding community, were only 500. Our coach entered us in every event. I was a low-hurdler, and the coach thought I was pretty good at that, so he entered me in the high hurdle. He entered Harry Thurmond, a junior and a good half-miler, in the mile event. Subsequently, we cleaned everybody's clock. We took a lot of seconds and thirds in the events we weren't practiced in, but we took firsts in those we were good at. Knoxville, Galesburg, and Abingdon were shocked. We tried our damnedest to do our best, and if that wasn't good enough to be first, the points we piled up helped our team. That's an important part of my youth I've never forgotten.

In my sophomore and junior years I took up Golden Gloves boxing. Our boxing coach, Eddie Rice, was a barber and also ran a pool hall, and our training was conducted in the rear of the hall. I guess I fought eight or ten bouts in Galesburg, and won all but two of them on decisions. In one fight my nose was bloodied, and as I wiped it and hit my opponent with that glove, the blood got all over him, and even though I won, the reason he looked so bad afterward was that he was covered with *my* blood.

When I wasn't in school or working the farm I enjoyed hunting and fishing, two activities I don't do anymore. I never was a good fisherman, but I was a good hunter. In those days hunting was more than just a sport, because the meat we'd bring home went into the stewpot, particularly in the winter. We'd shoot rabbits, skin them, and hang them on our porch. That was our "deep freeze" in the winter. Hunting supplemented our diet. While we had wild meat to eat we didn't have to kill a laying hen—they were for Sundays. We ate a lot of squirrel, too.

To this day the only food I don't like to eat is none, and I think the reason for that is that I *had* to eat what was on my plate when I was a kid. Today I'll eat anything that won't eat me. That stood me in good stead when I was a prisoner of the Germans. Why, I even like broccoli. If President George Bush knew about grated cheese he'd probably like it too.

For pure diversion we had card parties, mostly for adults, but we kids went, too, because there wasn't anywhere else for us to go. Normally we'd play pitch and 500 rummy.

The parties rotated among the homes of the participating families. Our mothers would take potluck suppers, and we'd drink coffee or tea—no booze, maybe eggnog at Christmastime but no nog. We couldn't afford liquor, in the first place, and drinking just wasn't something we did very much of, in the second. Because the parties would last well into the night, way past the bedtime of us children, by the time they broke up, we kids would be sleeping all over the place and the grown-ups would have to sort of peel us off the piles of coats, the sofas and chairs, and the floors in order to get ready to go home.

Entertainment in the country in those days was just what we could improvise, because we didn't have money to spend on amusements. But we enjoyed the movies. When I was a kid in grade school it was a great treat, if I could get away on a Saturday, to go to the movies. Galesburg had the Colonial and the West, and also the Orpheum. The Orpheum was beyond my pay grade at the time—it cost seventy-five cents to get in there, and the others only cost a quarter for adults and fifteen cents for kids. We used to see the serial westerns: Tom Mix and Lash Larue and Tim McCoy. They went on for what seemed like years. We never got to see more than about 25 percent of any of them, but that was enough to keep up on what was happening.

I still like movies, although I don't go too much—we don't have to anymore, with the VCR and all the movie channels on TV. Technology has changed our lifestyle in this century, and television is certainly a good example of that. We could never have imagined such a wonderful thing in those days. This is especially important when I recall the things we did to amuse ourselves as children. For instance, we'd build a T-bar out of two wooden building laths, and with the iron ring off the hub of a wagon wheel, we'd have races pushing the wheels down the road.

We didn't have electricity on the farm until well after World War II, but we did have a radio. It was powered by a six-volt wet battery, just like the one in the car. We had two batteries, one usually at the store, about a mile away, being recharged, and the other hooked up to the radio. If we were careful, one charge might last us about two weeks. We also had to make sure that the battery never got anywhere near Mom's furniture, because one drop of that battery acid would eat right through the upholstery. We could tell when the battery was running down—the quality of the sound or the volume deteriorated—and when the symptoms would begin to appear, my brother and I had to be ready to run up to the store and fetch the spare.

While we didn't have electric lights on the farm, we got by with kerosene lamps, and we did have "running" water: we'd run out to the well, pump the water, and run back into the house with it. We didn't get a telephone until around 1940 or '41. Our telephone switchboard operated out of Glen and Evelyn Smith's home. (They later became my in-laws.) Our whole network consisted of one line—a "party" line, because everybody on it was party to what everybody else was talking about over the telephone. When the telephone rang in one home it also rang in all the others on the line, so each customer was identified by a series of rings—I think ours was two shorts and a long—but anybody else on the line could pick up and eavesdrop on your conversation. That's how we got the news of the day.

I'll never forget the time I volunteered to run the switchboard for the Smiths when they went out for a picnic. It was a Sunday, and during the course of the afternoon I got one call and I told the caller the party was not at home. The caller wanted to know how I knew that without ringing the number. It just happened that this particular family had driven the Smiths to the picnic and I'd seen them drive off together, but the caller insisted I ring their home anyway. You operated the switchboard by pulling plugs out of one line and sticking them into the other, so I just pulled the plug and sat there for a few moments and then told the caller, "They don't answer." That was the sum of my career as a telephone operator.

I learned to swim in the Spoon River. We had a swimming hole just north of the Sante Fe railroad bridge in Dahinda. I learned to swim because I had to. My brother threw me out into the water, and it was sink or swim. We had little "dressing rooms" cut out of the horseweeds along the river, one for the girls and one for the guys, but most of the time there weren't any girls, so we would go skinny-dipping. That part of the river was only about thirty feet wide and just over my head.

I did a lot of reading when I was a kid. When I was in high school especially I would read a couple of books every month, in addition to everything else I was doing, and we had a small library at home. My brother had most of Zane Grey's books, because our mother somehow scraped the money together to buy them for him. We also had the Tom Swift series. We had an English teacher in high school, Miss Ellsberry, who made real literature seem interesting to us, and I think I got a lot out of my English literature in my junior and senior years in high school, but I'd rather read history and geography and cheap novels.

That's not to say that my teachers didn't have an effect on forming my character. One who impressed me was Miss Reed, my first-grade teacher. She was an "older" lady, maybe forty. I got my first licking in school from her. The kid who sat behind me in class, a good friend of mine, Dwayne Gibbs, was fooling around with a pair of blunt-nosed scissors and he reached up and cut the lobe of my right ear with them. It stung so much that before I could think what I was doing, I'd jumped up and knocked him right out of his seat. We both got a licking from Miss Reed for that. It didn't amount to much. When my dad found out that I'd gotten the licking at school, he gave me another for good measure, but after he understood what had happened, he was sorry, because he realized I was right to hit the kid.

Now that was my real dad. He died while I was in the first grade. He was a good father—a strict disciplinarian, but a good parent.

One of my best friends and a role model in those days was John Folger, who lives in New Jersey today. He had been down playing around his grandmother's place one day when he fell out of a tree and broke both his arms. He just hollered, "Grandma, I'm goin' home," and he proceeded to walk the mile and a half home, and as people met him along the road he'd just nod his head at them, because he couldn't wave back at them. When he got home his mother asked him what was wrong and he told her he'd broken his arms. "Which one?" she asked. "*Both* of 'em," he answered.

John taught me that you can take a lot of punishment if you learn not to complain about the little stuff.

I had a chance to imitate John's stoicism just a little while later. I had been raking hay with a team of horses and an old dump rake one day. At noon I took a break for lunch. After eating I felt like a little target practice, so I got out my .22 caliber semiautomatic pistol, filled the clip, stuck some extra rounds in my pocket, and went down to a draw behind the house.

I fired off the clip and then took one of those single rounds out of my pocket, stuck it into the receiver, closed the breech, and spun the pistol around my finger on the trigger guard. I don't have any idea what I was trying to prove with that maneuver—maybe I'd seen it done in a cowboy movie—but as the gun spun around the weight pressed it into my finger and it fired that .22 Long Rifle hollow-point bullet into my left leg, just above my knee, and knocked me flatter than a fritter.

I got up, not knowing exactly what had happened, but I discovered I could still walk. I went back to the house, put the pistol on the table, and walked up to the neighbors' place, Cecil Caldwell's. She was Hazel's cousin. Mrs. Caldwell was in the yard and asked me what I wanted. I told her I needed somebody to take me to the doctor because I'd just shot myself in the leg. By that time my trouser leg was soaked in blood and my shoe had filled with blood and it was running out onto the ground. She took one look at that mess and fainted dead away.

Well, I had to leave her that way and went on down to the Folgers' store. John's mother, Elizabeth, was tending the store, and jokingly she hollered out at me as I came in, "G'wan, g'wan, we don't want any bums in here!" She had red hair and a ruddy complexion, and when she saw what had happened, all the color drained out of her face, which made her hair seem all that much redder. She had a guy named Budge Hickman doing some carpentry work around the house, and he took me to Doc Overholtzer's office in Williamsfield, some eight miles away.

Budge was a pipe smoker, and evidently he'd tapped his pipe out on the windowsill of the car. As we pulled into town he asked me if I smelled something burning, and sure enough the ashes had started a fire in the backseat. The fire had burned clean through this hundred-foot coil of rope back there, and it got so hot a saw sitting underneath the coil lost all its temper. Budge said, "You go on in and see the Doc—I'll put the goddamn fire out!"

I walked around on crutches for a couple of weeks after that, but the wound's never caused me any trouble since. My dad kidded me about it, saying I was such a poor shot that if I'd pointed it at my head I'd have missed. Actually, I was a very good shot with a rifle and a shotgun, as much hunting as I did, yet ever after when someone warned about fooling around with firearms, I knew exactly what he meant.

Besides John Folger, another good friend of those days was Hazel's brother, Russell Smith. They used to kid me that I was going down to see Russell as an excuse to see Hazel, and that wasn't really true—I went down to see both of them. We're still good buddies today. In high school I ran with a really good crowd of young fellows: Barney Cole, Bob Tucker and his younger brother, Sam, Ken DeWolf, and Hollis Benjamin, a classmate of mine. Hollis was more bookish than the rest of us, but he was a good athlete; we all enjoyed sports. We enjoyed our own company and did things as a group. If one was in the wrong, we all were, but we never really did anything nasty or harmful to anybody else.

I'll never forget one Halloween, though. A fella in town owned a team of old, blind gray horses, and that Halloween we snuck them out of their barn, hitched them to their wagon, and led them to school. Our auditorium was in the gym, at one end of which was the stage. We must have spent half the night taking that wagon apart and reassembling it on the stage roof, which was maybe fifteen feet above the floor of the gym. To do that we had to build two ramps, one to the wings of the stage, about six feet high, and another from the wings to the stage itself, maybe another nine feet. When the kids came to school the next morning, there stood that old team, hitched to their wagon, right in the middle of the stage roof.

They never found out we did it, because none of us would tell, but we volunteered to get them down. It took us all day to do the job, but we didn't want to go to school that day anyway. We never did anything malicious, though—only things in good fun.

We were too close-knit a community for viciousness. For example, the teacher I had in the seventh grade, Eleanor Stevens, married a farmer by the name of Stanton Moore, after I'd graduated from high school. When I got back from the Army in 1945, I went to work for Stanton and Eleanor on their farm for $95 a month. I got a house with no electricity and worked for my former grade-school teacher for more than a year. Eleanor's sister, Georgia, had been my eighth-grade teacher.

Over the years I've visited Dahinda many times. When I go back I visit the local grocery store in Williamsfield, where I might see Eleanor again or some of the old gang and catch up on the news. When Bob Tucker was the barber I'd visit with him every two or three years and catch up while he cut my hair. Bob was also Williamsfield's mayor. That's how things are in rural America.

Most of my old gang has stayed right around Dahinda. Of the seventeen who graduated from high school with me, we've lost about eight over the years. At our forty-fifth class reunion a few years ago, I could still recognize every one of them—none had changed that much in the interval. The man who was principal the year we graduated, Kenneth Elliott, made the reunion that year, all crippled with arthritis, but he was there, as were Mr. Guyer, the biology teacher, and Shaw Terwilliger, the agriculture teacher.

I can't prove it with statistics, but my observations lead me to conclude that country people live longer lives than city folks. We ate bacon and eggs seven times a week, but cholesterol was no problem, because in those days we worked it off in the fields.

Of course, farming today is not as I remember it. For all the farms I can remember of 160 to 325 acres, there's only a few left. People no longer farm the same way we did, either. They raise and sell their crops. People still raise livestock, but now they breed them by the thousands and feed them in centralized feedlots.

The family farm in America is fast disappearing. I think Iowa today has the largest number of small farmers left, with Illinois second. Illinois still has the largest number of small towns—towns of under five hundred people—in the country.

The Midwest has always been a solid and basic part of America. In my youth the farmers never had enough machinery to do all the work around the farm that had to be done, so they relied on their neighbors to assist. During harvests the machinery that was available made its way from one farm to another as every hand pitched in to help his neighbor. The women helped by doing the cooking—

they prepared everything you could think of, and the men ate it. We really had a "groaning board" at harvest time in those days.

When people work together like that, they also learn to trust each other, and I think that experience was a great lesson in human psychology and sociology. People don't neighbor the way they used to because today they don't have to. It is not that people have become less neighborly, it's that technology has managed to isolate them. Now things that required many hands in my day can be done easily and more efficiently by one man and his machines.

Today the residents of Dahinda can jump in the car and drive to Chicago for the weekend. When I was a boy the highlight of our weekend was a ball game on the radio, a picnic with another family, going hunting, a card party on Saturday night, an ice cream social at the church on Sunday afternoon, a quilting bee for the women, or a plowing contest for the men. The county fair was a very big event in our lives then. People would take two or three days off and go to the fair. We don't do that anymore.

That way of life has left its impression on me, especially in how I view other people. In spite of the times we find ourselves in today, I am not cynical about mankind. I think there are still a couple of good ones out there.

As I observed earlier, when I was growing up the farthest thing from my mind was the idea of any kind of military service. Until my second year in high school, that is—when World War II came along.

On Sunday, December 7, 1941, I was listening to a Chicago Bears football game on our old battery-powered radio. I remember the game was being broadcast by a Chicago station. I was actually annoyed when they interrupted the game to announce the Japanese attack on Pearl Harbor. I didn't know anything about Pearl Harbor, and I hadn't been following the events in Europe either. I suppose I knew what war was in a vague sort of way, but the fact that now my country might be involved in one had no real meaning to me at that moment. Once the war was actually on and the full impact of it hit me, I just couldn't wait to get out of high school and into it. There wasn't a good Japanese in the world as far as we were concerned, unless he was dead, and it wasn't too long before we thought the same of the Germans.

One of the first changes the war brought to Dahinda was that it got very hard to buy tires or gasoline, and sugar and coffee and other things became rationed, although, living on a farm, we had no problem with food. Because Dad had a milk route, he was able to get a little more gas than the average driver. There were three gasoline ration categories. A was for the smallest amount, about enough to get you to town and back once a month; B was a bit more liberal; and C was for people like my dad, with his milk route, or the family doctor.

All the junk metal that people had been tossing into the washes and ravines over the years to help stop the erosion—oil and vegetable cans, tin pots and aluminum buckets—and all the broken-down farm machinery that had been parked in front yards to rust away disappeared rapidly as it was sold off for scrap to aid the war production effort.

World War II was the last time this country was really into something right up to its clavicle. If your father, husband, brother, or sister wasn't in the service, he or she was working somehow to support the war effort, whether it was at farming, as a mechanic in a defense plant, or whatever. We felt the country had been violated, as if someone had broken into our homes, and people were really hacked off. We hated everything about Japan and Germany. If there were any who didn't think that way, you had to look for them pretty hard. Those times weren't like the Vietnam era, when the protesters were running up and down in the streets.

Youth is eager, and I was afraid the war wouldn't last long enough for me to get into it. It wasn't just me—everybody was that way. Some kids got their parents' permission and quit school before graduation to enlist. Youth is also invincible. I graduated in mid-May, and on June 7, 1943, I was in the Army. My mother tried to talk me out of going. She already had one son in the Army, and mothers are the same the world over—they want to see their sons do their duty, but they don't want to see them go off to war. But she relented, because she knew I'd go whether she wanted me to or not.

So I went down to the draft board and asked how soon my number would come up. They told me five or six months. I asked how long it would take if I volunteered for the draft, and I was told it would be about a month before I could be inducted. After December 8, 1941, when the manpower of the country was fully mobilized for war, you couldn't enlist in the Army, but you could volunteer for the draft if you wanted to accelerate your call-up for the service. I volunteered, and seven days later I was on my way to become a soldier.

≡ 2 ≡

YOU'RE IN THE ARMY NOW!

You're in the Army now,
You're not behind the plow.
You'll never get rich
In a thirty-year hitch,
You're in the Army now!
                    —*Old Army song*

I went off to World War II early on a June morning in 1943, taking the train from Galesburg to the Chicago induction center. During the induction process a Navy chief talked to me long and hard to try to get me to join up. With a name like Bainbridge, he told me, I should go into the Navy instead of the Army. We bantered back and forth for a while, but I told him, no, I was going into the Army, because my brother was already in, and besides, I could always walk farther than I could swim. Later on I learned about William Bainbridge, a commodore in the Navy way back. I don't think he was my kin, because he had no direct descendants, but that's why the chief was arguing I ought to be a sailor.

I was inducted for "the duration of the war plus six months." I went through the usual tests, taken at the end of a long night in a strange place after having ridden a train to the induction station the day before. On June 7, 1943, we went to Camp Grant, Illinois, where I was processed, given a host of inoculations, and issued my uniforms. I was given Army Serial Number 36 752 604, stood five feet seven inches tall, weighed 128 pounds, had a "ruddy" complexion, and wore shoe size 6½ E. My base pay was $50 per month.*

*As of January 1, 1994, a private with less than four months of service was entitled to a base pay of $770.10.

Camp Grant was just west of Chicago, out by Rockford. It's all gone now, but it was a big place in those days. I spent two days there, processing, and on June 9, 1943, went to Camp Wallace, Texas, just north of Galveston, which was an antiaircraft training center.

I spent seventeen weeks at Camp Wallace in basic antiaircraft artillery training. We had a buck sergeant by the name of Simpson, from up in Pennsylvania, who was a great trainer. I became an acting corporal about four weeks into the training, wearing an arm brassard with corporal's stripes on it. Not that I really knew anything. I recall one session when we were practicing the manual of arms with the rifle and a lieutenant came by. I called my men to attention, put my rifle in my left hand, and saluted with the right one. I received a quick lesson from the lieutenant on how to do a rifle salute. I never forgot how to do that.*

One of my good friends during basic was Danny Russell, from Hereford, Texas. Danny and I got the only two weekend passes out of my platoon at the end of training, and we went to Galveston, Texas. I don't recall what we did, but I know it was an honor for the two of us to be able to go to town. I remember our first sergeant giving us a stern lecture on not getting VD, and that always stuck with me too. The old VD films and lectures we had in those days were pretty strong.

Afterward, in August, I got home leave for twelve days. During that time at Camp Wallace I'd volunteered to be an Army Air Corps cadet. I was going to be a hot pilot, as everybody in those days wanted to be. When I got back from leave I had orders to Sheppard Field, Texas, to be processed for cadet training. I'd been asked to apply either for officer candidate school or cadet training, and I chose cadet training. In hindsight I suspect OCS would have

---

*The hand salute is rendered when at sling arms or when unarmed. The right hand, fingers and thumb joined and palm extended, is brought smartly to the tip of the brow or edge of the hat or helmet while the forearm remains rigid at a 45-degree angle, the upper arm parallel to the ground. At sling arms the salute is done the same way except the left hand secures the rifle by its sling, whether the piece is slung over the left or right shoulder. There are three ways to salute with a rifle: at attention, with the rifle butt on the ground, the piece parallel to the left leg and grasped firmly by the barrel in the left hand, moving the right hand smartly to the muzzle; at left shoulder arms, moving the right hand smartly to the receiver of the piece; at present arms, where the soldier is at attention, the right hand grasping the rifle at the stock, the left by the upper handguard and the piece turned trigger guard outward and held perpendicular with the center and about four inches away from the body.

been better. However, I might have ended up a lot differently, and I have no regrets about how things did turn out.

I arrived at Sheppard Field in September 1943. One part of processing was an interview with a psychiatrist. He had a small office with a desk, and he sat there going through the papers of a previous candidate while I waited for ten or fifteen minutes. Then he looked up from his papers and said, "Bainbridge, are your mother and father married?" I shot right back, "Damned if I know, Doc, but they were when I left home." I passed the exam.

Sheppard Field was close to the Oklahoma border, and it seemed to me that Oklahoma sand blew in one day and blew back into Oklahoma the next. I wasn't there very long. In October I went to Grand Forks, North Dakota, to the University of North Dakota to get the equivalent of one year of college and learn to fly a Piper Cub.

We were put into a ten-man room in a dormitory, and since my name began with a B, I was the first guy to be "room monitor." The room monitor was responsible for everything that did or did not happen in that room. A cadet had an allowance of ten demerits in any month, but for each demerit over ten, you were punished by "walking tours"—one hour walking around with a rifle in the riding stable or field house. That gave you plenty of time to think about how you'd earned those demerits.

I got nine demerits the first *day*. None of them were mine, they were all from the other guys, but because I was in charge, they were heaped on me. So we had a meeting in that room, and I told them I wasn't getting any more demerits. I went over the list and we didn't get another demerit the rest of that week. I had great cooperation from those guys, and nobody in that room ever had to walk a tour. We all pitched in and helped each other.

Of the ten guys in that room, I was the only one who had had physics in high school. That goes back to my dad. I had said when I got out of grade school that there'd be no more math for me, because I didn't like mathematics. But Dad said, "I've got news for you. First, you've got to take general business, which is required, but as you move through school, you're going to take the rest of it, too." Well, I kind of got into it, and I took algebra, trigonometry, and physics, the whole works. The first year of college physics, to me, seemed like a repeat of the high school course. So I tutored the other guys in physics at night and got more out of it than they did.

We were regular college freshmen at the University of North Dakota except we were also there to learn to fly. In the three months we were there we got the equivalent of a year of college and enough hours of pilot training to solo in an airplane. It was an accelerated course because of the wartime need for pilots.

Those pilot instructors were tough graders. My instructor was Paul A. Anderson, and the highest grade he gave me was an 82, merely average by the system they used. My average grade was only 77, "below average" according to their system. But on my final check, Anderson wrote, "Student could solo."

In January 1944, I went to preflight training at Santa Ana Army Air Base, Santa Ana, California. I think that is now Orange County Airport, a very busy place. We were in a vast tent city at Santa Ana. That was the first time I ever saw Bob Hope. Well, I say "saw," but I must have been five hundred yards from him, back in the audience.

In March 1944, the situation was getting pretty bad for ground-force replacements, so they took 35,999 cadets and me, as well as other people who had had previous ground-force training, and assigned us back to the earth. At the last minute my orders were changed and I was sent to the 10th Technical School Squadron, Lowry Field (now Lowry Air Force Base), Colorado, to be an aircraft gunner.

We were all upset over these reassignments, because we wanted to be hot pilots, but we realized our feelings made no difference in the decision and we had to accept that.

The only thing I learned at Lowry was how to do kitchen police. They had a big consolidated mess* there that operated twenty-four hours a day. That required three shifts of kitchen police, but they had enough of us waiting to go to school to do two shifts. We were on eight hours, off eight hours, and on again for another eight hours. I did that for almost six weeks, and I've said since that I did both my share and a lot of other people's share of KP while I was at Lowry Field.

I was then reassigned again, because the need for gunners and other crew members had diminished, and that's why I ended up at Camp Atterbury, Indiana.

In April 1944 I was assigned to the 106th Infantry Division, 423rd Infantry Regiment, 1st Battalion, A Company, Camp Atterbury, Indiana. Atterbury was about thirty miles south of Indi-

---

*A rarity in those days, the consolidated mess was equipped with a large central kitchen and dining wings on both sides and could feed several hundred personnel from different units all at the same time. A company mess fed the men of only one company at each meal.

anapolis. It was a huge place, or seemed that way if you were company runner and had to take something up to the post headquarters.

In less than a year I'd gone from a potential hotshot pilot to a private in the infantry. But that was okay by me. I'd joined the Army to fight, and if the Army thought I could be better used behind a rifle than in an airplane, I was ready to try it.

While I was at Camp Atterbury some German POWs working in the laundry went on strike because they thought they were working too many hours. Our company happened to be designated to take care of the problem if they didn't go back to work. We were issued live ammunition and were told we might have to "straighten out" the laundry. But nothing happened, and the Germans went back to work.

The point of this story is that though it shows the anti-German sentiment that was widespread at the time, it also shows that those German prisoners were treated so well they thought they could buck the system. I also mention it here as a contrast to the way we were treated when the Germans were our captors a little later on.

I went through six or eight weeks of training there and on July 1, 1944, got my first big promotion—to private first class. My company commander appointed Jim Poole (who later became my assistant squad leader), Walter Ware, Jim Harper, and me acting squad leaders and assistant squad leaders. I think we were selected because of the aptitude we had for the training. We were all fresh out of cadet or advanced training, and maybe we appeared to be a little bit sharper than our buddies.

We were squad leader and assistant for a week at a time. I started out as squad leader and Jim was my assistant. We went through one week and then they switched us around. The third week I became the squad leader permanently. The rank of squad leader in those days was staff sergeant, three stripes with a rocker. In those days a company commander could make his own enlisted promotions, and subsequently, in October 1944, I, along with Poole, Harper, and Ware, was promoted to sergeant, skipping the grade of corporal entirely. That promotion upped my base pay to $78 per month. I was only designated as squad leader and didn't make staff sergeant until after I was liberated from prison.

There were twelve men in an infantry squad then, including the squad leader. All of us were riflemen except for the guy who carried the Browning automatic rifle. He had an assistant, who was also his ammo bearer. That was the only automatic weapon in the squad. My BAR man was a Cherokee from Oklahoma by the name of Robert L. Woods. He could move faster with his BAR than I could with a pistol. The BAR weighed about twenty pounds and required four times the ammunition of the M-1 Garand, which was the basic infantry weapon of World War II.

When I first came into the Army I was issued a British Enfield .303 rifle for training. The first-class weapons, of course, went to the troops who were doing the fighting. Later I was given a .30 caliber Springfield Model 1903 bolt-action rifle. And finally I got an M-1 Garand. The Garand was a semiautomatic, gas-operated, clip-fed weapon with a lot more firepower than the Springfield. It didn't have quite the range of the old '03, but the amount of ammo you could fire with the Garand, eight rounds to a clip, compensated for that. The '03 had a greater range because it was bolt-operated and all the expanding gas from the powder charge was used to propel the bullet. In the M-1, some of the energy was diverted to operate the rifle's semiautomatic mechanism. At the same time we got the .30 caliber carbine, which came in semi- and full-automatic versions firing fifteen- and thirty-round magazines.

From the Garand they later developed the 7.62mm M-14, a magazine-fed weapon that came in semi- and full-automatic versions but had basically the same operating system as the M-1. The M-14 put out more firepower, which increased the logistical problem of resupply. And then they developed the 5.56mm M-16, which is a smaller weapon but can produce more firepower still. It can't shoot quite as far as either the M-1 or the M-14, but it is much lighter and the soldier can carry more ammo for it. The Army's famous for redesigning weapons, making them lighter, reducing them by a pound and a half, and then adding five pounds of ammo to the soldier's load.

The big complaint against the M-16 originally was that it wouldn't stand up in the field because it jammed. The old M-14 and M-1 didn't do that. The reason why an M-16 would malfunction so often, in my opinion, was that it needs very careful cleaning. Its tolerances are not as great as those of the older models and it requires more attention.

Another difference is the weight of the projectiles. If a .30 caliber or 7.62mm round is fired through heavy brush, it'll clip away at the stuff and continue on its trajectory, but the M-16 round is easily diverted, because it's such a light, high-velocity, unstable bullet. On the other hand, the M-16 round is devastating when it hits the human body because it tumbles around inside; the M-1 and the M-14 rounds just go straight through.

But if I had to fight in another World War II–type war, I'd carry the M-14 into battle, because it's just as accurate as either the M-1 or the M-16 and it's got plenty of firepower. The M-16 would do well in the 40mm grenade-launcher version. You can throw a grenade maybe twenty yards, thirty if you're a real hoss, but you can shoot a grenade with that launcher two hundred meters, and you can take area as well as pinpoint targets under fire with it.

Of course, I've fired the old M1911A1 .45 caliber pistol. It was okay. It was developed as a man-stopper, of course, but you have to be pretty close to get a hit with it. I've never even had a 9mm pistol in my hand, but the replacement of the Colt .45 with the Beretta 9mm was a development that I think was bound to come.

In the days before World War II, a soldier could go through his whole career with only one type of weapon. During my career I went through five generations of infantry rifles. That just demonstrates how our weapons technology has developed over the last fifty years.

Those guys in my squad at Camp Atterbury stayed with me all the way through the Bulge. I recall in particular one guy named Smith, who came out of Chicago. He and I had our differences, and we settled them when we got to England. In those days we settled disagreements differently than they do now, and I'll come back to this later.

Then there was Cochran, who was my first scout, and Royal R. Merservey. His middle name was also Royal—Royal Royal Merservey, a Mormon out of Utah and a good soldier. When we got to England and we had rationing, he always gave me his candy bars. I told him I didn't want the things, but he insisted I take them.

We called Cochran "Pops," because he was thirty years old at the time, an old man by our standards. Somebody had given him a quart of Golden Wedding bourbon as a wedding gift, and his wife had put it in the cupboard to keep for their golden wedding anniversary. While we were at Camp Miles Standish, outside Brockton, Massachusetts, he got a pass and went home for the weekend before we shipped out, and they drank that bottle of bourbon. He'd had a premonition he wouldn't come back from the war. He didn't.

I don't remember the names of all the other men anymore, but they were good men. When we got to Camp Miles Standish the company commander did a little reorganizing, and my platoon leader, Lt. Jackson Behling, came to me and told me that I was going to lose Smith and Merservey. I told him no way! He explained that there were some "weaknesses" in some of the other squads in the platoon and the Old Man wanted my men to strengthen them. I told the lieutenant that I wanted to talk to the CO, to tell him that the reason my squad was a good one was that we all had trained together, knew each other, and worked well together, and if he took my men away from me he'd just wind up with another weak squad—mine. I never did get to talk to Capt. Donald W. Naumann, who was company commander, but Lieutenant Behling informed me later that I would be able to keep my men.

We went from Camp Atterbury to Camp Miles Standish in September 1944 by train. It took us two days to get to Boston. We were at Camp Miles Standish until October 1944, when we embarked for England. We were going to ship out from Boston, but at the last minute they sent us by truck and train down to New York, and we boarded a troopship there. Being a farm boy, I didn't understand too much about the sea, and I had no idea what a troopship was. After we got out into New York Harbor the captain came on the public address system and announced we were on "the largest ship in the world, the *Queen Elizabeth*." So there we were, the entire 106th Infantry Division, on the *Queen Elizabeth*, headed, as it turned out, for Glasgow, Scotland.

Our crossing was unescorted. We were told by her captain that the *QE* could outrun any U-boat that the Germans had. Not knowing any better, we took his word for it. As it turned out, he was right. While we were on the ocean the ship changed course periodically so that if we were being tracked by a submarine it couldn't get a fix on us long enough to launch torpedoes. As I recall, the crossing took about five and a half days. The reason we hadn't shipped out of Boston, I discovered later, was simply that the *QE* was too big to berth there.

A story that was current during that time had President Roosevelt and Winston Churchill, who'd both apparently died, standing before the Pearly Gates of Heaven, locked out despite much futile knocking and pounding. Finally, Roosevelt turned to Churchill and said, "I'll tell you what, Winnie—you kick it down and I'll pay for it." That was hilariously funny to us in those days because of the Lend-Lease program, which had furnished the British with so much of the matériel they needed to fight the war. In fact, the *QE* and the *Queen Mary*, both British ships, had been refitted in

U.S. shipyards to do service as troopships. Their taking us to the war was one way the British paid us back for Lend-Lease.

The food on that ship was terrible. We ate twice a day, breakfast and dinner; no lunch. We spent one day belowdecks in staterooms filled with canvas cots, just room enough between them to slide in and out of bed, and the next day topside. We got a freshwater shower every other day. To use the toilets you had to stand in an immensely long line. I thought the crossing was pretty calm, but still lots of men got sick.

From Glasgow we went by train to a temporary camp just outside London, called Cheltenham. I never got a chance to see London while I was there. We could get passes, but my policy was to let the other guys go first, and we shipped out to France before my number came up. We all could go into the local village, of course, to get fish and chips and beer.

Here is where Smith and I resolved our differences. He said he didn't like the way I was running the squad. I asked him what he wanted to do about it, and he offered to step outside and settle the matter with me. We did, and I remained the squad leader, and we became great friends after that. In those days often the first sergeant of a unit was the biggest and toughest guy in the outfit, and differences of opinion were settled physically. Sometimes whoever had the hardest fists got the squad. But after our settlement, Smitty decided that I was capable of running the squad after all. The friendship that developed between us lasted through our time as POWs and after the war was over.

Our cantonment consisted of little Quonset huts heated by charcoal stoves or coke stoves. Coke is hard to get going, but once it catches fire it's great. Well, one day they moved my squad to another hut, one that had a defective stove. I told Smitty he had the job of switching the stoves without anybody catching us doing it. He said, "How in the world are we going to do something like that? Ours is fired up and that one in the new hut isn't!" I told him *I* sure didn't know, but a good Chicago boy ought to be able to figure out something. He responded, "Okay. We'll take care of it."

When we moved into the new hut, it was nice and warm and the hut we left was cold. Lieutenant Behling came around later and remarked, "I thought you guys weren't supposed to switch stoves." I told him that as far as I knew, nobody had. Smitty and a couple of other guys had gotten a pair of two-by-fours, picked that stove up, and taken it, fire and all, over to the new hut and exchanged it with the broken one. This illustrates a lesson I've been preaching all my life: The American soldier, given just a little leadership and then left essentially to himself, can figure out how to do just about anything, short of interplanetary travel.

We were there maybe two or three weeks and then shipped out for France through Southampton, England, on LSTs. That crossing was my first exposure to "ten-in-one" rations—a box with rations in it to feed ten men for one day. We were used to K and C rations, but we ate those ten-in-one rations on the LST crossing the English Channel. Seems to me it took about six hours to get to France. The seas were very heavy and the crossing was miserable, but being an invincible eighteen-year-old, I couldn't wait to get there.

It was rainy and muddy when we landed in Le Havre, France. We were taken out of Le Havre by truck on the old Red Ball Express, up to the front. Now the Army pup tent consists of two halves, one issued to each man so each pair of men can pitch a two-man shelter. But whenever we bivouacked on the way up to the front we pitched our tents out of three halves. It was so muddy everywhere that we got straw and put it on the ground and then used the third shelter half as a floor, over the straw, then slept three men to a two-man shelter. Being fairly small, I volunteered to be in the middle. I wanted to be in the middle, because if you got up against the tent wall, the damned thing would leak all over you; I figured if anybody was going to get wet, it sure wasn't going to be me.

We didn't get to see many of the sights in France as we moved up to the front, but the few Frenchmen we did meet were friendly. When we'd hold out our canteens and pantomime that we wanted water to fill them, they always seemed to come back filled with hard cider. Although the countryside and the villages were torn up pretty badly in some areas because of the fighting that had passed over the place since D-Day, it looked a lot like the Midwest to me. The weather was sure different, though. We had rain and mist back home all the time, but that stuff in France in the early fall of 1944 was just overpowering. But we were there to fight a war, and we just accepted the weather conditions as they were handed out to us.

We relieved the 28th Infantry Division in the Siegfried Line. We spent a lot of time patrolling with very little artillery support, and what little we did have sometimes seemed wasted. For instance, there was a German bunker a little beyond our lines. Intelligence believed it was fully manned, and artillery would be directed against it every day. We kept telling the intelligence people the thing was empty except for one German soldier who came out on occasion and "waved the flag." So to prove it to them, we went out and got him.

We got one hot meal a day. Our quarters were in some old ammunition bunkers. We were really shaking down. Some of our noncommissioned officers turned out to be below average. My platoon sergeant, whom I'll call Jones, was nicknamed G.H. He couldn't pronounce my name—he always called me "Bambridge." I'd try to correct him and he'd just say, "Okay, Bambridge." One day he came up to me and asked me, "Bambridge, how come they call me G.H.? They know that's not my name." I told him, "The initials G.H. stand for Ground Hog, you son of a bitch, because you never come out of your hole."

That really upset him, so he volunteered to go out on a firewood detail. He came back in with one piece and his rifle, giving the password all the way, so no one would shoot him by mistake. He never went out again.

As I said, we did a lot of patrolling. We even managed to free some of our people who'd been captured by the Germans. In one incident an ambulance came through Woods's position with four returned American POWs and a German the boys had captured in the process of freeing our men. Those ex-POWs really wanted to kill the German, but we wouldn't let them, because we knew what the Geneva Convention was all about. One of those guys had had a sister killed in a bombing raid on London.

In those days, infantry doctrine dictated that a company front be 250 yards long. In our sector the front was 1,100 yards, because we were in what was considered a "quiet" sector. And on December 16, 1944, hell broke loose when the Germans commenced what turned out to be their final offensive of the war.

We knew the attack was coming, because it was preceded by a terrible artillery barrage that began about four o'clock in the morning. We suffered no casualties, because we were buttoned up in the Siegfried Line fortifications, and those bunkers were solid. The bombardment went on for two or three hours, until after daybreak. Then we could hear the rumbling of approaching tanks. But there were good fields of fire to our front, and that first day we held off everything the Germans threw at us. We began to take pretty heavy casualties from then on, because we couldn't stay in the bunkers and defend ourselves from them.

Of course, we'd been aware of the armor building up to our front for some time—we could hear the tanks, a lot of engine noises in the distance—but when the artillery bombardment started, it was a shock. It was the first bombardment any of us had been under, and it was terrible even though we were fairly well protected in those old ammo bunkers with walls eight and ten feet thick. We had one platoon sergeant who became a basket case—he could not get out of his bunker, even after the shelling was over, so he had to be evacuated. Overall, our casualties were relatively light.

It is difficult to describe what that bombardment was like. Their stuff was hitting the treetops just as if it were *raining* shell fragments.

In retrospect, I think we did a hell of a job, because we really upset the Germans' timetable. They thought they could get through us in twenty-four hours, but it took them four days. So we traded time for our lives, time for the heavy combat forces and more experienced divisions to get back into line. We did more than I think even our leaders expected of us in that situation.

In fact, the night before we were surrendered we actually *attacked* the Germans. There must have been about sixty of us left out of our company (normally 100 to 120 men), and the company commander was moving us toward what he thought was a friendly area. We spotted a German 88mm gun emplacement when it opened fire on somebody—not us. In order for us to get where we wanted to go, we had to take out the gun. Part of our group flanked the 88, which was dug in and not as mobile as the 88s usually were, and drew the crew's fire while the rest of us knocked them out. Afterward we destroyed the gun with a grenade down the muzzle. That attack was the first time any of us had ever used bayonets in real combat. We used them primarily because we didn't want to give our presence away.

I had to use my bayonet. We'd had a lot of training in hand-to-hand combat, but that could never prepare us for the shock of the real thing. I do not want to remember that fight, although it is impossible ever to forget it. You see in the papers all the time about murders where people are repeatedly stabbed. I don't see how anybody, having used a bayonet once, could ever repeatedly stab someone again unless it was an extreme case of self-defense. It's just a terrible feeling.

During that assault I'd chambered a round in my rifle and then forgotten about it. The next day that little oversight caused me some trouble.

The next day, December 19, just before we were surrendered, we got into a fierce firefight with the Germans in what had been a village, just a small church and two or three houses. There was a sunken road with sloping banks seven or eight feet high. My first scout, Cochran, and my second scout and I were in this sunken road, and the Germans were in front of us but also flanking us to our left. A machine gunner with an MG-42, one of those rapid-fire German machine guns, came around a bend to our left and sprayed the bank where we were. He hit every other man. That's where Cochran was killed. His premonition proved true. Another man hit was Robert L. Woods, who took about four bullets in his legs. He was captured later but lived through the war. Last I heard of Bob he was living in Colorado.

Now, when I fired my rifle, that damned cartridge I'd inadvertently left in the breach all night long stuck fast instead of ejecting, and I had no cleaning rod to punch it out. Right behind me and on the other side of the road lay a weapons platoon man who'd been hit, so I took his carbine. Royal Merservey, who'd stayed on my side of the road, kept muttering, "We're gonna get outta this."

The German machine gunner had taken refuge behind a log right along the edge of the road, but his feet stuck out from behind it. When Merservey kept saying we'd get out of this I said, "Okay, you cover this guy, because we're going to get him out from behind that log." One foot was clearly visible, so I told Royal I was going to shoot for that foot, and if the machine gunner's head popped up, Royal should plug him in the head. I shot that man in the foot, and he did exactly what I hoped he'd do, and Merservey got him.

Then we were able to move up the road toward the church. Behind the church was a house with the windows all shot out. As we moved up, we received fire from the second floor of that house. We maneuvered behind the church. I had Merservey cover me so I could toss a grenade into the house. I had five grenades. The first two fell short, but the third one went through a window. I don't know what the hell was up there, but whatever it was, it was powerful; the whole roof blew off. I knew the explosion wasn't just my little old grenade. They must have had some ammunition up there. Anyway, we didn't have any more problems with that place.

I think we acquitted ourselves very well, when you consider what we were up against. After our surrender, as we were being marched back from the front, the sight of the German heavy equipment coming up was so overwhelming that we couldn't believe we'd been able to hold out as long as we had. We must have been outnumbered thirty to one. And so far as combat was concerned, we really were green troops, no question about that. Of course, it doesn't take long—about five minutes—to become a combat veteran, if you last that long in your first firefight. The longer you last, the better you get.

A happier memory of those days, if there is any such thing, is that while we were in the Siegfried Line some of our farm-boy instincts came in handy. Merservey and I found a barn full of cows, and we milked our helmets and canteens full and had fresh milk for everyone. We also butchered a hog for fresh meat. A guy named Dacus, from Arkansas, and I and our platoon leader butchered that hog. We weren't allowed to shoot any livestock, but this one had gotten himself killed somehow and we willingly converted him into fresh pork for the platoon.

One thing we had no lack of at the Bulge was guts, no matter how badly trained and equipped we might have been. We proved that by holding off the German onslaught for four days when we were supposed to fold after only one. But after we'd been taken prisoner we faced another ordeal, and in some ways it was to test us more severely than combat had.

The Germans marched us for about five days. During that time we wore out several sets of guards. Of course, they were all older men who couldn't be used in frontline units and we were in pretty good physical shape, so the guards who started out with us didn't make it to our destination—a processing point at Bad Orb, just east of Frankfurt.

Although we were surrendered on December 19, 1944, my family didn't learn I was still alive until March 1, 1945. My mother received a telegram from the War Department dated January 11, 1945, that was almost cruel in its terseness:

THE SECRETARY OF WAR DESIRES ME TO EXPRESS HIS DEEP REGRET THAT YOUR SON SERGEANT WILLIAM G. BAINBRIDGE HAS BEEN REPORTED MISSING IN ACTION SINCE TWENTY ONE DECEMBER IN GERMANY. IF FURTHER DETAILS OR OTHER INFORMATION ARE RECEIVED YOU WILL BE PROMPTLY NOTIFIED.

My mother told me later that she refused to believe that I wouldn't come back. She really didn't know what to make of it. I told my mother before I went overseas that if ever bad news was to come to her about me, she shouldn't give up hope, because I was determined to come back from the war. She just took my word that I'd be back and hung on.

The weather on the way to Bad Orb was absolutely "scalding" cold—it was terrible. We had a lot of snow, and we passed a lot of wrecked American equipment and the bodies of our dead, which didn't do a hell of a lot for our morale. The Germans didn't feed us along the way, and we drank what water we could get out of roadside ditches. Jim Poole and I subsisted off the two chocolate bars I mentioned earlier, and whatever we could dig out of the farmers' fields along the way—rutabagas—when the Germans would let us off the road to forage.

At Bad Orb they interrogated us and separated the noncoms and officers from the rest of the men. Bad Orb was the final stopping point for the lower-ranking enlisted men of our group, but we NCOs were to be transferred out of there. That was also where they stripped us of the rest of our personal belongings. I had very few left. I lost a pen and pencil set, a cigarette lighter, some odds and ends, and what money I still had on me. We had "invasion" scrip as well as a few reichsmarks that had been issued to us. I might have had $40 all told.

The officer who interrogated me, a German lieutenant, gave me a receipt for all this cash. He told me the German government would pay me for the reichsmarks, but since my government had printed the invasion scrip, it would have to reimburse me for that money. I asked him where he was going to get the money to pay me back, and he asked why I wanted to know that. "Well," I answered with all the arrogance and assurance of my nineteen years, "if you guys lose the war, how are you going to pay me back? And you *are* going to lose this war." That was the end of my interrogation.

After about ten days or two weeks, they marched us NCOs out of there. My memory of those days is still hazy, because it was a very traumatic experience for all of us. All we did during that whole time was mill around aimlessly like cattle in a huge outdoor compound. We had absolutely nothing to do, and the place was crowded with several times more men than it had been built to hold. I think they fed us some very thin vegetable soup once a day. Soup like that, it turned out, was going to be our main fare for the rest of the time we were prisoners.

I fell through the ice over a sewage pit one day. I didn't go all the way in, because someone pulled me out, but one leg got immersed and my trouser froze solid almost at once. That soon became the warmest part of me, because the ice prevented the wind from penetrating my trouser leg. But my feet were constantly cold. The day we marched out of Bad Orb, Walter Ware, one of the assistant squad leaders from my platoon, accidentally stepped on my heel. My foot was so cold and being stepped on hurt so bad I almost wanted to cry. As we trudged along our feet warmed up a little and then it didn't hurt so much.

They loaded us on railroad cars, the old "forty-and-eights." I think that expression originated with French World War I troop trains that had *"Hommes 40, chevaux 8"* stenciled on their sides—forty men and eight horses. Since the German railroad cars looked like those old forty-and-eights, that's what we called them. I don't know how many of us they crammed into those cars. The Germans locked the doors, but we had one small window, probably a foot square, covered with barbed wire and open to the outside. There was straw on the floor, no toilet, and one stove with only the straw for fuel. We were packed in so tightly that nobody could lie down. We were in those cars for five whole days.

We were never fed, never got any water, and never once got out during that whole time to exercise or relieve ourselves. We voided our bowels in a steel helmet and then emptied the thing out that little window. Two or three helmets were passed around for that function.

We were almost reduced to the state of animals by the end of the trip.

The day before we reached our destination, the train stopped at a siding. Some other POWs—I believe they were Russians—were working on the railroad there, and they gave us water in steel helmets. To this day I remember drinking a whole helmetful by myself. We were completely dehydrated after four days with no food or water.

Nobody died in our car during that time, nor was anybody killed. But to add to our misery, twice during the trip the train was strafed by our own planes. Though I'm sure we must have lost some men elsewhere on the train, nobody in my car was hit.

Being under your own fire was no different from being under an enemy's, except you wished the son of a bitch shooting at you knew who in the hell you were. It was obvious the pilots had no idea ours was a POW train. The Germans are noted for being methodical and careful about everything, but the bastards had neglected to mark our train in any way. If they had, those planes would have left us alone.

We ended that trip at a place called Siegenheim, up by Giessen. There were prisoners of several other nationalities in that camp—Russians, South Africans, French. We were not all mixed together but in our separate areas of the camp. Siegenheim was where I spent the rest of the war.

The first thing we did was get organized. We had a little council with a commander and a first sergeant, just like a military organization. We appointed our officers from among ourselves based on our evaluation of their abilities and their actual NCO rank in the Army. The Germans did nothing but give us thin soup and keep us locked up.

This council proved very useful in our negotiations with the Germans, especially when they asked us to work in Siegenheim, at the railhead there. Allied planes would fly over almost every day and drop bombs, and the Germans wanted us to go down there at night and work to help fix up the yards. Through the council we told them no. We knew the Geneva Convention specifically forbade putting NCO prisoners to work. The Germans asked for volunteers with the inducement of extra soup rations. We refused that also, and told the Germans what they could do with their soup. We told them we weren't going to assist their war effort in any way.

The huge barracks they put us in held five hundred or six hundred men. In the center of the complex was a washroom with barracks on either end. The washroom itself consisted of stone troughs with the coldest damn washing water I've ever used—it was never heated. There were two toilets, one at each end of this building, each supposed to serve 250 men, but we never used them because of the numbers of men waiting to get in there; we used the outdoor latrine instead.

We were two men to a bunk, and there were four bunks to a stack. Jim Poole and I shared the third one up in our stack. The bunk was maybe thirty-six inches in width and six feet long, but that wasn't long enough for Jim, because he was a tall man. He couldn't sleep stretched out fully. By the time we got out of there, we could both lie in that bunk without touching—that's how much weight we lost.

We had soup once a day, primarily vegetables like barley and dehydrated sugar beets. I'll *never* forget them! It was a long time after the war before I could tolerate barley again.

We carried our soup from the kitchens in a big tub, and each man got two-thirds of a canteen cup. Very seldom was there any meat in our soup—once in a while a little fat. Occasionally a piece of real meat would be discovered, which would be proudly displayed to everybody. We used to joke that we were still doing something toward the war effort by eating the Germans' transportation—their horses.

On Sunday evenings we would each get one slice of German black bread. No butter. So for a couple of days before the Sunday meal we'd extract the solids from our soup and save them as a "spread" for that German bread. I still like that kind of bread to this day.

I went into captivity weighing about 140 pounds and came out weighing only 89 pounds. We suffered extremely from vitamin deficiency. After I was liberated and back at Le Havre, getting some real food after all those months, my tongue swelled up to twice its normal thickness and turned painfully raw because of my body's reaction to the sudden influx into my system of real food with vitamins and minerals. But to the best of my recollection, nobody died from malnutrition in Siegenheim. We were there only four months, and we were in good enough shape to start that we made it through to liberation before the usual diseases that kill malnourished people could really develop.

During those first days at Siegenheim I had the worst case of dysentery that ever happened to anybody. It was *uncontrollable*. I had about three days of terrible hygiene problems. During the course of the dysentery I received no medical care; the disease just ran its course.

We had hygiene problems anyway. We got a bath once a month whether we needed it or not. They would take us to a bath area, put our clothes in a heated room, and delouse them, and we'd get a hot shower with soap. We were allowed maybe ten minutes in the water and then had to wait an hour while the Germans were delousing our clothing. It didn't make any difference, however, because we then went back to the infested barracks and were lousy again before the night was over.

And then there were the bedbugs. How many times have you heard someone say, facetiously, "Sleep tight and don't let the bedbugs bite"? Well, at night the damn things would be lined up in the nail holes of our bunks, just waiting for us. We'd kill as many as we could, but their eggs hatched everywhere and we were always being bitten by them. Before going to bed, we'd take off our underwear and kill all the live lice we could find. I'd never lived like that before and I am glad to say I have never lived like that since.

On some Sunday mornings we got ersatz coffee. The rest of the mornings we had tea, or what they called tea. The coffee was close, but it still wasn't coffee. The tea was the only hot water we ever got, so that's what we used for barbering and shaving. We also used it to wash our socks. We'd pool the stuff and four or five men could wash their socks or a pair of shorts in it.

Our barracks had a long row of bunks, and at intervals there was a little alcove where you could sit around a stove. We were sitting there one night when a cat came waltzing by. We never knew where he came from, but there was a hole in the floor nearby and he probably had come up from underneath the building. I got him by the tail just as he was going down that hole, but he proved stronger than I was or we'd have had a little meat with our soup that night.

We did get into a carrot cache underneath the barracks. I don't remember who discovered it, but for a day and a half there were a lot of carrots floating around. Then the Germans found the hole and boarded it up. There was no punishment for our getting in there except a bawling-out.

During the time I was in Siegenheim we had one man killed, a black soldier who'd been captured from a tank destroyer outfit. He tried to escape about four weeks before we were liberated and was killed before he got very far.

The Germans shot that man because he was trying to escape, but on the whole our guards were not particularly sadistic or cruel. One I'll never forget we called Pop Kramer. I would guess he was nearly seventy years old. He had a son who was a POW in Jefferson Barracks, Missouri, and he would ask us about the treatment of POWs in the United States. I had been to Jefferson Barracks before I joined the 106th Division, so I was able to tell him a bit about the place. Subsequently, whenever Pop Kramer was on duty when we went to fetch our soup, he would always make the kitchen personnel fill the tub right up to the top.

Since the war there have been a lot of motion-picture treatments of what it was like to be a POW in the German camps. Well, *Stalag 17* is wholesome entertainment compared to places like Siegenheim: no lice, no bedbugs, no dysentery.

Of course, the Red Cross did send packages to us prisoners. We got one while I was there. Those boxes were intended to sustain one man for one week. We shared ours among twenty men. That was my introduction to M&M candies. Maybe they weren't called M&M's in those days, but these were little candy-covered chocolates. My ration was *seven* of them, and they lasted me a week. I ate one a day. I recall I also got four tablespoons of powdered milk, half a cracker, and probably two cigarettes.

Ah, cigarettes! I was a smoker in those days. Jim Poole traded a watch we'd managed to save during all the searches to a French POW for two and a half packs of cigarettes. They were the old Lucky Strike Greens. When the war started, they were a very popular brand of smoke. As the war dragged on they changed the package to white. There was a saying current in those days, "Lucky Strike Green Has Gone to War." Evidently the dye for the green packages became scarce and they had to change to white. Well, here it was, 1945, and we were getting cigarettes made before 1941.

Those two and a half packs lasted four of us for well over a month. We had a system. I had one of those pocket-size plastic humidors—and I still have it to this day—in which I'd carry my cigarettes, and so I was appointed Keeper of the Cigarettes, a very responsible and honored position. We'd light a cigarette and everybody would take one puff. Then we'd butt it, and save the butt. Later, when the butts were smoked way down, we'd roll another cigarette from the leavings, so not a shred of the tobacco was wasted. When one of us experienced a nicotine fit and it wasn't time for a smoke, I'd open up that humidor and let him *smell* it, and that would have to satisfy him.

One of our favorite pastimes was thinking about recipes that our mothers or grandmothers used. We had recipes for everything from chocolate cheesecake to chocolate-covered dill pickles, whatever anybody could think up, because we all thought a lot about food.

We had little by way of diversion otherwise. It was winter, and we had no sports equipment. Most of our time was spent just sitting around, talking or walking and talking. We'd pull pieces of tar off the sides of the building and chew them to strengthen our gums. Everybody had a couple pieces of tar he carried around to chew on.

Later on, when some new prisoners came in, we were joined by Philip J. W. Gleisner, a most remarkable man. He kept us up to date on the news. He was originally from New York, and I forget what unit he had been with, but he spoke I don't know how many languages. He'd talk to the different work groups as they came back into the camp and get news on what was going on outside. The Germans provided us with news broadcasts every day telling us of the great losses they were inflicting on the Allies. Other than occasional battlefield exaggerations, these reports were fairly accurate, because they realized our knowing the truth about events wouldn't really harm them.

Gleisner would take the daily news broadcasts and the information he'd get from people coming into the camp who'd been out to places where they could see the damage inflicted by the bombings and give us a pretty good idea of how the war was going. He was really our link to the outside world. I have no idea what happened to him after the war. The last time I saw him was at Le Havre, after we were liberated.

Then one day in March 1945 a tower guard fired on a passing P-47 aircraft. The pilot was just out there by himself having a good time, I guess. Our camp was not marked in any way to identify it as a POW compound, and when the guard fired on this P-47 it didn't set well with that pilot, so he did a job on our compound. The .50 caliber rounds came through the roof and we could hear them bouncing around inside the latrine, which had concrete walls. He shot up the kitchen, too. We didn't get any soup for four days after that while they were repairing the kitchen. He made several passes on us and killed about forty men, other nationalities, but never got one American.

Eventually he stopped strafing us. I don't know if he ran out of ammunition or if he finally realized what we were; men were running all around on the ground, wildly waving their arms at him. We were told later that when he got back to his base and they developed the film in his gun cameras, the analysts spotted GIs on it and they realized he'd attacked a POW camp. Six days later we were liberated by the 6th Armored Division. Because they knew we were there, the division made a push to liberate us. They would not have done that had it not been for the attack by that lone airplane. Otherwise, we might have been there another month or so. As it turned out, that trigger-happy tower guard did us all a real favor.

About three weeks before our liberation, we got a doctor, an Army captain who'd been captured. The Germans sent him to Siegenheim to be our medical officer. They provided him with some medical supplies to take care of us, but he was also sort of an activist and organizer. When the 6th Armored started advancing toward us, the Germans started evacuating. The doctor got us all together and announced that we had to move but we weren't going to do it until we absolutely had to. He told us everybody else would go before he'd let the Germans move any of us.

He told us to expect the Germans to bring him into the barracks several times to make us move out, but until he said "I mean it," we were to do everything we could to disrupt the process. It took him about five trips before he said "I mean it," and by that time it was four o'clock in the morning. We had guys fainting over here, injuring a leg over there, anything we could to slow things up. One fellow was going to pass out from weakness, which he did, but he fell into a puddle of water. Just below the surface of the water, unbeknownst to him, was a rock, and he cracked his head on it and wound up really unconscious. We had to roll him over right quick so he wouldn't drown in the puddle.

This went on until around noon, at which time the Germans got fed up, turned the camp over to us, and left.

The next morning, Good Friday, 1945, the 6th Armored Division arrived. Here we were, liberated at last, the war almost over, a good chance we were going home, and two things went through our minds: eggs for Easter and how soon could we rejoin our units. We were informed very quickly that there was no way we'd be going back to our units, because we were in no condition for active service. We gracefully accepted the inevitable and reconciled ourselves to the grim fact that for us the war was finally over.

The men of the 6th Armored Division were really moved when they saw us, their former comrades-in-arms, reduced to living beanpoles. I was so skinny by then I could put my boots on laced up and buckled. My foot was just like a bone. All I had to do was stick it in that shoe, never mind about unlacing it to put it on.

We were surprised to learn that they had rounded up a good number of the guards and the people who had run the camp (but not the commandant) and brought them all back to us. Now *they* were the prisoners. There was one of them whom we called Horseface. There's at least one jerk in every outfit, and this guy was a big one to us. He wasn't a war criminal, just a prick who liked to give us a hard time. Prisoners of war learn to hate the friskings and searches they're constantly being subjected to, so we turned the tables on old Horseface, and he must have been "searched" 250 times before we were done with him. It was probably upsetting, but I don't recall that any of us did any physical harm to the people like him.

We remained at Siegenheim for about ten days after our liberation, because everything was going only one way at the time— toward the front. Our ration continued to be soup, but all of a sudden it had meat, salt, and pepper in it, and we were getting bread from the field kitchens, little square loaves of white bread, all we wanted. I never tasted anything as close to angel food as that bread.

They tried to restore our strength gradually, feeding us three meals a day, adding a little salt to our soup, giving us butter for our bread and C rations in the evenings. When we finally reached Repatriation Military Camp (pronounced "RAMP") Lucky Strike at Le Havre, we'd gotten a lot of our strength back. Incidentally, all the RAMPs were named after cigarettes—Lucky Strike, Philip Morris, Camel, and so on.

The organization for getting us out of Siegenheim, once it got going, was the finest I'd seen in the Army up to that time. One plane would come in, up would come a truck, the men would be loaded aboard, the plane would take off, and then another plane would land. They moved us all out in about two days.

Back at Camp Lucky Strike we were deloused, given haircuts and new clothes, and fed. They fed us anytime we wanted, twenty-four hours a day. We ate *all* the time.

While we were there we got more immunizations. I walked through the line, got my shot, went on a few paces, and then asked the medic if I could have *another* one. He wanted to know what for. I said, "Well, you forgot how skinny I am. The needle went all the way through and the stuff is running down the inside of my arm." He told me to get the hell out of there.

It was then it really dawned upon us that we were out of the war at last. Being able to get something to eat whenever we wanted it was alien even to our army. But the word had gone out that whenever a returned POW wanted to eat there *would* be food available for him. You could go into the mess hall and get eggnog or breakfast at four in the afternoon.

As I recall, we were at Camp Lucky Strike a week or ten days and then we loaded onto an old Liberty ship and joined the convoy that was to take us home. I celebrated my twentieth birthday on the boat that took us home. We were told each ship had enough rations to take care of three times as many men as there were on board for about three months. When we got to New York eighteen days later, we 375 or 380 ex-POWs had eaten everything, including probably some of the paint off the bulkheads. When we went over on the *QE*, all we got was two meals a day. But coming back they fed us three meals, and all the time in between. On top of that, we competed for jobs in the galley so we could get a chance to eat even more often. Even after all that miserable KP I had at Lowry Field, I didn't mind kitchen duty on that old Liberty ship.

The crew was concerned about our getting seasick on the high seas, because those Liberty ships would roll around quite a bit. Well, we also had with us some Army Air Forces men who were rotating back to the States after completing their missions. Not one ex-POW got sick on that trip, but a lot of the airmen did. Maybe the reason none of us did was that there was nothing inside us to slop around—we were just filled up with good solid food all the time. That crossing was also bad for those airmen because we ex-prisoners didn't have to do *anything* while we were on that ship but eat. The airmen boys had to do all the cleaning up.

They had those stand-up dining halls on the ship, and I think I ate until I just couldn't reach over my stomach anymore to grab the food put out there. For the first three months after I got back, even when I had eaten to the point where I was full, I was still hungry. I guess my system was just craving food after all those months I had been undernourished, but I also think the urge to eat and eat and eat was partly psychological. Ninety days after I got back I weighed 175 pounds. I looked like a butterball. I'd never weighed that much before, nor have I ever ballooned up that much since. I had no eyesockets; my face looked like a basketball. My mother just fed me all the time, all the things I'd been yearning for, like amber pie—a beautiful custard-type pie made with sour cream and raisins.

Once back in the States, we were sent to Camp Kilmer, New Jersey. Again we had physicals and another complete uniform issue. We'd already had one at Le Havre, but the people at Kilmer had been told to issue us a *complete* uniform set, so now we had two of them, two duffel bags full of complete uniform issues.

From there we were sent to the camp nearest to our homes of record. For me that was Fort Sheridan, Illinois, 165 miles from home. At Fort Sheridan we were given still *another* complete issue of uniforms.

At Fort Sheridan they were using German POWs as KPs and landscapers and that sort of thing. They used the old steel compartmented trays in the mess hall there, and the first time through the serving line a German KP gave this one guy a small dollop of mashed potatoes. He asked for a second helping, and the German replied, "No, you only get one dip." The soldier banged his steel tray over that German POW's head, and from that point on it was mayhem in there. Whack! Down went the German and over the serving line went his assailant, who began to hack on the fallen POW with the edge of this tray. Well, we got him off before he killed the guy.

For the rest of the time we were there they stationed military policemen inside and outside the mess hall. The next day somebody who wasn't aware of what had happened asked if the MPs were there to protect us from the Germans. He was told no, to protect the Germans from the GIs.

The Germans had the run of the camp. They worked in the day and went to their barracks at night, just like regular GIs. That just shows how different the Germans' treatment of us was from our treatment of the Germans. A lot of those German POWs just walked out of the camps and never went back—they stayed here, married, raised families, and I suppose became citizens in time. Some of them might still be living here.

After some processing at Fort Sheridan, we were sent home on a ninety-day delay en route. In those days, delay en route was considered part of travel time and did not count as leave time. I think they probably did it that way to give us a little extra time at home. Obviously, none of us had many days of leave coming otherwise. That delay en route was on the way to Miami Beach, Florida, where the rehabilitation center for returned prisoners of war was located.

The policy was that married men could take their wives with them to Florida. I wasn't married at the time, so I was expected to show up down there by myself. Well, before my delay en route was over, Hazel and I got married. When I went down to Florida I left Hazel at home, because, since I hadn't actually been married when I filled out the application, I assumed that the Army still considered me single. Of course, when I got down there it turned out nobody gave a hoot whether I was married or not. Hazel's always chided me about that, and I guess my naiveté is proof that at that stage of my life in some ways I really wasn't much advanced beyond the fifth grade.

Well, I spent that ninety days at home fattening myself up. I'd eat until there wasn't any room left and then go right on eating. Then I'd go lie down and sleep for a couple of hours, wake up, and eat some more. I still like to eat, but I can get full now.

I spent three weeks in a hotel at Miami Beach, eating anytime I wanted to. One thing that impressed me at the time was that they had Coke machines in the restaurant with no coin slots in them. The Army had contracted with these hotels for our stay there. We were issued meal tickets, and anytime you went in to eat they totaled up your bill and took your ticket so they could be reimbursed by the Army. Young guys like us were amazed that we could get a Coke anytime we wanted—all we had to do was push the button.

After the second week there we had one formation a day, to see who'd come down on orders to go back under military control, but otherwise we were on our own.

The first morning there I made the mistake of making my bed. After breakfast the maid asked me if I'd made my bed that morning. I answered, "Sure. Why? I make my bed every morning." She said, "Don't do it anymore, because that's *my* job!" Her name was Caledonia, and one of the popular songs of that day had a line in it that went "Caledonia, what makes your big head so hard?" We used to kid her about that, and she'd say, "That song wasn't written about me!"

My young friend Smith, the one who had challenged me for squad leader back in England, wound up at the White House Hotel with me in Miami Beach. He'd stayed at Bad Orb when I was shipped to Siegenheim, but we were reunited at this recuperation center. One day we went to the dog races together and cleaned up. I bet on what they looked like and Smitty bet on them by their names. A couple of women observed us and asked us our secret. We told them and they tried it for themselves, but evidently the names they picked or the looks of the animals they bet on weren't quite right, because while we continued to win on every race, they continued to lose. We made $400 apiece that day. I've never been back to a track since.

I also recall making a long-distance telephone call back to Illinois from a telephone booth. I had a bunch of coins, and one of the nickels turned out to be a slug. It went through the telephone into the return slot, but it registered. When I realized that, I thought I'd try it again. I paid for that long-distance call, maybe $1.25, with that one slug. After I'd fed in about a dollar's worth the operator asked me, "Is that all you got is nickels?" I called Hazel about five times using that one slug.

After three weeks there, in the middle of July 1945, the Army sent me to Camp Maxey, right outside Paris, Texas, where I was assigned the duty of company armorer-artificer, issuing the weapons and keeping them secure and repaired. Hazel joined me there, and we rented a one-bedroom apartment in a private home with bath and kitchen privileges. I rode back and forth on the bus. I still remember that old red bus with a hole in the floor where you could see the hot manifold glowing in the dark.

That's where we were when VJ Day—August 14, 1945—came. I don't recall that at the time we had very many thoughts about the atomic bombs that were dropped on Japan. There just wasn't much speculation about that in our circle at the time. The big news was the capitulation itself, not what brought it about. Of course, we saw the pictures of the devastation those bombs caused, but at our level in the world that was not significant. What was important to us was that the war was over worldwide and now we'd all go home for good.

We closed up Camp Maxey—with the war over the Army's training requirement had been drastically reduced—and Hazel went back home, pregnant, while I went to Camp Roberts, California. That had been my brother's first station when he went into the Army at the beginning of the war, and it was my last station after the war was over.

I took the train from Texas to San Luis Obispo, California, and hitchhiked to Camp Roberts. I got a lift from a trucker. I remember we drove up this mountainside very, very slowly, and he said, "We don't make very good time going up this side, but I usually make it up going down the other." I didn't think too much about the remark, but he was right. We got to the top of that mountain and he reached down and took her out of about four different gears, then sat back and steered, wheeling around cars. I don't know how fast we were going when we hit bottom, but I was sure glad when that ride was over. That was a four-lane road, but it wasn't big enough for me, the way that guy was driving.

I was discharged in December 1945 at Camp Roberts.

There is no doubt in my mind that what this country did in World War II had to be done. From my level, our country had been minding its own business when the Axis powers jumped on us. I couldn't get out of high school quick enough to get into the Army.

I thought we'd done well in the war. We'd recovered from a devastating blow to our naval strength at Pearl Harbor, and once we got our act together we'd bounced back because of our industrial might and because we as a nation were determined to win.

I was naive—all of us were. I actually liked the Army. I've always maintained that the Army's never hurt anybody. In my view, it's not the Army that makes people turn bad. People who go bad in the Army are bad before they come in.

The draftee was the man who won World War II. We cannot maintain an army or a navy or an air force large enough to fight a world war without a draft. The men who fought and won were trained by a small professional nucleus.

In those days we thought the training we'd had to prepare us for combat was great. But compared to the training of today, it was terrible. Gen. William Depuy, one of the Army's all-time premier trainers, has said that we went into World War II trained just a tad "above the ridiculous." He's right. Of course, today we've had time to train, which we didn't have in World War II. We also have a better training system today than we did in 1943 and 1944, the Noncommissioned Officer Education System being just one aspect of this. I'll get into that more thoroughly later in this memoir.

We overwhelmed the Axis powers by the sheer weight of our unharassed industrial might. Even though we weren't trained very well, we had so many soldiers that we prevailed by mere numbers. As the war wore the Germans down, their supply lines lengthened and their manpower and matériel were destroyed or began to wear out, and we were able to overwhelm them.

I'd estimate that maybe as many as half the men in the 106th Division were just replacements sent in to fill up spaces, though my company was an exception. The Army Air Forces and special training program guys who'd been in school never even melded into their units, they just stayed in their own little cliques. So the combat effectiveness of our units, with replacements like those, was not as good as that of, say, the units we had in Saudi Arabia during Desert Storm. Everybody in those units went with his friends; everybody knew what he was supposed to do; some of those men had trained together for *years*.

I've been told that the largest division we employed in combat in World War II was 18,000 or 19,000 strong. An Army division of today, with two or three thousand men fewer, is much more lethal than any World War II division. Of course, the weapons are different, but I'm just considering how much better trained the men are today.

Remember old Ground Hog Jones, my platoon sergeant? Well, I was just reading in the paper a while back about a sergeant first class (E-7)* in Saudi Arabia who'd just completed a ten-mile race in one hour and sixteen minutes. He said he finished way back in the pack, but that wasn't his concern—he just wanted to finish in under one hour and twenty minutes "to set an example for my younger troops." He said he finished in between two buddies. One was thirty years old, the other twenty-eight, and he was thirty-four. The oldest man I had in my squad at the Bulge was thirty, and we called him Pops!

*The enlisted pay grades now range from E-1 (private) at the bottom to E-9 (sergeant major) at the top. Soldiers in grades E-7 through E-9 are considered "senior" NCOs. SFC falls just below master sergeant. See the charts illustrating the enlisted grade system 1942–1992 in Appendix I.

That thirty-four-year-old SFC went on to say that his unit had been deployed long enough to get rid of the effects of the Big Macs and the Miller Lites, knew exactly what it was doing, and was ready for any mission. That's the contrast between today's generation of soldiers and mine.

Even up to a short while before I retired from the Army in 1979, a lot of people in the Army thought training was just fixing bayonets and charging up a hill. Today the Army as an institution considers training to be anything that makes the soldier better equipped to do his job—better able to apply the rule of war. That rule is: to destroy the enemy in the quickest possible way with the least loss to your own side. That's a very simple rule, but without the training to get to that end we'd just be sacrificing ourselves in war.

Thank goodness that today the Army as an institution knows what has to be done and the nation has the wisdom to let it do it. The lessons we learned in World War II and since have been put to good use, and that's why the Army of today is the best force we have ever fielded.

The squad leader engaged in Desert Storm knew more about soldiering than my company commander did in World War II. That company commander of mine was also a draftee in one respect. He went to OCS and got a commission, so maybe he was a "commissioned draftee."

Now that the war was over, I wanted to get back to the farm. That was my whole focus in life. I had done my part, and that was it for me. I never gave a thought to staying in the Army. True, I was a staff sergeant* by then, but I just wanted to go back to farming. I went home to Knoxville, where my parents were living, and one week later I was working for the Chicago, Burlington & Quincy, unloading coal cars at Galesburg, Illinois.

In September 1991 I attended the 45th reunion of the 106th Infantry Division Association. That year it was a three-day affair held at Huntsville, Alabama. Over the telephone and through correspondence I had been in touch with some of my old buddies, Jim Poole, my assistant squad leader, Jim Harper, and Walt Ware,

---

*A decent grade for only three years of service, putting me between sergeant (4th grade) and first or technical sergeant (2nd grade). I was what was known as a "first three grader," or in the top three enlisted grades of the Army. In those days there were only seven enlisted grades. In 1958, pay grades E-8 and E-9 were added, giving us the system we use today.

and I looked forward to seeing them again. It was no small disappointment that they couldn't make it.

But the reunion was well done and I did see Bill Lane, who had been a platoon guide in the 3rd platoon of my company and who served with me as a prisoner of war. After the war he also went back to Bad Orb and visited Stalag 9B, where he kicked loose two of the cobblestones that line the road there, took them home, and turned them into bookends. Other veterans of the division have offered him large sums to buy those bookends, but he won't part with them. After the war he joined the Naval Reserve and retired as a master chief petty officer.

Since Hazel and I knew hardly anybody who was there, we set about getting acquainted. We sat at a different table for each meal and got to know quite a few of the other veterans and their wives.

Allen W. Jones, the son of our wartime division commander, was there. Al had been a first lieutenant in our battalion headquarters and later he was the battalion S3.

The 106th Division Association has held reunions periodically since the war, but somehow I was not aware they were being held, otherwise, I would have made an effort to attend a few. What struck me at this one was that the 106th is a "dying" division; it is no longer on the active rolls nor has it been since World War II. I'm 66 and many of the other vets are even older, so the time is coming when the Association will just cease to exist.

≡ 3 ≡

HENS AND CHICKENS

At the time I got out of the Army, in December 1945, nobody was hiring farmhands; January–February is the season for that kind of work. Of course, I could have drawn unemployment after my military service, $52 a week for as long as twenty weeks, if I remember correctly, but I wasn't having any of that sort of thing, not while there was work around, and I've yet to draw one day's unemployment compensation.

So I got a job with the old Chicago, Burlington & Quincy in Galesburg and lived with my parents in Knoxville, which is about six miles away. That job paid about $2 an hour. I knew I would never be able to buy a farm from the wages the railroad paid me, but it was something to do until the farming season began.

I unloaded coal cars. In those days there were still some steam locomotives, and they'd come in under the "tipple," as it was called, and fill up their tenders. We had a cable hooked to the cars, which we'd use to pull them up over a pit, and then we'd empty the tenders through the bottom of the cars. Usually the cars would be frozen and someone would have to get up under them to chip the ice away. That was really physically demanding work, unloading those coal cars, but by then I'd recovered from the ill effects of my time in the POW camp. I'd been back many months and was back in pretty good shape again.

I worked on that job until February 1946, when I learned that the husband of one of my old grade-school teachers was looking for a farmhand, so I went to work for Stanton and Eleanor Moore, down by Gilson, Illinois. Hazel and I got a house with no electricity and a garden and maybe fifty chickens. We worked that farm for $95 a month. It was general farming. I raised hogs and a few cattle, but primarily grew corn, oats, and soybeans. The oats were a "nurse" crop for alfalfa and clover to provide hay. You seed the clover or the alfalfa in with the oats. You harvest oats the first year, clover or alfalfa hay the next two years, and at the end of the third year, plow under the alfalfa or clover and raise corn for the next two years. It worked as a five-year rotational system: two years of corn, one of grain, and two more of clover or alfalfa.

I broke the ground using a plow and a tractor, and then I disked and harrowed and planted, and after that I tended the rows of crops. When it was a rainy day I cut weeds on fence rows, built fences, made repairs to buildings. Around a farm, when you can't get into the fields there's always something else to do.

Hazel and I worked that farm a year. Our first child, Kathy—Kathryn Lee—was born in June 1946. I remember the day Hazel thought she was ready to deliver Kathy. I was mowing hay, and I was about half or three-quarters of a mile from our house, north of the landlord's place. He and his wife were gone, so I told Hazel that if she thought her time was coming she should hang a dishtowel on the side of the corncrib. The crib was dark and the white dishcloth would show up on it. I mowed hay all day, watching for that signal, and it never did show. I had a stiff neck, constantly watching over that way. About maybe three in the afternoon I saw my car coming out to the field, and I thought that was mighty strange. My landlord was driving it. He flagged me down and told me that Hazel was ready and he'd brought my car out to see me so I wouldn't have to waste any time getting it started.

I asked Hazel why she hadn't given the signal we'd agreed upon, and she told me, "I wasn't *able* to get out there to do it. If I'd tried, I might have had the baby at the corncrib instead of in the hospital! So I toughed it out until the Moores got home and called them." We did have a telephone.

Later that evening, Kathy Bainbridge appeared. That was quite an ordeal for Hazel, but everything went well.

In February 1947, I got an opportunity to go to work for a guy named Roy Taylor. His farm was about five miles from the place the Moores owned. I got a big pay raise, from $95 a month to $110. I also got a house, and this one had electricity. It was a small place, kind of a "shotgun" house: a kitchen, living room, and bedroom in a row. The bedroom had been built on; I think they built that place on three different tries. But it did have a basement. We also got fifty chickens and a place to keep them, a cow, a half of beef, and a hog to butcher. We were literally living "high on the hog" at that place, compared to our previous situation.

All this time I was going to school, studying agriculture. I started school when I was working for the Moores and continued for two years. I went to classes two nights a week, in my old high school at Williamsfield. The thing that kept us going those two years was the GI Bill, which paid me $90 per month. Without that, life would have been really tough.

Then when I went to work for Roy Taylor, we sold the eggs from those fifty chickens, for which he provided the feed, and the cream from the cow, and that was enough to keep us in groceries the two years we worked for him.

I remember that we had a glass coffeepot and were always breaking the damn thing, one way or another. I went to Knoxville shopping one day and bought an Ekco stainless-steel vacuum pot. I think I paid $20 for that thing. When I got home, Hazel exclaimed, "Twenty *dollars* for that coffeepot?" I knew the price was exorbitant, but we'd broken so many of the glass ones I thought in the long run the stainless-steel version would pay off. I kept that thing until 1988.

I also tried to convince Roy he should change the way he fed his chickens. He fed his birds egg mash and I fed mine a protein supplement. He had three hundred layers and I had fifty, and I'd get forty or forty-five eggs out of mine per day and he'd get only 150 out of his. That was something I'd learned in night school. But Roy was an old-time farmer and it was pretty hard to get him to change anything.

Yet Roy and his wife, Esther, were good people. Esther took Hazel under her wing and helped her out a lot.

You might be surprised to know how much attention farm work requires. I have a story to illustrate just how absorbing it can be.

Roy had two tractors, an Allis-Chalmers, which he drove all the time, and a Massey Harris, which I drove. That Massey Harris didn't have a muffler on it, and it was the noisiest damn thing you can imagine. It's a wonder I can hear anything today, all the time I spent on that tractor. Well, in the summer of 1947 I was cultivating* corn one day, the first cultivation, in fact, and the corn was no more than three inches high. I had to really watch what I was doing, to drive that tractor at the right speed so as not to cover the corn up.

Kathy was about a year old at the time, and she caught her little finger in a cedar chest hinge and cut the tip of it off. Hazel

---

*This is done by using a cultivator, a machine with metal sweeps that go along each side of the row of corn removing the weeds while leaving the corn standing.

walked out to the field, carrying Kathy, and I drove by her three times before she was able to get my attention. That tractor was so noisy I couldn't hear her hollering. Finally I caught her out of the corner of my eye and stopped. She'd been standing out there twenty or thirty minutes while I'd made three circuits, so intent on what I was doing I hadn't seen her all that time.

We got Kathy to the doctor and he sewed the tip of that finger back on. Kathy has the cedar chest today.

Farming also consumes every moment of your life. The Christmas of 1947, I wanted to have Christmas morning with Hazel and Kathy, so I got up at two-thirty and did the chores. It took me two and a half hours. I left a note for Roy that I'd been by early so I could have Christmas with my family.

Milking cows is an aspect of life on the farm in my day that's a thing of the past now. It was really very easy. You sit to the right side of her, shut off the flow of the milk back into the udder with your thumb and forefinger, and squeeze it out of the teat with the other three fingers. It probably took ten minutes per cow, once you became used to the process. It really builds up the muscles in your forearms.

Once you milk the cows, you run the milk through a separator, a machine that takes the cream out of the milk using centrifugal force. The cream is actually the butterfat of the milk, and it was a continuing source of cash for farm families, because it could be sold in town.

We were always dependent on little cash projects like eggs and cream, but that money was a mere trickle that paid for incidentals. The real cash-generating activity was the two or three times a year when we sold the hogs or the grain. That was when we paid off the major bills and the mortgage.

After about two years with Roy, I began looking for a farm of my own. The word was out in Knox County that I was looking for my own place, and one September day a fellow by the name of Probst came to the milk barn and asked for me. I finished up the cow I was working on, and he told me that his father-in-law, Noble O. Crissy, had a farm at Victoria and was looking for somebody to take it over for him. He said they'd heard about me and wanted to talk to me about taking it.

I told him I was really interested in the proposition but I had no farm implements, and once I got my own place I'd need a mortgage and some money to get the necessary machinery to farm it. He told me he didn't think that would be a problem, because the bank in Knoxville was willing to back Hazel and me on a loan if we would take the Crissy place. The farm was right next to the Victoria cemetery and consisted of 193 acres with a large house on the property. The deal was that Crissy's daughter, Catherine, and her husband, this Probst fellow, were going to move up there. She was a drama teacher in the Tulsa, Oklahoma, schools and he was an oil man out of Oklahoma. We would go halves on the equipment and everything else.

This farmhouse had about twelve rooms to it and a full basement. It also had an automatic stoker-fed furnace, which was really unusual on a farm in those days. We also had our first indoor convenience at that place, with a septic tank. The place had a gas stove too, so Hazel was able to cook with bottled gas.

We shared the place with Catherine, who had an apartment in the upstairs half of the house. She spent a lot of time in the garden, for two reasons. She loved fresh vegetables, and this was a new experience for her, communing with Mother Nature. She also gathered eggs, and we shared and shared alike, and she got a portion of the crop. Her husband never did live there, and they finally split up. The last we heard of Catherine, ten or twelve years ago, she was living in Lake Worth, Florida.

So we got a loan from the Farmers and Mechanics Bank in Knoxville and bought an old Farmall F-30, and some other farming implements. The tractor I bought to start was ten or twelve years old, but I got a new Ford tractor the second year. We started with a loan of about $15,000.

Besides the equipment, we bought some hogs and some Brown Swiss cattle. I wanted the Brown Swiss because they sold well as beef and as veal calves, because they're big calves and produce beef pretty quickly. They were not registered cattle; they could have been, but we didn't go into that business. A registered cow means it's a purebred—there's nothing else in that animal but Brown Swiss. Registering cattle is just like getting an AKA registration for a dog—it assures the purity of your breed. I didn't want to get into that at the time, but I had what is called "graded" cattle, which means there weren't any Hereford bulls in my cattle for at least a generation.

Registered Brown Swiss would have cost us about $275 or $280, so we saved about a third by going with them as graded cows. They produced good milk.

I raised hogs, too, and chickens. Most farmers don't want to mess with chickens, by the way. I bought sexed chickens, pullets. They cost a little bit more, but I got all females to lay eggs. I also bought 150 or 200 roosters, and I'd caponize them. Neutering

roosters is a good rainy-day or evening activity. That's done by
going under the bird's wing, between the second and third ribs,
plucking out some feathers, and making a little incision. They
make a little stainless-steel tool for that purpose with a small eye
on the end of it. You run the tool down inside the body cavity, run
the testicle through that eye, and pull it out. I learned how to do
this on the GI Bill. The bird squawks a little bit during the procedure, but it is a fairly simple operation. It takes about two minutes. I'd mark each desexed chicken with a spot of dye.

We'd sell those capons for their meat. They can get up to seven
or eight pounds, and you can still fry them, because they don't get
tough. Once in a while you get what they call a "bloater"—the
chicken swells up like a balloon. It swells up so much you can
hardly see its feet, and it can't even walk. If you don't do something, it dies. You correct that by taking your scalpel, punching a
hole in the bloater, and squeezing the gas out until it returns to its
normal size.

The next year they developed a chemical method of caponiza-
tion. The chemical came in the form of a pellet that you inserted
in the skin at the base of the neck with an injection gun. The
chemical prevented the sex from developing. A rooster has a
wattle down under his beak that normally gets real red and much
bigger than the hen's wattle, but when you caponize him that
never develops. But this chemical form of desexing was only temporary. At the end of four months the effect would wear off and
the testicles would redevelop. So what you did was to butcher
them during that four-month period. You threw away the head and
neck because of the chemical, but most people don't eat the neck
anyway. This process was much easier to perform and took less
time than the older method. I could do a hundred in an hour or
so, whereas with the scalpel it took me up to two days to do that
many birds, doing them in my spare time.

I made some good money off of those chickens. I used Auster
Whites, a cross between the black Minorca rooster and a white
Leghorn hen. The white Leghorn is an egg-laying machine, but
flighty. If you startle Leghorns you can reduce their egg production significantly. Lots of things can upset their laying, like getting
their feet cold, which will result in their going a day or two without laying an egg. In those days you expected six eggs per bird
in an eight-day cycle.

Hogs, as I mentioned before, were the real money-makers, our
"mortgage lifters." The sows come in different categories. There
is the "gilt," a pig that has never had a litter; a "tried sow," which

has had one litter; and the "proven sow," which will produce a good healthy litter of pigs.

How you bred and butchered your hogs made a big difference. Roy Taylor had proven sows many times over. He would keep sows up to four or five years, and they'd get to weigh six hundred pounds. They'd produce big litters and good ones, but the problem with this method is that you have to feed the hog all that time. The scientific way to do it is to have the gilt, and if she produces a good litter the first time, you breed her again, but if she doesn't come through the first time, you sell her. If she produces a good litter the second time around, you sell her after that. That way you keep good hogs coming around and you don't have to feed them for four or five years in between their productive cycles. And as they get bigger they lie on their piglets and squash them and so on, so it just doesn't make any sense to pay out a lot of money for their feed when you can raise almost as many my way and sell them off.

Roy would castrate his hogs when they got to be sixty-five or seventy pounds. It takes two people to castrate a hog that big. I would catch and hold and he would operate. That makes the boar hog into a "barrow." You can't sell boars for very much, because the meat gets strong, but barrows have good sweet meat. But if you wait until they grow to be over sixty pounds, they lose four or five pounds when you castrate them. I did it by a technique I learned at school, which I could never get Roy to follow. When the pigs were a week old I'd let the sow out of the farrowing house and then sit down with a razor, put that little guy's nose down between my knees, and castrate him. He'd go "wheek, wheek," and it'd be over. He never lost an ounce and never knew anything was missing, and best of all, I could do the operation myself while saving the money I'd have spent on feeding him if I'd waited until he grew bigger. That became a Sunday-morning chore for me.

Another thing. Once in a while you'd find a ruptured testicle, and if you took that out, the intestines would come out along with it. On a hog weighing seventy-five or eighty pounds, you'd lose him if that happened, but with a little guy, I could use a plain old needle and thread, stuff it back in, put two or three stitches in him, nip it off, and he'd be okay. Considering that I usually had about forty sows producing litters of seven or eight piglets each, I'd have a hundred or so twice a year, so you can imagine the labor I'd have had to put into it if I'd waited for those hogs to grow bigger.

I liked working with hogs. One night I happened to go by one of my tried sows who'd just had a pig, and it was dead. The piglet comes in an enclosed membrane, a little sack, and sometimes that membrane is so strong the pig can't get out of it. His mother, unlike many other mammals, won't help him out. As I was checking this dead one, she had another, and I took it out of the membrane and the pig lived. I came back about an hour later and she was just having a third one. So after that I took a book and a lantern and sat with that sow all night long, and every hour, like clockwork, a pig would come out. She had twelve pigs and we saved eleven of them. If I hadn't sat out there with her she'd have lost all of them, and then we'd have fed that sow for nothing.

Cows are demanding farm animals, also. When they're calving and there's some difficulty and the cow can't get up almost immediately, you have to be there to make her, because if she doesn't get up within an hour, she just isn't going to get back up ever again.

And you cannot afford to miss milking them, either. Once I was taking a tractor down for some new rear tires and the front end of that old Farmall hit a chunk of frozen mud and the steering wheel spun in my hands and I cracked my elbow on one of the spokes. I mean, I *really* cracked that elbow, and it hurt like hell. After I got my business in Galesburg done, I went to the doctor, and he advised me not to use that arm for two or three days, until the swelling went down. I asked him what I was supposed to tell my eight cows. So even though that elbow should probably have been in a sling and ice packs, I went ahead with my ordinary chores, painful as it was for me to use that arm. I just had to or I'd have lost those cows.

When I wasn't taking care of my animals and all my other chores, there was the maintenance of the structures to be attended to. The man who'd owned that place before me ran it with a hired man, his father, and himself—three men. The fences were run-down, the barn needed work, the corncrib was falling apart. They'd just let everything go. The manure hadn't been cleaned out of the feeding shed in three years. The fences around the feedlots were gone. In the time I was there I repaired all those things besides farming 193 acres, and that was just with Hazel to help me.

Mr. Crissy couldn't understand how I'd managed to do all that when the three men who'd had the place before me had let it go so badly. It wasn't easy, but it was just a matter of staying at it. I'd learned a lot from Roy Taylor, a lot of techniques that saved time and effort, and I got the buildings repaired because I didn't go to the tavern and spend that extra time drinking beer.

And believe me, farming is hard, physically demanding work. I remember the first year a neighbor just to the east of us, a guy by the name of Clark Nelson, had a combine and I didn't. That's a big, expensive piece of equipment, and most young farmers starting out in those days couldn't afford one. Clark had been farming for thirty-five or forty years at that time. So when Clark combined his grain I hauled it to the granary and put it into the bins with a shovel, and then he'd combine mine for me and I'd shovel my own in too. So in a three-week period I shoveled two farms of grain. I'd go through a whole wagonload and never straighten up, and by the time we'd get to the end of a field I'd be throwing that stuff up over my head to get it into the wagon. It was very hard work.

The next year I bought an elevator, and when we did Clark's fields I took it along. That was not an expensive piece of equipment, but it permitted me to do much more work. We had one field that was forty-three acres in extent. I was cutting stalks in it one day in the spring of the year. You cut the stalks from the year before with a disk before plowing, that way it's easier to turn them under. We had a dog, just a mongrel we called Squirt—Kathy couldn't pronounce "Squirt," so she called him "Firt." That dog stayed with me as I cut those stalks in that field, and it took me all day. Hazel brought me my supper, and I just kept on going. About eleven o'clock that night, Squirt looked up at me like he was thinking, "You fool! I'm leaving!" And he went back to the house. I finished up a little after midnight. The dog was on the porch, and as I walked by he opened one eye as if he were saying, "Well, you finally came in!"

That's what farm work was like in those days. When you're farming, you're never your own boss. It's a little like being in the Army, actually. You get up early and go to bed late, and there's always something dictating to you—the weather, your animals, and so on.

That dog, by the way, was one smart critter. When we were working for Roy Taylor, Hazel would put Kathy out in the yard on a blanket, so she could get the sunshine and air. Whenever Kathy started to crawl off that blanket, the dog would put her back on it. One day Hazel had to go into the house for something and she glanced out the window to see Kathy crawling off the blanket again. Well, Squirt ambled over there and lay down in front of Kathy. She wasn't big enough to climb over him, so she turned around and crawled off in another direction, and Squirt walked over and lay down in front of her again. After about ten minutes of that Kathy decided that Squirt just wasn't going to let her off that blanket, so she stayed in the middle. We never taught that dog a trick. He learned just from watching Hazel. Some people say animals can't think. Sometimes I wonder.

In September 1949 our second child, Mary, was born. It was a Sunday morning around six and I was milking. Usually you do the milking much earlier, but this was a Sunday. I was on the second cow and Kathy came out and said, "Daddy, Mama says she has to go to the hospital." I told her to tell Hazel I'd be in as soon as I finished my milking. I did about three more cows and Kathryn Lee appeared again. "Daddy," she said, "Mama says you'd better hurry!" So I did just enough on the remaining cows to relieve some of the pressure and headed for Galesburg with Hazel.

As it turned out, I could have milked the cows all day long, done the chores, and probably built a couple of yards of fence, because it wasn't until early the next morning that Mary Elizabeth Bainbridge finally appeared. Hazel said, "Oh, my, you wanted a boy! We'll just have to try again." Here she'd just come through an all-night labor and she was willing to try again. Is there any wonder why I love that gal so much and we've stayed together so long?

While we were at Victoria, my old platoon leader, Jackson Behling from Tulsa, Oklahoma, came by with his wife. We'd had a chain letter going among some of the old members of my platoon, and we'd all get one about every eight months. When they got to our place, about two o'clock in the afternoon, we had chickens ready for the frying pan and fresh vegetables from the garden, and we really fed them. The next letter that came around, old Behling couldn't get over how well he'd been fed and that it was all fresh.

We pasteurized our own milk to give to the girls. We bought a gallon-size home pasteurizer, which was the thing in those days, because people worried about TB in the milk. The pasteurizer was just a little bucket with a heating element, and it kept the milk at a certain temperature for a certain length of time.

I worked hard and I ate hard. I could eat as much for breakfast then as I eat all day long now, working all those calories off during the day.

We stayed at Victoria until 1950, when the Korean War broke out. While I was there I joined the Army Reserve. Don't ask me why. I just went to Galesburg one day and dropped in at the armory. The lieutenant there asked me if I wanted to join up, told me what the Reserves were all about. I mentioned that it would be pretty tough for me to get to the meetings because I was so busy all the time, and he advised me to join up anyway, so I did. I went to one meeting and this lieutenant asked me to apply for OCS. I wanted to know what was in it for me besides a little higher pay, and I never did fill out that application. I never went to another meeting, either.

When the war broke out in Korea I was called to active duty. That was a surprise, but the Army was calling up all those who did not participate in their Reserve unit's activities. They didn't call up units, only individuals who hadn't made the meetings. I would never have been called if I hadn't gone down there and joined up. As it turned out, it was the greatest thing that ever happened to me. Maybe instinctively I knew something was coming.

The war broke out in Korea on June 25, 1950, and in September I got the call to report to Camp Breckinridge, Kentucky. I went to the Fifth Army Headquarters in Chicago. I had no problem with being called up, really, but I had to do some serious planning, because I was right in the harvest season and I had no idea how long I'd be in the Army this time around. I just wanted a temporary delay in my reporting date. I'd have been ruined financially if I'd gone before I could get my crop in and livestock sold, and my share from the sale of the equipment. We'd just gotten to the point where our heads were a little above water and bang, here came another war.

Fifth Army Headquarters gave me until January 4, 1951, to report. I got the crop in—the neighbors helped me with that—and got our furniture sold or stored away, and we raised enough money to make a down payment on a Pontiac house trailer, because we knew there'd be no quarters for us. In those days if you were only a sergeant, like me, you had to be really lucky to be assigned a set of family quarters on an Army post.

We got back about twenty-five cents on the dollar on our investment in that farm. We lost our hat and chewing tobacco, as they used to say, but we paid off the mortgage and we got enough cash to make a down payment on that trailer. The loss we took on the crop because we had to sell at the wrong time was devastating. So there we were, going back into the Army with two little kids.

In the meantime, my orders got changed and instead of going to Camp Breckinridge, we went to Camp Atterbury, Indiana. I was an infantryman and they sent me to be the information and education (I&E) NCO at a food service school. The service school at Camp Atterbury was an Army/Air Force school where they trained cooks, bakers, butchers, and mess sergeants.

I was called back in my World War II grade of staff sergeant and in June 1951 was promoted to sergeant first class. That was pay grade E-6, because in those days the enlisted pay grades did not go beyond E-7—master sergeant. The chevrons for SFC, E-6, were three up and two rockers, same as they are today for SFC (which is now pay grade E-7). If that sounds confusing, it *is*, but it got worse, of which more later.

When I came back in I was given a new service record. My old one, which covered my service from June 1943 to December 1945, was actually a book, DAGO Form 24, which I still have. The new service record was a four-page form on heavy paper, the DA Form 20. The version I have was remade in 1973, all the old information copied over from the previous form. Under civilian occupation it lists "Farmer General (Agric)," and it describes my "Duties Performed" like this: "Operated a 193 Acre farm raising corn, oats hay also 12head ofcattleand 180hogs milked cowsbyhand, Performed General duties of a farmer such as planting and operating farm." Somehow over the years my old herd of cows got inflated.

We lived at first in a trailer park in Columbus, Indiana. I'd hitched the car, a 1949 Nash, to the trailer and hauled it down there from Illinois. That was some trip, because the car wasn't made to pull a trailer.

I commuted between Columbus and Camp Atterbury. That was where Hazel first learned what a "GI party" was—a general scrubbing and cleaning of the barracks. I never thought to explain to her what it was, and I suppose thousands of Army wives went through the same learning process at that time. She couldn't understand why she had to stay home with the kids while I was out at this "party," where I stayed all night. In those days even married men who lived off post had a room or a bunk in the barracks, which they were supposed to keep straight, and when the Friday-night scrubbing and cleaning for Saturday-morning inspection came around, we were expected to participate.

I was a platoon sergeant* in addition to being I&E NCO and was responsible for a little cadre room right at the top of the stairs. I'd clean—"GI," it was called**—my floor and three

---

*This was a school platoon with sixty men; an infantry platoon has about thirty men.

**The term "GI" comes from "government issue," and often is used to mean an American soldier. "GI" is also used as an adjective, as in "GI can," a galvanized-steel trash can, and "GI brush," a wooden brush with stiff bristles. Thus a "GI party" is where GIs—soldiers—use GI brushes and GI cans to clean up their barracks.

boards outside my door and tell the men that when the rest of the floor matched those three boards, we were done. I really set the standard, and after a few times we had the best barracks around.

That's how I got to be the company first sergeant. As such I was responsible for the cleanliness of the barracks and the company area, the conduct of the troops, presentation of the unit for inspections, and company administration. Administration included preparing the morning report (the daily report that documented the status of the men in the unit), making up duty rosters (kitchen police, charge of quarters, etc.), and posting various work details (cleanup and other duties).

But a good first sergeant is much more than just a noncommissioned jack of all trades. I saw those three hundred men in that school company much more frequently than their commander did, and it was my job to know how they felt about things, what was going well with them and what wasn't. When there was a disciplinary or morale problem in the company, I always knew about it first, and it was my duty to keep bad situations from growing worse. I tried to fix things at the source, before the company commander had to take action. This is just what any good NCO does, whether he or she is responsible for a squad, platoon, or an entire company of troops.

As I mentioned earlier, the school was split between the Air Force and the Army, so I became the first sergeant on the Army side. A guy by the name of John Knox was first sergeant on the Air Force side. John was as big as a barn. That was in the days before weight-control programs became so common in the military. He kept a bucket by the side of his desk full of ice water wherein he'd stash eight or ten bottles of pop, and he'd drink all that pop before the day was out. He'd sit at his typewriter in the mornings doing his morning report, using two fingers, going along tat-a-tat-a-tat, making forty words a minute, and soon you'd hear him slow down and eventually stop entirely, and in a few more moments he'd be snoring away, sound asleep.

That was where I ran into Col. "Monk" Meyer, one of a colorful and eccentric breed of officer that was still around to some degree after World War II. An All-American at West Point and a real jock, he had been an assistant division commander in World War II. But when I encountered him his passion in life was the fire lights we had over the doors of the barracks. He was buggy about fire lights. Monk Meyer and his fire lights—sounds like a good name for a band. If those lights weren't out when the sun came up, old Monk would let the offending unit's orderly room know about it. He lived in one of those sets of colonel's quarters, small bungalows actually, that used to be so common on Army posts. His happened to be right at the end of our company street.

Well, Colonel Meyer raised sand one day with my company commander, and I told the CO I'd take care of the problem. By then Hazel and I had moved our trailer onto Camp Atterbury. That reduced our rent from $22 a month to only $6 a month, a big deal in those days, especially on my pay of only $191 a month plus $77.10 a month for quarters. And living on post, I was able to walk to work. I arrived this one morning before dawn in the company area. I told the CQ—the charge of quarters, the man assigned to stay on duty in the orderly room overnight—to get a cardboard box, and before the sun was up, I had the bulbs from all those offending fire lights stowed behind my desk in the orderly room. I knew damn well none were still on in my company area that morning. It was a pain in the neck to put them all back in at the end of the day, but it kept old Monk Meyer off the CO's ass.

The third morning we'd been doing this, Colonel Meyer called the CO and informed him, "Your goddamn fire lights are on again!"

The captain came running down to the orderly room and confronted me. "I thought you said you were going to take care of those fire lights," the captain said.

I assured him there were no fire lights on in his company that morning. He wanted to know how I was so sure, and I showed him all the bulbs in the cardboard box behind my desk. "How about letting *me* go talk to the colonel?" I suggested.

"Be my guest!" he replied.

So I reported to the colonel. "We've been on this fire light business long enough. You guys ought to be able to get them out in the mornings."

I said, "Sir, there are no fire lights on in my company."

"Don't tell me that! I can see one, right there," and he pointed out his window. I told him what he was seeing was not a fire light. He said, "Look. I know what a fire light looks like, and *that's* a fire light!"

"I beg your pardon, sir, but it is not a fire light. I *know* there are none on in this company. That's the light in the shower room." I invited him to walk down there and see for himself.

We got about a hundred yards down the street and he admitted he was wrong. "How were you so sure the light was out?" he asked, and I told him. He never called us again and we didn't have to take the bulbs out anymore.

This story illustrates a principle I've followed all my life. When you know you're right, never back down. You'd be surprised how many powerful and autocratic people cave in when confronted by someone who stands up for himself.

I stayed at Camp Atterbury about two years and then was transferred to Fort Sheridan, Illinois. While I was there, the time came for me to get out or reenlist. If I went back to farming, I'd have to start all over again, from scratch, because I'd lost everything when I was recalled. And in the intervening years the cost of establishing a new farm had also risen way beyond my means. I told my CO I wanted to reenlist in the Regular Army. I was a Reservist, remember, and a Regular Army enlistment would indicate to the Army that I wanted to dedicate myself to a military career.

Fifth Army Headquarters told me I could reenlist in the Regular Army, but as a *corporal*. I told my company commander how unfair I thought that proposal was. I explained that every promotion I'd ever gotten had been while on active duty. I had never been a corporal—I'd gone from private first class to buck sergeant, back when the company commander could do that—and I wasn't about to be one now. I wrote a letter to Fifth Army, and he endorsed it for me. I told them the whole story and how I felt about their proposal, adding that I'd never been a corporal and thought it was too late to start now. Fifth Army approved my reenlistment in my then current grade. My total pay as an SFC E-6 was about $268 per month.

Because I wasn't too sure how long I'd stay at Fort Sheridan, I took Hazel back to Williamsfield and we parked our trailer behind her mother's house. Every weekend or two I'd go home from Chicago. I remained at Fort Sheridan a year and a half, with the Fifth Army Food Service School, where I was by then the personnel sergeant. After a short while I moved Hazel and the girls up there with me, and in August 1953 we were transferred to Fort Riley, Kansas.

So that is how I got into the Regular Army. At the time, if I thought any about staying in the Army for a career, I probably considered myself a "twenty-thirty man"—that is, I was going to stay in twenty years and thirty minutes, the thirty minutes being all the time it would take me to grab my retirement and run.

As it happened, things turned out a little differently.

≡ 4 ≡

SEAGULL SUPPERS AND CPXs

In August 1953 we traveled from Fort Sheridan, Illinois, to Fort Riley, Kansas, in a convoy of house trailers. Ten or twelve families who owned mobile homes at Fort Sheridan and had orders to go to Fort Riley got together, as soldiers will, and traveled in a group.

Before leaving we looked around for the best deal on trailer licenses. I found that the cheapest license was offered by the state of Mississippi, $2 for a mobile home trailer license. I picked out a county at random and wrote to the sheriff and tax collector there—in Yazoo City, Yazoo County, Mississippi. I got a form letter back that informed me that since I was not a resident of the state I couldn't register my trailer there. But down at the bottom somebody had penned in, "However, send $2 to the Sheriff and Tax Collector and we will register your trailer." About fifteen of us registered our trailers in Yazoo County. I kept that $2 license for the next eight or nine years. I found out later on that being a resident of Illinois, I could have gotten a free one, since I was moving on government orders.

We closed up the school at Fort Sheridan, and Fort Riley became the Fifth Army Food Service School, where we trained cooks, meat cutters, mess sergeants, and bakers. I was the school first sergeant. As first sergeant I worked for and reported to the company commander, while as sergeant major I was responsible to the school commandant.

We had twenty-four master sergeants (pay grade E-7) on the staff as instructors, and I was only a sergeant first class (pay grade E-6). All those sergeants were cooks, bakers, butchers, etc., and they didn't want the first sergeant's job. The school sergeant major was Jimmy Wagers. He was a master sergeant, because in those days the Army didn't have a special grade for sergeant major—that didn't happen until 1959. Sergeant major was only a temporary title that the man left behind when he left the unit or got another job within that unit. When Wagers transferred out, I became the school sergeant major.

I gradually came to regard my grade—SFC, pay grade E-6—as permanent, because I was to hold it for the next ten years. Lest anyone think I was some kind of dud in those days, at least thirty different times during that period my recommendation for promotion to master sergeant was forwarded to the promotion authorities, but there just weren't many allocations for promotion to master sergeant in the Army at that time. The Korean War was ending, and the Army had more master sergeants than it knew what to do with, so there were few promotions.

We did have what were called "blood stripes," or promotions that occurred when someone in a unit lost a stripe and it was then given to the man next in line for promotion. The company commander could promote men up to the grade of corporal (E-4) or sergeant (E-5). The "top three grades"—staff sergeant, sergeant first class, and master sergeant—received their promotion allocations from the Department of the Army through the numbered army—Fifth Army, in my case—and what was available then passed to the post commander, who convened the promotion boards at his level.

We lived in the little town of Ogden, Kansas. In the 1950s, there were family quarters at most posts, but not nearly enough. That's why Hazel and I had bought the trailer in the first place. At the trailer court where we lived, I managed the place for the owner, who was an Army lieutenant colonel named Stillinger. This got me free rent and free utilities, and all I had to do was collect the rent from others, make sure the grass got cut, and keep the area policed.* In those days, there were very seldom many empty spaces in a trailer court. This particular one abutted the post boundary, so it was a prime spot. As mentioned before, as an SFC with over five years in the service, my total pay was $268 a month, so the break on rent and

---

*"Police" is a basic Army word meaning to clean or to clean up. Originally it extended to camp sanitation and the general control of the living condition of the troops, but since World War II its use has been narrowed to such mundane activities as picking up the trash around the barracks or a living area. Thus a "police call" is a formal detail of troops formed for the purpose of removing trash from a designated area.

utilities was very important to us, even if it did require some extra work after duty and on weekends.

I was at the Fifth Army school for about five years. We had about three hundred students enrolled in the various courses at any given time. I did everything expected of a first sergeant, including arranging for transportation for the students—getting their tickets and so on.

We graduated most of the students who came to us. For the most part, they were educable men who did well; many of them were already cooks and mess sergeants in the units they had come from anyway. We figured that if the units in the field sent these men to us to train them, the least we could do was get the job done. Whenever a man did have trouble, the commandant would convene a board to review his case.

That was a good time, and I learned a lot there. We had a records keeper by the name of Cornelius Bradyhoff. Cornelius was an old-time master sergeant who'd been in the Army twenty or twenty-five years at that time. A couple of the instructors, as a joke, phonied up a grade sheet for a fictitious student named Mickey Mantel, and they ran that grade sheet all the way up to the sixth week of the course, when the board had to meet to review Mantel's academic standing, because it was so low. Old Bradyhoff produced Mickey Mantel's grade sheet and announced, "I knew this SOB wasn't going to be a good student when he first got here." He really didn't know one student from another, but the guys who pulled this stunt thought for sure he'd catch on before the phony grades went to the board. Fortunately, the full board never got to review Mickey's record.

That story also illustrates the quality of the noncommissioned officers the Army had in those days. We had a guy by the name of Jim Paulus, a dryly humorous guy from Missouri somewhere, who was a master of repartee. Those were the days of a uniform the Army called Bermuda shorts—they were knee-length khaki shorts worn with long, sand-colored knee socks and were probably one of the most useless and ugly uniforms the Army's ever had.

Well, one day Jim was wearing them and someone said, "Jim, you've got the ugliest knees I've ever seen. Why do you wear those shorts?"

Jim just turned around and looked at him and said, "Well, I'll tell ya, you got the ugliest face I ever saw, but I just got my knees out during the summer and you got your face out all year around." No more comments about Jim's knees.

It was at Fort Riley I received the worst ass-chewing I've ever had. One day we had a sale bill come through the office. In that part of the country, every winter somebody goes out of business or somebody dies and they have a farm sale. The sale bill is just a list of things that are available for purchase. Well, this particular bill was a fake with political overtones. I remember one item on the sale bill was a farm mower listed as "Dulles hell," a play on the name of John Foster Dulles, then our Secretary of State. Eisenhower was President at the time.

Coming from the farm, I thought it was pretty funny, but I made a real strategic error: I put the distribution stamp on the thing and sent it through the company commander all the way up to the commandant, a lieutenant colonel named Crocker. I got a lesson on politics in the service.

Colonel Crocker appeared before my desk at about a quarter to one that day and let me know that politics and soldiering don't mix. I don't know if he was a Democrat or a Republican, but he told us there was no room for politics, even as a joke, in his unit. Needless to say, no more sale bills, fake or otherwise, ever got across my desk again, particularly with an official distribution stamp on them.

I really felt sorry for my company commander, Capt. Robert A. Berg, a hell of a fine young officer. I've kept in touch with him all these years. He and some other officers had initialed the thing and sent it on, and when it got to the commandant's office, they were in trouble too. I felt bad about it because I thought I'd let my CO down.

Captain Berg, incidentally, replaced a man whom we called Captain Clink. Captain Clink was an alcoholic. He kept at least two bottles of vodka in his desk drawer. Every Monday he'd bring in this little canvas bag, which would clink as the bottles in there knocked against each other. Three or four times a day he'd come to the door and say, "Hey, Top,* I've got a couple of things I've got to go over here, so I don't want to be disturbed for a while." He'd close his door and everything would get real quiet in the orderly room. I could hear his desk drawer open and his mess cup hit the desk, and we wouldn't see him for the next half hour or so. That was one of those sad situations that happen every so often. He didn't last long; within a few months he was forced out of the Army.

*Short for "top sergeant," a traditional nickname for first sergeants and sergeants major—the "top" sergeants in an outfit.

Captain Berg was an ROTC officer. He was one of those people who fall in with a unit as naturally as if they'd been born there, but there's never any doubt they're in charge.

After I'd been first sergeant for about four months, he came out one day and said, "Top, I've noticed that the company punishment has fallen off dramatically. What do you attribute that to?"

I reminded him that when he'd appointed me as first sergeant he'd told me to handle things, and I said that I'd been taking care of company discipline ever since.

He said, "Shut the door! Top," he began, "do you mean *you've* been giving out company punishment?"

"No, sir, I have not," I told him, "but what I have been doing is telling the men, 'Look, you can work for me for seven days or fifteen for the Old Man, so take your pick.' "

Well, of course they'd all been taking my informal seven-day punishment tours.

In those days, company punishment, which could only be administered by the CO, consisted of two hours of extra duty every day for seven to fifteen days, and a record of the action was made and filed in the company punishment book, which was kept for two years or until the man departed, whichever happened first. I'd offered the men a real bargain. I figured if I could straighten out errant soldiers without putting anything in their records, then that's what I ought to do. That worked very well. We got all the little details done, but we did it in seven days instead of fifteen, there wasn't any administrative work to it, and Captain Berg was satisfied.

Here's an example of how that informal system worked. In those days everyone had a pass and we had a pass board on which to hang them that covered a whole wall. It was a job just to keep them up. The men would have to come in and return their passes to the proper place on the board, or if they happened to return after the orderly room had closed, put them in a slot in the door. Then next morning the charge of quarters would have to take those passes and put them up on the board himself. And if a pass wasn't put back in the right place, finding it again was another problem.

Well, I was never able to get rid of the pass board, but I did use it very effectively as company punishment. In those days we had bed check every night. The CQ would go through the barracks after lights out and report the name of any man who wasn't in his bed and had no excuse for being elsewhere. Missing bed check was automatic company punishment. The first time we gave the man a verbal reprimand; second time we'd give him a little extra manual labor in the company; but the third time he had to bring his bunk down to the orderly room and set it up right after dinner *under the pass board.* All night long, guys would come in and put their passes up there, and needless to say, the offender didn't get much sleep. But he never missed bed check again either.

We also knew how to educate our officers. Sergeants teach young officers all the things really worth knowing in the Army, especially at the company level.

In those days you were supposed to report in to your new unit in uniform. Well, one Thursday afternoon here came this young fellow in civilian clothes. I was busy trying to get transportation for a group of graduating students when this guy came in and asked if he'd found the service school. I looked up and said, "Can't you see I'm busy? And besides, didn't you see the sign on the door that says 'Knock and Wait for Your Turn'? So just move back out into the hall."

Finally I called him in and discovered that he was a lieutenant, reporting in for the officers' course. I reminded him of the requirement to report in uniform. "And second, you didn't act like an officer when you came in here, and third, if you think I'm going to apologize for jumping on you, forget it, because you were wrong. Now what can I do for you?"

Monday he walked in again in civilian clothes and wanted to know what the return address of the school was. He asked Sergeant Major Wagers the question, and Jimmy said, "Obviously, you can read, young man, and it is posted on the bulletin board— that's why we have one. So move back out there to the bulletin board and it'll give the address to you."

When this lieutenant went to the supply room to draw cook's whites for a practical exercise, he was again in his civilian clothes. There was a sign above the counter announcing that soldiers had to report in uniform to draw supplies. The supply sergeant, SFC Vernon Reed, told him, "You can read the sign. Now get your ass out of here, and when you come back looking like a soldier, I'll talk to you."

At the end of the course, students were given a critique sheet and asked to list the things they liked and didn't like about the school. This lieutenant was a good officer. He wrote: "I found out one thing around here. Just because it's a school, you'd better not forget your military courtesy and bearing *and do what the signs say!*"

* * *

In 1956 SGM Wagers retired and I became the school sergeant major. In January 1958 the whole school was transferred to Fort Leonard Wood, Missouri, about 120 miles southwest of St. Louis. We became a company-size operation within a battalion of the 4th Training Regiment at Leonard Wood. That was the regiment that trained all the specialties. We had dropped the meat-cutting course by then and only trained cooks, bakers, and a few mess sergeants.

To make the move I borrowed my father-in-law's pickup truck. The unit itself trucked down, and some of the cadre flew. A lot of our equipment we left behind at Fort Riley, and we were issued new stuff at Fort Leonard Wood.

Since there was no position for a sergeant major in a company-size unit, I was transferred to the 3rd Battalion as the operations sergeant. This battalion taught what were referred to as "common subjects," such as the food service course, field wireman course, truck driver's course, and mechanic's course. This was my first experience on a special staff.*

As the operations sergeant, I did class scheduling and coordinated all the lesson plans—the POIs, or programs of instruction—for all the courses. Each POI was different, and my job was to ensure that they followed the manuals. At least once a week I'd monitor every course being conducted. I got along very well with the instructors. We had a battalion sergeant major by the name of Markham who made it clear that everything would come through me as operations sergeant. The most I knew about cooking was how to eat, but I handled the administration of those courses well.

In the Army, loyalties run deep, and just because I was up at the 3rd Battalion now didn't mean I'd lost all interest in my old company. One day my old company, Company K, got a new commander. The guys all began complaining about him, how he just didn't have any feel for the soldiers, and they just didn't know what to do with him. The cadre asked me to figure some way to help them communicate with this officer. Well, one day I was driving down to the mess hall to pick up the guys who shared the car pool we'd formed at our trailer court, and I saw the new com-

---

*The Army staff is designated as either special or general. The special staff assists the commanders of battalions and regiments; the general staff is found at division, corps, and army level. The special staff consists of a personnel officer (S-1), intelligence officer (S-2), operations officer (S-3), and supply or logistics officer (S-4). The general staff is organized in the same manner except the respective staff sections are larger and are designated G-1, G-2, G-3, and G-4.

pany commander standing out there. He jumped in my car and asked me to drive him around the block one time.

During that little spin he gave me the other side of the story. To him it seemed his first sergeant wasn't supporting him and the instructors were down on him and he couldn't get any cooperation from anybody. I asked him if he'd ever considered that maybe he was the one who was out of place. I reminded him that he had twenty-five or thirty top-notch NCOs in his outfit and they were all down on him. I suggested he listen to what they had to say, because, I told him, "They think you're a no-good SOB." He said, "Drive around the block one more time!"

About three weeks later I had another session with this officer. In the meantime, the NCOs had already told me how he'd turned completely around—they could talk to him now and he was listening to what they had to say. "Whatever you said to him, we appreciate it," they said. Their CO, for his part, told me how much better he was getting along with his cadre since we'd had our little talk.

To be an effective noncommissioned officer you've got to be honest and straightforward with your superiors as well as with your peers and subordinates. My feel for the soldiers helped my old outfit and this new company commander too. He just wanted to be king and he couldn't be, without listening to the jacks and the queens too. I never saw him again after I left Fort Leonard Wood—he was Quartermaster Corps, and I never served with the QMC again after that assignment—but I was happy that I could help that young officer at a time in his career when he needed help badly.

I got my first award coming out of that battalion—my first Army Commendation Medal, after ten years in the Army. In those days you had to have at least a year in the unit before you could qualify for an award for meritorious service, and I was a couple of months shy of meeting the requirement. But my battalion commander wrote up an outstanding recommendation and it went through anyway.

Awards like that were a big thing in those days, because they were hard to get. The Army Commendation Medal, which then ranked between the Good Conduct and the Bronze Star medals, was about the only peacetime award for achievement an enlisted man could get.

I spent about a year at Fort Leonard Wood. We lived in a trailer court outside the post. There was this master sergeant who'd bought a place up along I-66, and for developing it for him—

clearing the land, taking out the tree stumps, and building the forms for our patios—he gave us two months' free rent. That was a big deal. So we built our own trailer court.

There wasn't a heck of a lot for Hazel to do around Fort Leonard Wood, because we were really out in the sticks. She went out with the Girl Scouts on one occasion and got into chiggers so bad that she was in bed for a week. They get up under your skin and die and then cause infections. Poor Hazel looked like a beet. The doctor gave her calamine lotion, but the only thing that gave her any relief was Aqua Velva shaving lotion. The alcohol base helped dry up the bites, and it had a soothing, cooling effect on the itching. The doctor had warned her that there wasn't much he could do and she would just have to tough the thing out, and that's what she did, without making a big fuss out of it. If it had been me, I'd have been raising hell all the time during those miserable days.

Both the girls were attending public school in Waynesville, Missouri. Mary had started grade school at Ogden, Kansas, and as it turned out, when we got back from Europe three years later, she finished grade school there.

We went from Fort Leonard Wood to Europe in February 1959. My turn had come up for an overseas assignment, and I was ready to go. We had to report to Fort Hamilton, New York, so we went home for Christmas of 1958 and moved the trailer to my brother's place in Oquawka, Illinois, down on the Mississippi, and stored it on his lot there.

We made the drive to Fort Hamilton, our port of embarkation, in our old 1953 Buick. Before we left I took it down to the Harvey brothers, who ran an auto shop in Galesburg—still do, but they've moved to the outskirts of town now—and asked them to time the engine so it'd burn the 80-octane GI gas they sold to us in Europe.

The winter weather during that trip to New York was sloppy and dirty, and I promised myself before it was over that the next car I got would have a windshield washer. The muddy, slushy muck that the trucks and other cars threw up on the windshield solidified there, and my wipers just couldn't handle it. Hazel had a Lilt home permanent bottle with her, and I filled it with water and at intervals I'd stick it out the window on my side and squirt the water on the windshield, and that's the way we traveled down the Pennsylvania Turnpike to New York.

This was our first long trip as a family, and the girls traveled well. They fought with each other all the way, but that's universal among kids.

While on the road I wore a greasy old hunting cap I'd used when working around the car. It had earflaps and I thought it would be useful on the trip. When we checked out of our hotel in New York after turning the car in to have it shipped overseas, I decided to get rid of that hat, so I kicked it under the bed. Well, when they brought the luggage down to the desk as we were checking out, there was that hat, sitting on top of our suitcases. The porter told me he always checked the rooms thoroughly whenever GIs stayed there because they were constantly leaving things behind.

I said, "Thank you very much."

In the taxi, on the way to the ocean terminal, I stuffed that cap under the driver's seat. After we'd paid the cabbie and were walking away with our bags, he called out, "Wait! Wait! You forgot your cap!"

I said, "Thank you very much."

After the ship got out into New York Harbor, I finally got rid of that damn cap—I took it out on the fantail and tossed it as far over the side as I could. It may have polluted the ocean a little, but I did get rid of it at last.

We sailed to Europe courtesy of the Military Sealift Command's troopship the USNS *Goethals*. There were a number of these ships that plied the Atlantic between New York and Bremerhaven in those days, among them the USNS *General Simon B. Buckner, H. W. Butner, William O. Darby, Walter H. Gordon, William A. Mann, Alexander M. Patch, G. M. Randall, Maurice Rose,* and *Nelson A. Wilker.* Our ship was named in honor of General George Washington Goethals, the man who built the Panama Canal. Hardly anybody flew to Europe or the Far East in those days.

Our passage took us five or six days on the North Atlantic route, and it was really messy. At that time of the year, February, the North Atlantic has heavy seas. A couple of days there were times when it was so rough they wouldn't even let us out on deck. Poor Kathy was seasick all the way across, although none of the rest of us was.

We had a stateroom down around the waterline of the ship. We didn't even have a porthole to look out of. I didn't have any troop details to perform, though, as you might expect an NCO to have, since I was traveling with my family. Each of us had a single bunk, and there was a sink in the stateroom. We traveled pretty fancy, compared to the unaccompanied soldiers.

About the last day out, Kathy thought she could choke down some solid food at breakfast. Mary was sitting right across from her. The stewards served us the cereal by putting the milk in the bowl first. Mary picked up her bowl of milk, sloshed its contents around, and said, "Look, Kathy, back and forth, back and forth," and poor Kathy jumped up and almost didn't make it to the head.

I'd eaten standing up on my World War II crossings, but now we ate sitting down, and we had a steward who really took care of the girls. When we had chicken he'd tell them it was seagull, to try to get them to eat, because he knew if they had something in their stomachs they were less likely to get seasick. Since our stateroom was right at the waterline, the center of the ship, the motion was minimized, and Kathy only had bad spells when she moved around. She was able to sleep all right. Kathy still suffers from motion sickness.

There wasn't much to do aboard ship except read and watch the occasional movie. The kids had Freddy the Freeloader, a pet turtle they'd brought with them from Fort Leonard Wood. We carried him in a little matchbox, got him through customs, and had him with us for several years before we finally sounded Taps for him. The girls buried him in the yard of our quarters at Patch Barracks with "full honors."

From Bremerhaven we took a train to Stuttgart. I was assigned to VII Corps. My family, however, was placed in temporary quarters in Munich, three hours by car from Stuttgart. I had three or four days to take them to Warner Kaserne in Munich, where I got them settled into Building 1745, which I'll never forget, because that was my speciality number* as an infantry rifleman.

On the fourth floor of those quarters, we had a kitchen, two bathrooms, a little sitting area, and eight bedrooms. We'd been put up in what had been the maids' quarters when the structure was built after the war. We were there about ninety days. I was very fortunate, because I got to travel back and forth on the weekends. It was about a three-hour drive on the autobahn—you could drive just about as fast as your car would go. Going along the straightaways or down the hills, all the Volkswagens would pass me, but going up the hills I'd pass them. Of course, I made the trip by train the first three or four weeks, until the car arrived. I traveled

---

*This is the number code used by the Army to identify each soldier's job skill. Today the codes are alphanumeric, i.e., 11B for rifleman. Other numbers are added to the basic designator to indicate skill level and special qualifications.

with Walt Irish, who was the corps G-2 sergeant major. We were to become great friends with Walt and his wife, Ilse.

After three months we moved to Patch Barracks in Stuttgart, into the same kind of temporary quarters as we'd had at Warner Kaserne, about twenty minutes from my duty station, Kelley Barracks. It wasn't until about nine months after we arrived in Germany that we finally got permanent quarters. I've dwelt on this subject because family housing is very important to soldiers of all ranks, especially the younger ones. In the eight years since I'd come back into the Army, Hazel and I had moved five times and then twice more in the first nine months we were in Germany. You get used to it, but it's never easy, and once you finally get settled someplace you know that after two or three years at the most you'll have to do it all over again. Although it does alter your routine and place a hardship on school-age children, it can also strengthen the family as a unit and is definitely a character-builder.

During the time we spent in Europe we had very little disposable income, like most military families of the day. We made a decision we wouldn't buy any of the trinkets that seem to fascinate so many Americans in Germany. Although we did buy a few Hummels, we spent most of our spare money on trips all over Europe. We visited Holland just before Easter one year, when all the flowers were in bloom, but there weren't the crowds that flock there during the tulip season. We had a hotel reservation in Amsterdam on that trip, and right outside the city we asked a passing bicyclist for directions. He volunteered to take us there, but took us to a place that wasn't our hotel at all. He'd been guiding us to get a tip, which he didn't. But as luck would have it, we drove along another two blocks, made a turn, and stopped right in front of the place.

On these trips we'd always get extra ration stamps for gasoline. Gas was so expensive in Europe in those days that GIs were authorized to purchase their fuel from U.S. Army quartermaster supplies. We got an extra twenty gallons and carried them in the trunk of our car. We could never get the cans sealed very tightly, so we were always accompanied by the smell of raw gasoline as we drove along. It was dangerous as hell, but it was the only way you could travel around in those days without spending a fortune for gas.

We discovered afterward that we'd done the right thing to see Europe that way. The girls were able to experience a lot of things while they were young but old enough to remember all the wonderful sights.

Also, Hazel worked with the Girl Scouts, and during that tour she took her troop to England, Switzerland, and other places, including Berchtesgaden in Bavaria.

Our quarters were located at Vaihingen, a suburb of Stuttgart, where Seventh Army Headquarters was situated. VII Corps Headquarters was over at Moehringen, another suburb of Stuttgart. That was where I had my first run-in with a billeting office. I was in temporary quarters, my second set of temporaries at Stuttgart, and I was trying to find out where I was on the list for permanent quarters assignment.

My name had finally worked its way up to No. 2, and I told Hazel it looked like maybe a week or so and we'd be in permanent quarters at last. Two or three weeks passed, and still nothing. I called the billeting office, and the clerk asked me to wait while she checked the list. She came back on a moment later and announced that I was No. 21 on the list. I pointed out that I had been No. 2 only a couple of weeks ago—how could I now be No. 21? I was told, "That's just the way it is." I thanked her and hung up the telephone.

I got permission from the corps G-3 to go over to the billeting office at Robinson Barracks. I saw the same clerk I'd talked to on the phone and asked her again why I'd gone from No. 2 to No. 21 on the list.

"Well, this guy is ahead of you," she explained.

"Why is he ahead of me?" I asked.

"Well, because he was . . ."

I told her that sounded contrary to the rules to me, and I asked to see her supervisor. I wound up going all the way to the billeting officer. I told him the same story.

He admitted there seemed to be something wrong. "You should have been in quarters long before now," he said.

"That's why I'm over here to see you," I replied. "Fair is fair. If somebody is supposed to move in ahead of me, that's okay, but I just don't believe all those people were supposed to be jumped up the list ahead of me."

He did some checking while I waited, and when he came back into his office he said, "You'll be moving next week, Sergeant Bainbridge. You're No. 1 on the list as of right now."

I never did find out what was going on, but I suppose some clerk was juggling the names at his or her convenience. The clerks were German civilians. Anyway, I got that squared away, and I'm sure it stayed squared away. I don't know how many other families got cheated as we did, but the lesson here is that in the Army, if you think you're being treated unfairly and you're willing to stick to your guns, you can always find somebody high up enough to redress the situation. But you've got to stick to it, be polite but firm, and just not take no for an answer.

Our permanent quarters were located at Patch Barracks, and that put me only twenty minutes from work by car. We had a three-bedroom apartment on the second floor of a four-floor apartment complex that contained probably thirty or forty apartments.

The ranking guy in each stairwell was designated the "stairwell coordinator" and the ranking NCO in the building was appointed "building coordinator," so there was a kind of chain of command. It worked very well to solve the minor problems you always have in such places, problems with children, wives, and husbands, the normal events of community living.

The building had a basement, and each stairwell had its own washing-machine room. There was a drying room upstairs. I bought a Norge washing machine from the corps G-3, Col. Ellis "Butch" Williamson. It was a 110-volt machine. In Europe the current was normally 220 volts at 50 cycles. In the washrooms the outlets were wired for 110 volts, but the rest of the electrical outlets in the building were for 220 volts at 50 cycles. In order to use American appliances you had to have several step-down transformers, which seemed to weigh ninety pounds each. But these transformers couldn't change the cycle, and that was bad for things that ran on motors designed for 60-cycle current, like tape recorders, and clocks. The Norge had been rewired to operate on 50-cycle current.

That Norge washer was a great machine, but you almost had to chain it down when it was in use, because it vibrated so much it would walk right on the floor on you. Damnedest thing I ever saw.

We were at VII Corps three and a half years. I started out as the noncommissioned officer in charge (NCOIC) of classified documents. You talk about a bear of a job. I don't know how many documents we had in the G-3 shop,* but there were lots of them. Right across the hall was the top secret control officer, a

---

*The G-3 in an Army headquarters is the general staff officer responsible for training, plans, and tactical operations.

warrant officer, but I had all the secret and confidential material. In those days you had to log everything. We had half a dozen different branch offices checking those documents out all the time. Some of those things were huge volumes with appendices, annexes, tabs, maps, and enclosures.

There was this one major named Forbes, a hell of a good officer but an impatient man. One time he checked out a secret plan from me, and when he wanted to return it a few days later, he was missing Annex C. I remember it was Annex C because it was the last one in the document, and when I signed them back in I had to check each page, because every page classified secret had to be accounted for. I told Major Forbes I couldn't accept the document because it was missing the annex.

"Well, it wasn't there when I signed for it," he said.

I pointed out to him on the receipt he'd signed that it said "w/Annex A, B, C." "C is missing," I told him. "You got it. I am not taking the document back, sir."

He said, "I'm telling you, take it back, *now*."

"Major Forbes, I'm sorry," I said. "I do not want to be disrespectful or insubordinate, but I am not taking that document back. You know the rules, sir."

At that moment Colonel Vogelsang, the G-3 executive officer, called out from his office nearby, "Hey, Forbes!"

Forbes answered, "Yes, sir?"

"You don't need to come in—just go back and find that Annex C," Colonel Vogelsang hollered out.

Forbes stomped back to his office, and about an hour later he came back with the missing annex. I know he found it after only five minutes, but he just had to wait the extra time. I asked him if he'd found it on his desk. "Yeah, on the desk," he grumbled as I signed for the document. I never had another problem with Major Forbes.

We were right down the hall from the corps chief of staff's office, and it always seemed that the G-3 executive officer was going in there for something or other, usually late in the afternoon, and I would wait until he got back before locking up the office. One day Colonel Vogelsang came back from up front and found that I had rearranged his desk for him. I'd installed three boxes, one labeled "Look at This Before You Go Home," another "Look at This Anytime," and the third "Don't Bother." He'd been back maybe half an hour when he came back out and told me, "Sergeant Bainbridge, you continue using those boxes. That system will save me a lot of trouble, and maybe from now on we can get out of here on time."

I did that on my own, figuring that if someone screened his incoming minutia for him it would save him work. I knew enough about what was going on, what the G-3's concerns were, that I could make those judgments, and he bought the concept.

I spent a year as the document control NCO and then became the operations sergeant in the operations division, working for Lt. Col. Paul A. Baltes. He'd been an enlisted engineer in World War II and had decided that wasn't what he wanted to do, so he got a commission in the cavalry. He still lives up around Indiantown Gap, Pennsylvania. I had a great working relationship with this officer. He had a son as a cadet at West Point during this time, and the boy was really having problems. His tactical officers were writing to the colonel, asking him to advise the lad. Colonel Baltes made a couple of trips back on leave to West Point from Stuttgart, and Paul Jr. graduated.

I also doubled as the G-3 air NCO, and when we went to the field I doubled as the G-3 air officer, because we didn't have an officer to do it. The G-3 air is the staff officer who coordinates the Army operations with the air liaison officer, an Air Force officer, and they plan the air strikes and how the Air Force is going to support the ground troops. So when we had an exercise I'd run my shift, and invariably the air annex to the operations plan would come in from Seventh Army after I'd gotten off and I'd have to get up and write the annex to the VII Corps operations plan.

We performed two types of exercises, field and command post. A command post exercise (CPX) doesn't involve the deployment of any troops, only the headquarters, but VII Corps would always go to the field anyway. That could be anyplace—Hohenfels or Grafenwoehr training centers or just into the local woods. We'd set up the headquarters out there, just as we would if we had troops in the field too, but all the maneuvers were done on the maps. We'd "jump" the command post from one spot to another, just as we would have done it in wartime. It always seemed that the jumps came just as I was getting off a shift and I'd have to run the jump command post to the new location. In other words, I'd have to run to the new location, set up the communications, and get everything ready for the main body to catch up and settle in.

A field training exercise (FTX) involved the whole corps and actual troop maneuvers with equipment. We'd run CPXs three or four times a year and FTXs a couple of times a year. We spent probably four months out of the year in the field on one kind of exercise or another. What determined the frequency of those exercises was the availability of money, particularly for gasoline, and logistical support.

VII Corps always went to the field, but V Corps set its CPXs up in Frankfurt. We used to call them the "Paper Corps." It was not until 1975, when I was Sergeant Major of the Army, that I learned that there were front gates to the Grafenwoehr and Hohenfels training centers. I thought you had to get to them through the woods. I had never made it to the cantonment or main post area at either place.

We made several innovations while I was at VII Corps. We initially went into the field using two general-purpose medium-size tents (GP mediums), one for the G-3 (operations) and the other for the G-2 (intelligence). A big metal-framed tent, intended for work on trucks and tanks and stuff in the field, was used as our war room. Then we graduated from that setup to a hospital tent with two end modules and as many other sections as were required.

Later we went into expandable vans mounted on two-and-a-half-ton trucks. We could have all our communications inside and could drive out to the field in them, phones all set up. They were heated, really first-class field headquarters accommodations. All we had to do was plug them into the communications net and we were ready to start work. The only problem with those vans was that they were underpowered and top-heavy, so you had to be careful how you drove them. They made CPX/FTX life better for all of us.

We used three of those vans, one for the G-3, another for the G-2, and in the center would be the war-room van. That was so much better than moving those tents. When I first got to VII Corps we would have seven or eight truckloads of equipment—tents for living and working accommodations, office equipment, everything needed to operate the headquarters sections for an indefinite period—just for the G-3, so the tail was really wagging the dog. We'd haul wooden duckboards by the truckload, so people would be up out of the mud when we set up. In actual wartime the practice is to take over whatever buildings are available, but we couldn't do that in Germany, so we had to take our accommodations with us on exercises. By using those vans and preloading a few trucks, we could move out quicker and set up a lot faster.

We also had operations alerts at least once a month. When they were called we never knew if we'd be in the field for a few weeks or come right back into garrison, so when we moved out on alerts we had to take everything. Alerts would usually come between eleven-thirty at night and three in the morning. We'd move to the assembly area and wait for further orders, and then if it was decided we wouldn't go to the field after all, we'd return to the garrison, but it would take us until about seven that night to get everything unloaded and back into place. We were working "half days" in those times—that is, fifteen-hour days.

I finally was promoted from sergeant first class, E-6, to sergeant first class, E-7, in August 1960. I had to appear before a promotion board, and that was the first time for me. What you have to do when you go before such a board is convince the members you're the best-qualified guy in your job to get the grade. They asked me a series of questions about what my position entailed, how I would handle certain situations, and so on. The board president was either a major or a lieutenant colonel, and there were two or three other officers sitting as voting members. The questions were pretty straightforward, designed to find out how well the candidate expressed himself and how well he knew his job. You knew within a day or so if you'd made the stripe.

Making SFC, E-7, did not mean changing my chevrons, but it did give me a little more money—I went from $255 to $285 a month (not including $96.90 for quarters)—and I thought the promotion would also get me off company details like charge of quarters. But wouldn't you know it, at that very moment they changed the rules so that only master sergeants (E-8) and sergeants major (E-9) were excused from those duties. However, on July 15, 1961, eleven and a half months after I made E-7, I was promoted to master sergeant, E-8. I was finally off the duty roster and was now making a base pay of $330 a month.

At that time in the Army the enlisted grade system was very confusing. It confuses me even today, although at the time those of us involved in it *thought* we understood the system pretty well. I'll try to explain it.

From 1920 until 1959, the enlisted grade structure was composed of seven distinct pay grades that ranged from recruit at the bottom (E-1) to master sergeant at the top (E-7). The chevrons for those ranks were pretty much as they are today for the same pay grades. During World War II, starting in 1942, there were technician grades, T-5, T-4, and T-3, which were pay-grade equivalents of corporal, sergeant, and staff sergeant. These grades were abolished in 1948.

Then in 1956 the Army introduced specialist grades. The specialist grades paralleled the noncommissioned officer grades, corporal through master sergeant. Specialists were experts in various technical fields, such as electronics, languages, maintenance, administration, and so on, but they were not expected to be troop leaders—that was the noncommissioned officer's job. The specialist insignia was composed basically of a spread-eagle device and a certain number of arcs above it to denote pay grade—a spread eagle with three arcs over it was a master specialist, pay grade E-7, for instance.

In 1958, in order to give enlisted soldiers in the top grades a chance for further advancement and allow the Army to retain its best and most experienced noncommissioned officers, the "supergrades" were introduced—master sergeant, E-8, and sergeant major, E-9.

Thus overnight the Army had a noncommissioned rank system that consisted of master sergeants in pay grade E-8 *and* E-7; sergeants first class in pay grade E-7 *and* E-6, and staff sergeants in pay grade E-6 *and* E-5. So now you'd look at a man wearing five stripes, SFC, and not know if he was pay grade E-6 (old system) or E-7 (new system). At the time this order was implemented, July 1, 1958, there were some 200,000 men wearing the old chevrons. The Army leaders thought that instead of making everyone change at once, they would permit soldiers to continue using the old chevrons until they either got promoted to the new grades, left the service, or retired. This dragged on until June 30, 1968, when all those men who were still in the pre-1958 NCO grades were required to change chevrons, and even then, about six thousand of them were still around.

The view in the field at the time was that instead of extending this situation on and on the Army should have just made everyone change to the new chevrons. The other services did it that way. We'd have had anguish for sixty days as men lamented "losing" a rocker, and then the whole thing would have been just another barroom war story—"Remember when we had to take off our stripes?" Of course, there were those individuals who said, Well, if I go home they'll think I've messed up. In reality, the home folks didn't even know what the stripes meant, unless the soldier told them, and the guys who counted already knew the difference anyway, so they wouldn't be asking any questions.

I guess I changed my stripes a dozen times in thirty-one years in the Army, and the best system we've ever had is the pin-on metal insignia the Army's got today. But the entire system of sew-on chevrons was just poor planning on the Army's part, and we went ten years when the only way you knew what a soldier's real grade was if you went up and asked.

Now this was my first experience of life on an Army general staff, and I found out a couple of things about it.

In order to do your job efficiently, you had to learn what your boss wanted. The operations officer, Lieutenant Colonel Baltes, was a down-to-earth guy. You could talk to him, and when he talked to you he always made a lot of sense. We were constantly giving briefings, and it seemed all of them were needed yesterday.

We had a draftsman by the name of Cleatus Boyer. That guy really knew his stuff and could make up map symbols and charts to perfection. One day we had to put on a briefing on very short notice, and we found ourselves worrying whether Cleatus could come up with the graphics in the little time we had to prepare.

I finally said, "Colonel Baltes, we have a new chief of staff. Why don't we run this one by him. Let's just get some butcher paper and draw the charts by hand. All he's interested in is the information, anyway—he doesn't care whether it's pretty or not."

Colonel Baltes said, "Good idea. Let's try it."

We had eight or nine large sheets of the brown paper that used to be found in meat markets—butcher paper. We used it for everything. We threw pieces of these brown sheets of paper over an easel and went in and did the briefing. Not a complaint was heard, and when Colonel Baltes came back he said, "Let me tell you, Sergeant B., let's don't *ever* make up another chart except on butcher paper for these quickie briefings. We'll save our good stuff for when we go to the field. The chief said that's how he wants it—he doesn't care how pretty it is, he got the information, and we're in business."

You've got to be able to read what your boss wants—you have to know his style. You also have to learn to tolerate some mighty difficult personalities.

Colonel Baltes had an officer working for him who I will call Maj. Foghorne P. Swithers. His name was just about that ridiculous. With the name his folks hung on him, there was no reason to expect the guy to be civil—he'd be bound to be pissed off all the time just because of his name. And he was a bear to get along with. It didn't make any difference what you said, it was wrong.

One time Colonel Baltes went away for a few days and left

Swithers in charge. The first thing he wanted to do was move a clerk back into his office, so he could just hand him stuff to type. I advised him not to do that, because the clerk would only distract him in his work. "Don't you worry about whether I can do my job or not. You move that clerk back here."

I moved the clerk. It wasn't two days before Swithers roared, "Get him out of here, it's so goddamn noisy I can't do nothin'!"

I said, "I told you . . ."

"Don't tell me what you told me, Sergeant Bainbridge, just get him the hell out of here!"

He demanded impossible things. Once he wanted a stencil eighteen inches high. I told him we didn't have them that big. I offered to have Cleatus freehand the sign he wanted made, and he exclaimed, "How's come I can get anything I want out of the E-4s down at control headquarters but when I come back up here to talk to the operations sergeant I can't get nothing?"

I guess I lost my temper then. I said, "Because I'm a hell of a lot smarter than those E-4s," and shut the door in his face.

He came through that door like he'd been shot through it and hollered, "Don't shut the door in my face when I'm talking to you!"

"I thought you were finished, sir—that's why I shut the door," I answered.

Finally I went into his office and told Major Swithers that he should wear spurs. "You've got me saddled. You've been riding me like a goddamn horse. I don't understand it. I'll do what you want, but I'm telling you, when Colonel Baltes gets back, one of us has got to go or you've got to change."

When Colonel Baltes did come back, I told him he had to do something with Major Swithers, and he admitted that he knew when he'd left that I'd be under the gun during his absence. He called Swithers into his office. A little later, Colonel St. Clair, the G-3, came in and asked where Colonel Baltes was. I told him he was having a private meeting in his office. He looked at me for a moment and then asked, "Who's he got in there? Swithers? Ask him to call me when he's finished."

We never had any more problems out of Major Swithers. He settled down and did exactly what Colonel Baltes told him to do.

Well, bless his heart, when I became Sergeant Major of the Army and he was a full colonel, he came by the office one day and chatted amicably. Apparently he didn't remember our difficulties, and I didn't bring them up.

* * *

One day I decided to revisit Bad Orb, where I'd spent such a miserable time as a prisoner of war, before they shipped us to Siegenheim. I'd have visited Siegenheim too, except that try as hard as I could, I never did find it. It must have disappeared in the postwar destruction or construction boom.

Bad Orb was up in the Frankfurt area, and it happened that Hazel and I had a friend up there, Roy Morrow, a person we'd served with in the old food service school. So we went up there to visit him and his wife, Jo, had lunch with them, and then drove on out to see Bad Orb. Hazel asked me if I thought I could find the place again, and I wasn't sure I could, but I wanted to try anyway. I drove to the place as if I'd just been there the day before—down into the town, made a left at an intersection, drove up a hill, right up to the camp. I'd walked that route back in 1944 and it just came back to me.

The place was a *Kinderheim*, a children's home, then. They had a guard on the gate who spoke no English, and I spoke no German. He wouldn't let me in. I pointed to myself and said, "In 1944, I was a *Krieg* prisoner here, Stalag 9B."

"Ach, gut!" he said, and let me in, though he wouldn't let Hazel in. I took pictures of the mess hall, the sleeping area, and other places. As Sergeant Major of the Army I got back there two or three more times.

I felt pretty good about going back. I felt better toward the Germans by then. I was particularly pleased to take photos of the place where I had *survived*, the place where it was so cold the day they marched us to the trains that when Walt Ware stepped on my heel it hurt so bad I almost cried. I think the good Lord has arranged it so that we can forget bad things because if He hadn't, we'd all be crazy.

You cannot live with miserable memories forever. It's like some of our men who're mentally still in Vietnam and they're never going to get over their war until they get out of Vietnam. I could have "stayed" in Germany, and I know some who did, and they're still miserable after all those years. Life has to go on, and there are too many good things in this life to ruin it by dwelling on the bad ones.

We enjoyed our stay in Germany, but at last it was time to go home, to Fort Riley.

≡ 5 ≡

TOP SERGEANT

Because I extended for six months before we came back from VII Corps, I did a three-and-a-half-year tour in Germany. The day in 1962 when my orders came through, the corps adjutant general sergeant major came up and said, "Hey, Bainbridge, I got your orders. Betcha you don't know where you're going. You're going to Fort Riley. How's that grab ya?"

"That's just great," I said. "Riley's great."

"That's a terrible post," he said. "Why'd you want to go there?"

I asked him if he'd ever been there, and he told me no.

"Well, I've been there, and it's not terrible, so I'm sure glad you got me orders to go back there." I ruined his whole damn day.

You'll recall that when we went over to Germany our older daughter, Kathy, was seasick most of the way. When we came back we flew on a C-118, an Air Force four-engine prop job with seats facing the tail. We had to buy box lunches for the flight. Kathy was airsick all the way back and couldn't eat a thing. She was apologetic about it, because she thought the food would go to waste, but Hazel, Mary, and I ate her lunch for her.

We flew into McGuire Air Force Base, New Jersey, picked up our car, and drove back to Fort Riley, with the usual delay en route to visit our families in Illinois.

Fort Riley is about a 120,000-acre post these days, but it was about 60,000 acres when I was there the first time. It sits between Junction City and Ogden. Both towns butt right up against the post. At that time it included Camp Funston, Camp Forsythe, Camp Whitside, and the Main Post. I was assigned to Funston. About then they started building another cantonment on Custer Hill, which today is the main part of the post. There's also Marshal Field, where the air cavalry is located.

Riley is an old post. It was first established in May 1853 and is named after Maj. Gen. Bennett Riley, a hero of the Mexican War. The famous 7th Cavalry was formed there in 1866. The post daily bulletin* used to reprint old post orders in every issue, and I remember one that stated, "Officers who shoot buffalo on the lower parade ground will refrain from firing in the direction of the commanding officer's quarters." Those quarters were once occupied by George Armstrong Custer.

The weather at Riley is terrible. It's colder than hell in the winter and hotter than hell in the summer. Just what GIs like to train in. What makes duty there so great is that some of the greatest folks in this country live in Kansas.

We lived in a trailer park at Ogden. In fact, we would not occupy government quarters again until Fort Benning, after I came back from Vietnam in 1966. Troops at Fort Riley lived in old brown sandstone barracks built in the 1920s and in the World War II cantonment-type wooden barracks that up until very recently were such a familiar sight on Army posts all over this country. Whitside, Forsythe, and Funston had those wooden barracks for the troops. The older stone buildings were up in the Main Post area.

Originally my orders had me assigned to the 12th Infantry Regiment. In the meantime, the 12th had already deployed on Operation Long Thrust to Europe. Long Thrust was the code name for the battle group or infantry unit rotation we'd started as a show of force, to reinforce our troops in Berlin after the Wall went up. We had the 2nd and 3rd battalions** of the 6th Infantry Regiment in Berlin, and the idea was to augment them with units rotated in from the States, just as we'd do on a much larger scale if actual war ever broke out.

So since the 12th Infantry was already in Europe when I left there, my orders were changed to assign me to the 28th Infantry Regiment of the 1st Infantry Division. Lo and behold, when we at last got to Fort Riley, neither was the 28th Infantry there at the

*An official publication containing information on post details such as staff duty officer, staff duty NCO, special events, and announcements of general interest to all military and civilian personnel assigned to an Army installation.
**The terms "battalion" and "regiment" are used here to avoid confusion. Under the combat arms regimental system (CARS) of 1957, the battle group concept was introduced but abandoned in 1964 under reorganization of army divisions (ROAD) concept. Today infantry divisions are composed of brigades, regiments, and battalions, and although technically anachronisms, these designations are used to avoid long and confusing explanations.

time—it was at Little Creek, Virginia, going through amphibious training. I began to think maybe the 1st Infantry Division didn't want me. So my first duty as a member of the 1st Battle Group of the 28th Infantry was as the noncommissioned officer in charge of the logistical effort to return the unit from Virginia.

I was assigned to the rear party, commanded by the personnel officer, a warrant officer, and worked directly with SFC Bill Landgraf, who was being assigned to the S-4—that is, logistics—and who'd also just returned from Europe. There was a requirement for one of us to be at Fort Riley and the other at Topeka. He looked at me and asked, "Guess who's going to Topeka?"

I answered, "Well, since I'm the master sergeant, I guess that's you." I'd been promoted to master sergeant, E-8, back in July 1961.

The unit flew into Forbes Air Force Base at Topeka and returned to Fort Riley from there by bus. Landgraf and I made a pretty good team; we never lost anybody's baggage and never lost any of the soldiers either.

My first job with the 1st Battle Group, 28th Infantry, was as the S-3 operations NCO. In August we were preparing for our Army Training Test (ATT), and we were moving into a staging area before going into the field for the test when I had to return for some additional maps. On the way back to the assembly area I ran into the battle group sergeant major and the group commander's driver, headed back toward the cantonment area. The sergeant major had gone to the NCO club early that morning and gotten himself severely under the influence of alcohol. We'd just gotten a new commander, Col. Joffre Boston, who'd previously served as the division trains* commander. The former battle group commander had been "carrying" the sergeant major, who just could not handle John Barleycorn. Colonel Boston relieved him.

The purpose of the ATT was to see how well prepared the unit was to accomplish the mission and to find out what mistakes the unit might make before the real thing. That is the purpose of all training, to prepare for war during peacetime. We were just getting ready to deploy to the field when Colonel Boston informed me that I would be the acting group sergeant major. However, my philosophy has always been that if you have the job, you're never "acting"—you're the one responsible for everything.

So I did two jobs for the ATT. I was the battle group sergeant

*A very old military term for those elements providing transportation, maintenance, supply, and other types of support required to keep a combat command operating in the field.

major—a new experience for me—and also the operations sergeant for the S-3. A battle group was like a regiment. It had seven companies—A, B, C, D, and E, a headquarters company, and a support company. We had our own personnel office. The battle group was a self-contained "minidivision," if you will.

We went on our ATT, and under our new commander, Colonel Boston, we passed with flying colors. At the time the battle group commander knew, and I was to know it before the test was over, that we were headed back to Europe on the Long Thrust unit rotation program. We finished our training in the last part of November and early December and then moved to Germany on December 28, 1962. I took the advance party along with the deputy battle group commander, Lt. Col. Ernest Bell, and we flew over in a C-135 out of Forbes.

Our job was to ensure that all the prepositioned equipment the battle group would need (already in place in the Kaiserslautern area) could be located and allocated before the arrival of the main body. We arrived at Rhein-Main Air Base, at Frankfurt, and while we were eating breakfast in the mess hall, a general from VII Corps approached us and asked who was in charge. Colonel Bell reported to him, and he asked who the sergeant major was, and Bell told him it was me. When I'd been assigned to VII Corps they'd had a party or a reception for this general, and when he saw me he asked, "Don't I know you, Sergeant Bainbridge?" I recounted our meeting at the party and reminded him of my assignment at VII Corps. He turned to Colonel Bell and said, "I was going to tell you about the pitfalls your soldiers should be warned about, but you've got a man here in Bainbridge who knows more about it than I do, so just ask him about the problems your soldiers can have while they're here in Europe."

I went back to VII Corps for New Year's Eve that year, to visit some friends of ours there, and also I visited the corps headquarters. The chief of staff was walking down the hallway, and he passed by me, turned around, and exclaimed, "Sergeant Bainbridge, what are *you* doing back here?"

"Sir, I'm here on Long Thrust," I replied, and showed him the middle finger.

"I don't think it'll be quite *that* bad," he responded.

After the battle group arrived and all the equipment had been signed for, we performed a road march into a place called Wildflicken, one of the best training areas in Europe. I wrote a letter to Hazel from there telling her we were so far up in the hills that when we opened our windows large birds and small airplanes would fly through if we weren't careful.

When I told Hazel we were going back to Europe, she said she didn't realize "we" would be going back that soon. I explained *she* wasn't going, the battle group was, for six months' temporary duty, and she and I would have a chance to go home before Christmas. We did, but in order to make it back to Riley in time to ship out, we had to drive through a blinding snowstorm.

The problem was that I'd be gone for six months, we had the girls in school, and Hazel had never learned to drive a car. I took Hazel out to a nearby driving range in our 1953 straight-stick Buick Special and she learned to drive that car. But to this day she'd rather drive from the passenger seat than from behind the wheel.

At Wildflicken we went through another ATT that began in December/January and lasted through March. We had several visits from the V Corps commander, "Iron Mike" Michaelis. He was quite a character, and I'll mention him again later on.

One of the things I remember best about this time was all the snow we had at Wildflicken that year. There was snow on the ground when we arrived, and I recall it snowed the first fifteen days we were there. We actually had to scoop out pathways into the buildings. Before the snow melted, those pathways had become tunnels. It snowed and snowed and snowed. Before we moved to Berlin in March, the thaw had started, and then we had the most concentrated police call I've ever been in charge of. We couldn't clean up the area during all that snow, but once it started to melt we hauled truckloads of trash out of there.

One of the highlights of my career occurred at Wildflicken. On February 26, 1963, I was officially promoted to sergeant major by Colonel Boston. The sergeant major of the 555th Engineer Battalion, right across the street from our battle group, provided the chevrons used in the ceremony.

I felt pretty good about that promotion. It increased my pay by about $60 a month, for one thing. I always knew I'd be promoted to sergeant major someday, because I'd had a lot of experience filling the position. I'd been a sergeant major before, you will recall, back at the old food service school, and then I'd been battle group sergeant major as a master sergeant, so I had ideas on how troops should be treated, and I felt pretty good about this, especially since Colonel Boston picked me for his sergeant major, because I was not the senior master sergeant in the group at the time. There were a couple of E-8 first sergeants who were senior to me by date of rank, but in the eyes of Colonel Boston I was his man. First sergeants and master sergeants are both NCOs in pay grade E-8, but the first sergeant is the senior noncommissioned officer in company-size units. The grade of first sergeant has existed in the Army since 1825, when it was designated by a red sash worn about the waist. Today the grade is identified by three chevrons over three rockers with a diamond or lozenge in the middle. The lozenge has been the distinctive heraldic badge of the first sergeant since it was first authorized by Army regulations in 1847.

My base pay as a newly minted sergeant major at that time was $455 a month plus quarters allowance of $120 a month.

After we got to Germany on Long Thrust, Colonel Boston tried to get the sergeant major of the 2nd Battle Group, 28th Infantry, which was stationed at Augsburg, to take over as the 1st Battle Group sergeant major. This man's name was Bill Wooldridge. Wooldridge was about to rotate, but he extended to stay in Europe, instead of becoming our battle group sergeant major and rotating back with us to Fort Riley in June 1963. If he hadn't done that I would not have been promoted into the job, at least not at that time.

When Colonel Boston promoted me he made a man we'll call Sgt. John Bull the operations sergeant. John really knew his stuff, but it went to his head. He was a flaunter. He had an ego as big as a barn, and later it was to get him in real trouble. When Colonel Boston appointed him he said he knew the man was a good ops sergeant but added, "I know your personality, Sergeant Bull, so don't test me—just do your job."

I had no problems with those ranking master sergeants. There could have been problems, but I had a meeting with all the first sergeants and reminded them that I'd been the acting sergeant major since before we left Fort Riley and we'd worked well together up to then, so all I asked of them was to do the job they were supposed to do and I'd do mine.

Maj. Billy Don Church, the battle group adjutant when I was promoted, had to send back to Fort Riley to get a waiver because I lacked six or seven months of time in the service to qualify for promotion. Fifteen years' service was then the minimum requirement for promotion to sergeant major. So even though I had already pinned on the stripe, Major Church had to get a waiver. In those days messages weren't always sent electronically but by mail, to save money. Just before we left Wildflicken to go to Berlin, Major Church received a reply from division headquarters back at Fort Riley, and as he opened the envelope he saw the word, "rescinded," and he put it back without reading any further.

He told me later, "I did not have the guts to call you in here and tell you your promotion had been rescinded."

Well, we'd been in Berlin about six weeks when one Saturday morning old Billy Don Church hollered out, "Top, come in here! I really got something for you!" When I walked into his office he showed me the letter and recounted the story. What the message from Fort Riley said was: "Waiver of time in service is granted. Promotion orders to sergeant major will not be rescinded." That night we shared a beer together.

General Michaelis was the V Corps commander, and Wildflicken was situated in his area. We got a message one day he was on his way to see Colonel Boston, who was in the field at the time. I had heard a lot about General Michaelis—he had a reputation of eating people up when he was unhappy with something. The guy who gave me the message refused to tell General Michaelis he wouldn't be able to see Colonel Boston when he got to our HQ. "*You* can tell him when he gets there," he said.

I met General Michaelis and reported to him. I explained that Colonel Boston was in the field and it would take a couple of hours to get him out, but said that I would be glad to help him in any way I could. "All I need is to make a telephone call back to my headquarters. Can you handle that?" he asked. After he finished making the call he asked me if we were having any problems at Wildflicken he could help us with.

"We've got plenty, sir," I told him, "but none you can help us with. You can see it's piled up outside there, and we'll take care of it as soon as it starts to melt."

He laughed, slapped me on the back, and said, "Carry on, Sergeant Major." We never had any problems with him.

In March 1963, we moved to Berlin. In those days when you got ready to go to Berlin by road you really had to have all your equipment ready. There was an ordnance unit at the border crossing point at Helmstadt, because if anything happened to your vehicles once you crossed over into East Germany and you had to abandon them by the roadside, you not only lost the use of them, but it could create diplomatic problems. The night we moved into the assembly area before we began our road march, that ordnance company overhauled many vehicles, changed the engines in several jeeps, put new transmissions in trucks, and so on. They did all that overnight. They were a fantastic outfit.

Right at the last minute, one of our trucks conked out. In twenty minutes here came another truck from the ordnance company's reserves, bearing, in chalk, the bumper numbers of the vehicle that had fallen out. All we had to do was put a tarp on it and we were on the way again. That showed just how well the Army could work when the chips were down.

We moved without incident into Berlin, where we spent the next three months, training with the two battalions of the 6th Infantry. We were split between two kasernes, Andrews and McNair; I was at Andrews, where they had an indoor Olympic-size swimming pool. It also had one of the first bachelor enlisted quarters (BEQs) I'd ever seen, quarters reserved for senior enlisted men. Of course, that was for local permanent party. We visitors lived in the barracks, where I had a room to myself.

While there I made several trips into East Berlin. There was quite a contrast between the Eastern and Western sectors. The Eastern side was all a facade. A lot of people didn't like going over there, but I went every chance I got. I found out where all their armor was. We were always tailed by either the East Germans or the Russians and sometimes both. We had to be in uniform and in a marked vehicle, and we were checked in and out of Checkpoint Charlie whenever we crossed the border between the two cities.

In those days the Berlin Wall was still a pretty primitive structure. They kept improving that thing right up to the time they finally tore it down. But it really was a scourge to mankind. That was the first fence complete with dogs, guards, and watchtowers I'd ever seen to keep people *inside* a country. I think one of the highlights of my tour there, possibly of my entire career, was when President Kennedy visited and made his *"Ich bin ein Berliner"* speech. The 28th Infantry was part of the security force, and I was fortunate enough to be right across the street from where he spoke that day. It was a real experience for us to see the President of the United States on what turned out to be a very historic occasion.

I never thought the Berlin Wall would ever come down in my lifetime. The Germans were no longer my enemies—those who had been were long gone by then anyway—and I guess in the back of my mind I realized that someday the people themselves would take the Wall down. I'm an optimist, but at the time, when the Wall was fresh in 1961, it was a real blight.

I'd been VII Corps G-3 NCO when the Wall first went up. The day it happened, the G-3, Colonel St. Clair, came in and announced that I was staff duty NCO* that night. I exclaimed that couldn't be

*A noncommissioned officer, generally grade staff sergeant through master sergeant (excluding first sergeants), who assists the staff duty officer or SDO. The SDO is literally the unit commander's alter ego during his tour of duty, handling

so, since you really keep your eye on that duty roster. He told me I wasn't on the roster for that night but still I would be the staff duty NCO, and he would tell me why later. About ten o'clock that night, he came into the office, where I was up to my ears in secret and top secret messages that had been coming in all night long, grinned, and said, "Now you know why I wanted somebody from S-3 on staff duty tonight." That was the night they began building the Wall. I spent the next three days on staff duty.

We were the lead battle group in the Armed Forces Day parade in June 1963. The battle group commander whose unit we'd replaced in Berlin had made all the arrangements for the parade, but our battle group performed the duty. He sent Colonel Boston a letter giving him all the details about the things he was committing our battle group to do. Colonel Boston, a man who wouldn't say "crap" if he had a mouthful of it, brought me that letter and with a crooked grin on his face said, "Look what this guy wrote to me!"

I read the concluding paragraph: "And on the 15th, a military ball will be held. Just whose, at this time, we are not quite sure."

That is where it became evident that my good friend, and my replacement as operations sergeant, Sergeant Bull, could not stand prosperity. We held reveille formations every Monday morning, and one Monday, Sergeant Bull had lingered downtown and was reported missing from the formation. The operations officer, Capt. John B. Cottingham, came up to me and said, "Top, you know what I think of Sergeant Bull—he's a topnotch operations sergeant. But he wasn't at reveille formation this morning, he came to work late, and on top of all that, he lied to me. I can handle his missing reveille and being late, but not his lying to me. You've got to get him out of here."

That was about ten o'clock in the morning. Shortly before noon, Colonel Boston called him in for an Article 15.* Bull said

all activities within his area of responsibility during off-duty hours. The staff duty NCO and officer receive and act upon all incoming messages, emergency personnel actions, alerts, and other actions normally handled by a commander's staff during normal duty hours. Soldiers are assigned these duties by roster rotation.

*Company punishment or nonjudicial punishment authorized under Article 15 of the Uniform Code of Military Justice. Under this article, a commanding officer may impose certain degrees of punishment upon soldiers without recourse to a court-martial proceeding, provided the soldier agrees to this. A soldier has a right to demand a trial by court-martial, but a finding of guilty by a court can re-

he needed time to get some witnesses to speak on his behalf, and
Colonel Boston gave him until two that afternoon. Sergeant Bull
produced no witnesses. Colonel Boston reduced him from sergeant first class (E-7) to staff sergeant (E-6). He was on his way
back to the States the next day. In those days in Berlin you didn't
have to fool with bad apples; they shipped them out at once. The
irony of all this was that at that very time, in the personnel office
was a set of master sergeant's chevrons that he would have gotten.
Within days he would have been promoted.

The adjutant told me about this and complained that he was going to have to turn that promotion back in, now that Bull was no
longer eligible. I said no, he didn't have to do that at all. "But
they were for Bull," he said.

"They are for anybody in this battle group who can qualify for
master sergeant," I told him. I recommended that Hank Weir, who
was the S-2 (intelligence) sergeant, and eligible for promotion, get
them. He deserved the stripes.

We called Hank into the colonel's office. In those days we liked
to make a production out of promotion ceremonies, so we cooked
up a little ruse. Colonel Boston was a stern commander. He said
to Hank, "I understand that you're missing a confidential document and you can't find it. What do you propose I ought to do
about it?"

Hank asked which document that might be, and Colonel Boston
told him. "But I gave that to the sergeant major only yesterday!"
he stammered.

Colonel Boston smiled and said, "Well, if the sergeant major
has it, we know it's in good hands. By the way, we've got a new
set of stripes for you here, Sergeant Weir."

You could have knocked old Hank over with a feather. He had
no idea the chevrons were even in the command, let alone that
they'd settle upon his sleeves. Hank's dead now, but that was
probably one of the best feelings I've ever had, recommending
him for that promotion.

John Bull wound up with the inspector general of the First
Army, got that Article 15 overturned, and got his SFC stripes
back. Later I saw him when he was with the ROTC detachment
at a university, and he made master sergeant before he retired. It

sult in much stiffer penalties than a company commander can impose under
Article 15. When soldiers are faced with making this choice, the code authorizes
them time to seek legal counsel before making up their minds.

was John's personality that got him into trouble, but he knew his business.

We were in Berlin until June 1963. Long Thrust was a good experience, moving an entire unit overseas. It was a good logistical operation, too, because we got the necessary equipment out of storage and worked the bugs out of it while we were over there.

One of our biggest problems was getting all the potential family problems worked out back at Fort Riley, ensuring that families' allotments continued while their men were in Europe. We had very little trouble in that regard. Another problem was that some of our soldiers couldn't cope with being footloose and fancy free in Germany. Some men ruined their careers. We lost a couple of first sergeants to heavy drinking, for example, and other men, like Bull, couldn't cope with having a curfew. We had to have that curfew in Berlin, because we had to be ready to go into battle. The enemy was only four streets away from us and we couldn't afford to have our men running all over town at night.

I think heavy drinking was much more common in the Army in those days than it is now. It was not that a lot of men drank, it was that those who did really had a problem with it. I can recall half a dozen such guys in the battle group. The sergeant major whom I replaced as battle group sergeant major is an example. His commander was also remiss. He should have straightened him out instead of carrying him along. Had he handled the problem right it might have gotten fixed.

The officers also had their problems. That is why a captain was doing the S-3's job instead of the major who was assigned to it. In this case the difficulty wasn't drinking, it was medical problems and incompetence.

Once we were back at Fort Riley, we went from the battle group concept of organization to the ROAD concept. ROAD stood for Reorganization of Army Divisions. We went back to having brigades and battalions once again. At that time the division table of organization was changed to create for the first time a position for a division sergeant major.*

The 1st Battle Group, 28th Infantry, was split into two battalions, the 1st and 2nd. I got the 1st Battalion and the S-4 sergeant, Cliff

---

*Division sergeant major is a title. The soldiers who filled this position were in the same pay grade, E-9, and wore the same chevrons as any other sergeant major.

Weatherby, got the 2nd Battalion. The 1st Battalion became the mechanized battalion, and was commanded by Lt. Col. George Fleeson. We were at Camp Funston, and the 2nd Battalion stayed at Camp Forsythe. That's when we got the first M-113 armored personnel carriers and the M-114 command vehicles. The M-114 turned out to be a real bomb. It was a full-tracked vehicle but underpowered.

I set up a promotion board at the battalion level at that time. I told Colonel Fleeson what I wanted to do, and he appointed me president of the board. I took my S-2, S-3, and S-4 sergeants, personnel staff NCO as the recorder, and one first sergeant, rotated among all the company first sergeants, to sit on the board with me. We couldn't promote anybody to sergeant first class, E-7, but we determined who went to the brigade board.

That system worked to perfection. When our candidates got to division we were sure they'd get their share or better of the promotions handed out, and they did. When we got a new battalion executive officer in, of whom more later, he told Colonel Fleeson he wanted to be president of the promotion board. I don't recall how many of these boards had met up to this time, but enough so that they were working well. The colonel compromised and asked him just to sit in on the next board and then he'd talk further about the subject if the major wanted. The major sat in for only three candidate interviews, then got up and said, "Sergeant Major, I'll see you," and left. Later the battalion commander told me the XO said that he wouldn't have wanted to go before one of our boards because he wasn't sure he could make it.

We examined the men to see first of all how well they could express themselves. Whatever you know, you've got to be able to communicate it to your men. We tested their job knowledge—how well they were qualified in their specialties—and what they knew about the Army organization. We tested them on troop knowledge. Other battalions weren't doing that, and we were coming away with most of the promotions up through the grade of sergeant first class.

That board system continued even after we got to Vietnam and I'd left the battalion. I visited the battalion one day in 1966 and had lunch with Lt. Col. Robert Haldane—whom I'll mention later—and the S-1 of the 1st Brigade. The battalion had just cleaned up on the last promotion board, and the brigade S-1 said to the colonel, "You really G-2'd* my promotion board. You guys really cleaned up."

---

*G-2, Army slang for getting over on someone or some circumstance by figuring out all the angles and thinking things through in advance. The G-2 or intelligence element of an Army staff is charged with predicting the enemy's maneuvers, etc.

Colonel Haldane pointed to me and said, "No, no, I didn't do it. There's the guy that G-2'd it, and he had you G-2'd before we even left Fort Riley! That's why those guys did well, because they were well screened before they even got to your board."

When we reorganized under ROAD, we had our first experience with the Davey Crockett forward-unit (infantry battalion) tactical nuclear supercaliber rocket launcher. We had some real backbreaking safety inspections to handle with that weapon. I doubt if there's anybody in the Army today who remembers it. I know my predecessor as Sergeant Major of the Army, when he visited the museum at Fort Benning, Georgia, didn't even know what a Davey Crockett was when he saw it on display there. Of course, he was an engineer, but very few people ever knew much about that weapon. We got rid of it before we went to Vietnam.

When we were getting ready to go to Vietnam in late 1964, the division commander, Maj. Gen. Jonathan O. Seaman, arranged for the 26th Infantry sergeant major, Theodore Dobel, "King" Dobel as he was called, to be transferred to West Point. Ted Dobel was a legend in his time. He was an old 1st Divisioneer who'd spent almost twenty-five years with the 26th Infantry Regiment. General Seaman did not want Ted to go to Vietnam, because he was afraid the Army would lose him in combat over there. But Ted had been quite a warrior in World War II—he'd won several Silver Stars—and was just a tremendous person all around.

When we held the farewell parade for him, the troops marched past the reviewing stand, and when the 26th Infantry passed by, they didn't do an "eyes right," as is the custom when passing in review. You could just see old Ted bristle. He just knew his beloved 26th Infantry had really screwed up. But when the full battalion was centered on the reviewing stands, Col. Jack French, its commander, halted them, gave them "right face," and they *all* saluted Ted. His eyes filled with tears at this gesture by his "Blue Spaders."

The 2nd Brigade was the first unit to depart for Vietnam in July 1965. When that brigade started getting ready to go, the division picked the best people we had to fill it up. They went with every position filled with the right man by specialty and grade. That stripped the rest of us, and we had to get replacements when it came our turn to go. We were so short-handed in some units that we didn't get the replacements we needed until only a week or ten days before we departed for Vietnam.

That's when quarters became available at Shilling Manor, in Salina, Kansas, forty-five miles west of Fort Riley, where our older daughter and her family live today. In the former housing area for the closed Shilling Air Force Base, the family of anyone who was going to Vietnam could get quarters while he was away. They had a commissary and a post exchange and all the other conveniences there.

In my battalion—and I say "my" because it was as much mine as it was the commander's; we saw eye to eye on that—we got a new battalion commander, two new company commanders, a new S-1, and a new S-3, all just before we went. Our new commander was Lt. Col. Robert Haldane, who later retired as a lieutenant general. He was class of 1947 at West Point. He and the brigade executive officer had been classmates at the Military Academy, he told us. When I found out that the XO had graduated in 1948, I asked him how that could be. In his own inimitable way he replied, "He's one of them dumb shits, Top. Took him four years to get through." Haldane had taken an accelerated course, which they had in those days, and made it through in only three years.

Until Haldane came in, we'd had an acting commander—and this guy was really "acting"—who'd been executive officer, and he just wasn't the commander we needed to take us to Vietnam. Under Colonel Haldane we really worked, but we got that battalion in shape in time to go to Vietnam. We trained hard, we spent most of our time in the field, and Colonel Haldane really honed us to a sharp edge.

I was in pretty good shape in those days, but to get ready for Vietnam I played tennis at noon every day instead of eating lunch. This was "jungle" tennis, if you will. About three hundred meters from my battalion headquarters was a tennis court. We had a clerk who'd played in college. My personnel staff NCO, my S-4 sergeant, that clerk, and I would go over there and play doubles. We just stripped down to our T-shirts and played in our combat boots. I'll tell you, we were in good physical shape when we went to Vietnam.

I didn't fly over to Vietnam with the advance party, I went with the rest of the battalion on a troopship. So in October 1965, twenty years after I finished my first war, I was on the way to my second one.

≡ 6 ≡

VIETNAM

My troopship sailed from the West Coast. We flew out of Manhattan, Kansas, in the old Super Constellations into San Francisco. As a unit, we were ready for Vietnam. Nobody *wants* to go to war, but Lieutenant Colonel Haldane got us believing that we had a job to do and we were going to do it.

Colonel Haldane had shaped us up, physically and mentally, for that job. We learned about punji stakes,* how to operate in the jungle, how to handle the water supply—you drank as much water in the tropical heat as you could, so we were taught that water discipline in Vietnam would be just bassackwards from what it had been in World War II, when you were expected to get by on just one canteen of water a day instead of four or five.

We dyed our underwear and hankies green—at home, to ease the burden on the quartermaster. We had guys walking around with green dye all over their skin because of the amateurish job they'd done on their underwear.

We had to alter our thinking on marksmanship, because in the jungle, under the heavy cover, you fire at area targets more than at point targets. We were taught that because of the heavy cover we wouldn't be able to rely on our mortars as we were trained to do in open country. Our orientation was aimed at getting us into the best mental state for the conditions we were expected to face in Vietnam.

At Oakland Army Terminal, we boarded the USS *Mann*. In addition to my battalion, the *Mann* accommodated the 121st Signal Battalion; the 1st Battalion, 16th Infantry Regiment; an explosive

---

*Sharpened, barbed wooden stakes used to line pits of different sizes designed to act as mantraps. When the victim fell through the camouflaged cover of one of these pits, he was impaled on the stakes.

ordnance detachment; and some other small units, probably close
to three thousand men all told. The authorized strength of my battalion at that time was around 870 men. I shared a cabin with the
1st Division G-1 sergeant major. The 2nd Brigade of the 1st Division was already in Vietnam, and while the whole division was
moving there, only a portion of it was on the *Mann*.

I was the troopship sergeant major on the crossing, and the brigade executive officer, Lieutenant Colonel Plummer, was the
troopship commander. In fact, he had picked me to be his sergeant
major. We split the ship in half. The forward half went to the
1/16th Infantry sergeant major and the other half went to the 121st
Signal sergeant major. Between them they were in charge of all
the troops fore and aft, whether they belonged to their units or
not.

We inspected the ship every day. The ship's captain would do
the front half one day and my boss and I would do the back half,
and then the next day we'd switch areas. We made sure the troop
areas were clean and that equipment was being properly cared for
and stowed away. There was training going on—rifle instruction,
physical training, stuff that could be done on a ship—so we
checked on how that was proceeding.

The troops were quartered in large open bays and slept on canvas cots. There were "heads" or latrines at either end of these
troop areas. We occupied two or three decks of the ship. We also
had some of our unit's equipment aboard the vessel.

When we stopped at Guam, to take on water, fuel, and provi-
sions, we discussed the possibility of letting the men off the ship.
We were to be there only eighteen or nineteen hours, but the
troopship commander and I decided that because our soldiers
were mature individuals with good officers and noncoms, we'd let
them off. So we made arrangements through the Navy to get the
chiefs' club to cater a cookout in a picnic area. They had beer,
soda, hot dogs and hamburgers, and some music, and they opened
the club for the senior NCOs. It was just a fine old picnic for the
troops, and our faith in the men proved correct, because we never
had a serious disturbance, everybody got back on the ship without
incident, and we sailed on time. Here we had three different battalions and odds and ends of other units, draftees and volunteers,
knowing they were headed to a war in a strange place a long way
from home, and they all got back on that ship without any problem. I think that says something for the discipline of those men.

I don't think I've ever seen another body of water as smooth as
was the South China Sea. There didn't seem to be a ripple any-

where as we moved up the coast to Vung Tau, where we landed. The surface of the sea was like glass. We sure didn't feel we were headed into a combat zone. Maybe it was a good thing the sea was so calm—perhaps it had a good effect on the troops. I know it sure did on me.

We were moved to shore in LSTs and were met by the division band, the division commander, everybody; my battalion commander was there, and the brigade commander. The trucks were waiting on shore to take us to Di An, where the division headquarters was located and where we'd get acclimated to Vietnam.

By that evening, everybody was in a tent somewhere, sides rolled up, getting ready to eat. After supper the Old Man said he thought we ought to take a shower and he'd show me where it was. That was one of the greatest disappointments I've ever had, coming into a new theater. It was dark, the place was covered with mud, and it was a job to take a shower and get your clothes back on without getting mud on your feet and everywhere else. Well, I thought, here we are, ten thousand miles from home, and at least we've got freshwater showers. But that shower point really left something to be desired.

On the way back to our tent I told Colonel Haldane that I thought we could do better. The monsoons were just starting at that time of the year, and you could just about count on it that around four every afternoon it would rain. I told the Old Man that we could use nature as our shower point. "The Good Lord's bringing it to us—why go to that one down the road? Let's see how many showers we can get right here in the battalion area."

So the 1/28 became the "jaybird" battalion about four o'clock every afternoon—everybody out in the rain taking a shower. The water was fresh, and if you could manage to catch some of it in a container, you could rinse off if it quit raining before you were done.

We spent about three weeks getting our equipment and preparing to move to our base camp along the Song Be, up in War Zone C, near the town of Phuoc Vinh, north and west of the Saigon area. We made the move in November 1965. When we got up there we were situated near a laterite pit, positively the worst area in Phuoc Vinh. There had been a battalion there before us—1st Battalion, 18th Infantry—and we relieved it. They really hadn't set up a campsite, because they were just on a search-and-clear operation in the vicinity.

Their battalion commander was Lt. Col. Karl Morton, and his sergeant major was Jim Knox. Colonel Morton was later to become my boss at the Sergeants Major Academy. Later on, Jim became the curator of the 1st Division Museum in Wheaton, Illinois. I was to attend Jim's funeral at Arlington some twenty years later.

So we set up in this area by the laterite pit, near an old airstrip, out in a place where the Vietnamese had been manufacturing charcoal, judging by all the little charcoal ovens around. Colonel Haldane freely admitted to me that this was probably the worst position in the entire brigade area, for comfort and convenience, but he said he'd picked the spot because he knew everybody else—the 1st Battalion, 26th Infantry, and 1st Battalion, 2nd Infantry—in the lush positions would have to move. "Meanwhile," he said, "we'll improve this place and make it livable, but you mark my words, all those other guys will move before long." He was right on the money. We both knew our position had to be manned if we were to have a secure base camp, because there was a VC-controlled village just north of us. It was the typical VC hangout. They had the church as their sanctuary and we couldn't shoot at it, but we sure got mortars from them.

So the 1/26th and 1/2nd Infantry Battalions moved two or three times, using our battalion as the "anchor." We also had a little stream inside our perimeter, where the fresh water and shower points for the brigade were located, so we knew we wouldn't be moved out of there, because it was essential that the water supply be secured.

The first night in that location I slept in a foxhole. It started raining just about dark, and it rained all night long. About midnight my hole was so full of water I decided to stop bailing and find high ground. When they prepared our vehicles for shipping back at Fort Riley, they'd protected the windshields with two pieces of plywood banded together around the glass, and these sheets were lying all over the place after we got the vehicles. That night I lay on one of those boards. I was still wet but it wasn't cold.

That was still a very miserable night. You know how your hands become if you immerse them in water too long, all wrinkled with little feeling in your fingers. Well, my fingers were so soft from being wet all night long that the next morning I couldn't even wind my watch. By the time darkness came the next night, we all had a dry place to sleep in our base camp tents.

One of the first things we did was to build an NCO club—I call it that, but it was for all ranks. It was in a tent to start, and then we bought tin from a local dealer in Phuoc Vinh for the roof and we bartered I don't know what and took up collections to buy the things we needed. So when we were back in base camp we could enjoy a cold beer or a cold soda.

We had a buck sergeant in the communications platoon who was probably the world's best scrounger. For a three-day pass to Saigon, that guy brought back a Chinook helicopter loaded with beer and soft drinks to stock the club. I asked him what it cost and how he got a Chinook to fly him up from Saigon with that beer. He said for three or four cases of beer those pilots had no trouble veering a little bit off course to deliver us some pallets of beer.

One day Robert Mitchum visited that club. He had his hat on as we went inside, and I warned him to take it off or according to the time-honored custom of military clubs, he'd have to buy everyone a round. He said, "Fuck it, Top, it's for the troops," walked in with his hat still on, and bought everybody a beer. That really cheered the guys up. Most of those people never came out to the battalions. The Bob Hopes spend their time at the division base camps, and I understand why that happens, but this guy's coming out to our little old battalion camp really boosted morale.

We conducted our field operations out of that place, and we probably spent more time in the field than the other battalions. Colonel Haldane figured the best way to keep the troops busy was to keep them out looking for the enemy. Soldiers do better when they do the things they're trained to do as opposed to "beautifying the area" and fortifying the base camp. When we kept the men in the field we had fewer problems. That is not to say we didn't have problems, but they were the difficulties associated with being in a combat zone.

Phuoc Vinh wasn't the kind of place you could go to and do some shopping. There were some Vietnamese entrepreneurs who did our laundry for us, and periodically we'd take truckloads of laundry down to them and get our fatigues done. We didn't have our own quartermaster laundry set up at that time. Once in a while somebody'd buy a bamboo mat to lay his sleeping bag on or a piece of plastic, a loaf of bread, a bottle of beer, down at the little market, but we didn't spend much money in that little village. We never went there at night, and during the day nobody had the time to wander around down there. We had no venereal disease in our battalion.

We were the only battalion that did not have a Vietnamese barber, and we were the last battalion to have mortars dropped on us, and that is exactly why. Our hair was a little more ragged, because we only had a "shade-tree" barber, but our tents had fewer holes in them from mortar fragments. We didn't allow any Vietnamese except our interpreter inside our wire, and that interpreter never went anyplace without an escort.

We didn't get hit until we started showing movies. As I recall, that night we were showing a John Wayne movie, and about a third of the way through we had our first mortar attack. That was also our last movie. Evidently that little old screen reflected just enough light for the VC to aim at. We didn't suffer any casualties that night.

Those mortar attacks were so infrequent and ineffective that sometimes they were even a source of amusement to us, if there's anything funny about a mortar attack. I remember that Colonel Haldane had very poor night vision, so after dark he never struck a light if he could help it. He also had no hair in those days (still doesn't). We'd dug a prone shelter beside the small tent that served as his quarters and placed sandbags around his bunk, to give him protection during mortar attacks. Every morning about six-thirty or seven we'd have a briefing in the S-2/S-3 tent on what had happened during the night. One morning after another little mortar attack, there was a big red gash down across his skull, just the hide scraped off, and I said, "Good God, what happened to your head?"

He said, "That blankety-blank trench you dug for me—I was going into it last night and I tripped over one tent rope and hit my head on another."

I told him we'd move the trench.

"Goddammit," he replied, "don't move it now, Top, I know where it's at!" He'd been in that tent almost ninety days at the time, and that was the first occasion he'd had to use his slit trench.

But camp life was not all laughs. One night we lost a young private first class from our water purification unit, killed by "friendly fire," an accidental weapon discharge. He wasn't even a member of our battalion, just ran the water point for us. There was a court-martial, but the man who shot him was acquitted. The PFC had been wandering around in the dark without identifying himself. I think the court-martial was handled very professionally. We did lose a soldier, but we didn't lose the soldier who shot him. That is just one of those things that happens, particularly when you have hundreds of people running around with weapons.

Colonel Haldane was very strict on wearing steel helmets—

"pots," as we call them. The only time a man could get by without wearing one in the cantonment area was when he was in the shower. We wore our pots all the time because he wanted to save soldiers. We always stood out around Phuoc Vinh, because we were the ones wearing steel helmets everywhere. But I think we had the best battalion in the camp, and I think that was because we had Colonel Haldane. There are a lot of men who owe their lives to that man. When people talk about a person's "sixth sense," I remember Colonel Haldane, because he must have had eight or nine senses.

I like to think I was one of them. Wherever he went, I went too. I saw myself as the liaison between him and all the first sergeants and sometimes the company commanders in the battalion. I always tried to get Colonel Haldane's word down to everybody and to make sure we had the right NCOs in the field. When we went on an operation, *all* our noncommissioned officers went—we had no stay-behinds in that battalion. When the Old Man went, I went, and when I went, all the first sergeants went. I tried to hold the noncoms together in that battalion so the Old Man got the best out of them.

We had a captain who commanded B Company, Terry Christie, an Oklahoman, a wiry little guy. He had bad knees. On operations his NCOs would sometimes have to carry Captain Christie, his knees would get so bad. But that's the kind of officers and NCOs we had in that battalion, that's the *esprit* we had, where we supported each other, quite literally sometimes.

We got our first bloody nose the day before Thanksgiving 1965. We were coming back in from an operation and were about twenty kilometers from base camp when we ran into one hell of a firefight. After about an hour, Colonel Haldane radioed back to base, "Hold the turkey." We didn't get back in until that Saturday. We were out looking for a fight that day and we found one. I think we ran into a regiment of VC. We lost about eight or ten killed and maybe twice that wounded, but we ran them off. We figured they were on their way to hit Phuoc Vinh, but they never got there. Our men acquitted themselves very well, and I was proud of them.

At one point on the return trip we had to cross a little stream over a log, and when the companies came over the Old Man and I were there with the lead company. B Company—Captain Christie's company—was the last one. We were about eight kilometers out of base camp by that point. When they got up to us he said, "I want to tell you, Sergeant Major, you and Colonel Haldane did something for my company today that I didn't think could be done. They were really down. We were tired and we'd been kicked around, but when they saw you and the battalion commander standing there, already across the stream they would have to cross, word went back down through the ranks, 'If those two old bastards can make it, by God, so can we!' "

Colonel Haldane at forty-one and I at forty were the two oldest men in that battalion. But that made me feel good. I had the respect of the men and their company commanders. One of the traditions in the battalion when someone griped about how much he had to carry in the field was to suggest he change packs with me. I used to carry extra stuff, because when we stayed overnight in a position I'd need just about two of everything. I'd dig a prone shelter for the Old Man and me and lay down two poncho covers. I also carried two wool sweaters for sleeping at night. Actually they were the upper halves of two pairs of old World War II GI wool underwear. The troops used to laugh at me until they found out how damp and miserable it could get at night in the jungles of Vietnam.

By the way, it was about this time that I got a telegram from home informing me that Kathy, our oldest daughter, had given birth to Kristine, making me a grandfather. I think that made me the only grandpa in that battalion. Now Kristine has a five-year-old son. Boy, pretty soon I'll be an old man.

When General Seaman asked for me to be his sergeant major at II Field Force, Colonel Haldane told him, "When you replace this guy you've got to give me a man who can carry the heaviest pack in the battalion, walk all day, shoot as straight as anybody, dig a foxhole for the two of us, and still be able to walk the line to see if the troops are ready." That was one of the finest compliments I've ever gotten from anybody.

We conducted many village sweeps, where we would start out toward a village at three in the morning to get there at daylight—and that's a real experience, going through that goddamn jungle at night. You can't see *anything* under there. There's no light under that triple-canopy jungle in the daytime, much less at night. You've really got to have your stuff together to keep two or three companies of infantry—two to three hundred men—where they need to be in order to surround a village in the dark.

My reenlistment came up in December 1965, and Colonel Haldane decided to reenlist me in the field. We happened to be conducting an operation in War Zone C and they'd just prepped the area we were to assault with artillery, and when we came into the landing zone in our helicopters there was still some smoke in the impact areas.

Colonel Williams, the aviation battalion commander, was flying the ship Colonel Haldane and I were on, and when we disembarked, he climbed out on the pilot's side at about the same time the brigade S-3 asked Colonel Haldane and me what the hell we were doing.

"We're going to reenlist the sergeant major," the Old Man told him.

"You're going to do *what*?" the S-3 exclaimed, one foot on the ground and the other still inside the chopper. He just stood there, frozen in that position.

I had my right hand up, taking the oath of reenlistment, and Colonel Haldane had his up giving it to me, and Colonel Williams, for some reason, was also holding one of his hands up in the air. When it was all over, Colonel Haldane said to him, "I don't know what in the hell *you* had your hand up for, Willie, but you just reenlisted in the Army."

After the brief ceremony was over, Colonel Haldane said, "Okay, Top, we'll see you." I asked him what he meant by that, and he informed me that Colonel Williams was taking me back to division headquarters with him. I said no, I was going on the operation with him. "No, you are not," he told me, "and that's an order. I know you want to go on this operation, but this is one time you ain't going. You get on that goddamn helicopter and get all your paperwork together so you can send your reenlistment bonus back to Hazel and she can meet you in Hong Kong." He knew I was planning to meet Hazel there on leave.

So I went back to Di An, got all the paperwork done and the money on its way to Hazel, and spent a couple of nights with Bill Wooldridge, the 1st Division sergeant major, before returning to Phuoc Vinh. That was the only operation I missed with that battalion while I was with it, and that was only by the direct order of my commander.

In December 1965 and January 1966, the 3rd Brigade, our battalion, and the 173rd Airborne Brigade cleared the area around Cu Chi for the incoming elements of the 25th Infantry Division. We really didn't clear it out, we just established a toehold for the 25th. We had a hell of a fight about two days before they were supposed to arrive. They were coming up from the coast the same way we had, by road. We got hit and hit hard. In my battalion we lost about twelve or fifteen men that day. We had the entire battalion committed with support from the 173rd. So we didn't really "clear" the area, we just jumped out of our foxholes and the 25th jumped in behind us, but at least we had the holes dug for them and they were ready to assume the position.

I think that time we were up against about four regiments of Vietcong with some North Vietnamese Army units mixed in. The enemy didn't want the 25th Division in the Cu Chi area. The 25th used to kill more enemy in their perimeter than a lot of other units got out in the jungles looking for them.

In 1965 the 25th Division commander was Maj. Gen. Fred Weyand, who later, as Army Chief of Staff, was to select me as his Sergeant Major of the Army. In 1968 the division was commanded by Gen. Ellis "Butch" Williamson, the guy I bought that peripatetic washing machine from back when I was assigned to the VII Corps in Germany.

We talk today about how news in the war zone is instantly transmitted back into our living rooms, but even in those days the news was quick to reach the folks at home. Well, during that clearing operation, one night Hazel was watching the news back in Ogden, Kansas, and I walked right into the living room. A CBS cameraman got me. She said it really shocked her—suddenly I was there on the TV screen and then I was gone—but at least she knew I was still making it at that point.

I must now confess that at one point I probably caused CBS a little problem during that particular operation. The brigade S-3 was with our battalion when he was hit by one of those little "Bouncing Betty" plastic mines. It took off the heel of his right foot and sprayed fragments all up through his buttocks into his groin, and a CBS cameraman was right on him. I told the cameraman, "Don't take that picture! Hell, his wife's gonna see it in the next couple of days, and you don't want that to happen!" He said no, no, this is what I'm over here for. So I told him, "You are either gonna get rid of that film or I'm gonna take it away from ya." He got rid of the film.

The brigade S-3 made it all right, and he wound up being the project officer for construction of the new Walter Reed Hospital building. But he was in dire straits at that moment. His name is Bill Crites. Because of that wound he was transferred from the infantry to the Medical Service Corps and eventually became project officer of the new hospital. As a matter of fact, he gave me a tour of the place after I took over my job at the Soldiers' and

Airmen's Home (now the Soldiers' and Airmen's Branch of the Armed Forces Retirement Home).

It was also during this operation that I witnessed another example of Colonel Haldane's sixth sense. On this occasion we were reoccupying a position we'd been in several days before, and I remember it was just before the Tet 1966 holidays. Tet is the Vietnamese New Year celebration, and everything just comes to a halt for them during that time—supposedly.

We couldn't have church services that Sunday, because for some reason I cannot recall now the division chaplain, Col. Harry Hathaway—"Harry Chat Away," we used to call him, because he talked so much—couldn't make it out to officiate. So on the next day, Monday, we had our services. We were also expecting a hot meal later in the day that was being flown in to us on a chopper. When we got up that morning, Colonel Haldane ordered that we fortify our positions, because the Tet holidays would be over the next day and he wanted us to be ready in case we were attacked that night or early the next morning.

Well, church services started at about eleven o'clock that morning and they were about halfway through when suddenly I knew that we were going to move. Something just told me. I guess I'd started thinking the same way or along with Colonel Haldane, and as soon as the services were over, he gave the order to saddle up and move out.

You know those soldiers were hacked off. They'd just finished doing extra work on their positions and were looking forward to spending the night there, and now they were ordered to walk away and leave them. We left behind one gun jeep and four men to meet the chopper that was scheduled to bring in our hot meal. The chopper was late, and we were probably six or seven hundred meters out of that position when all kinds of hell broke loose. The VC hit our old position with everything they had. We didn't lose a man. The gun jeep had one man wounded. We didn't get our hot chow, but if we'd been twenty minutes later in moving we'd have been hit hard.

We set up that night in another position maybe five kilometers away from the old one, and at three o'clock in the morning they hit us again, but they made a mistake—they hit four hundred meters to the west of where we really were, one of our outposts instead of our main perimeter, and we really knocked their socks off that morning. We took half a dozen men wounded, but we kicked the hell out of a bunch of VC. I think they were still angry because they'd missed us the previous afternoon.

* * *

But that particular operation did have its light moments.

Colonel Haldane's driver and radio operator was a guy by the name of Ertelt. He was working shirtless on putting up a tent at one point during this clearing operation when he brushed up against a rubber tree and a whole bunch of these ferocious red ants dropped right down the back of his trousers. I remember these creatures because it seemed they carried their tails folded up over their backs, like scorpions. He was dancing around trying to get his trousers off, and I couldn't help laughing at him, not because I thought it was funny he was getting stung like that, but because his antics were so hilarious. When it was all over and we'd gotten him de-anted, he said, "You know, those are the toughest insects I know of. Anybody who can carry five times his own weight and run around with his ass up between his shoulders has got to be tough."

I got my first Chinook* ride on the trip back to Phuoc Vinh, after that operation. I still to this day don't like to ride in a Chinook. It seemed to me that the pilot flew one end of the thing for a while and then the other end for a while and then didn't fly either end the rest of the time.

In March 1966 I was getting ready to go on leave, to meet Hazel in Hong Kong, as I've mentioned previously, and I'd sent her the reenlistment money. Colonel Haldane's wife, Alise, had sent me the address of the Carleton Hotel in Hong Kong; she had stayed there one time and recommended it to us. So I wrote for reservations. But in corresponding with Hazel I asked her to make reservations also, just in case. She made them at the Holiday Inn, on Hong Kong Island; the Carleton was over on the Kowloon side. Well, I never heard from the Carleton, and after Hazel had made reservations for us at the Holiday Inn, we decided to stay there instead.

When the battalion surgeon found out that I was going on leave, he asked Colonel Haldane if he could go with me. His name was Isaac (Ike) Goodrich, and he'd been married about four

---

*Officially the CH47 medium-transport helicopter. It could move up to four tons of cargo or thirty-three troops. Cargo or artillery pieces could be sling loaded and transported underneath. The CH47 used twin rotors and could cruise at a speed of 150 MPH with a range of about 250 miles.

days before he went to Vietnam. I also thought it was a good idea that we go together.

Every soldier in Vietnam was authorized during his one-year tour a seven-day rest and recuperation (R&R) at a variety of special centers in Southeast Asia and the Pacific. This was not leave but essentially one week off from the war. But when Colonel Haldane found out that I was going to spend my R&R in Hong Kong with Hazel, he told me if I was going to spend all that money to bring Hazel over there, R&R wouldn't be good enough, and he authorized me to take ten days' leave instead. So I took ten days and we had a full week together in Hong Kong.

In the meantime, Maj. Gen. Jonathan O. Seaman, 1st Division commander, was being transferred to command II Field Force Vietnam, which was just setting up at Long Binh. The IIFFV had been activated at Fort Hood, Texas, in January 1966 as a redesignation of XXII Corps, which had seen action in World War II. Eventually IIFFV became the largest Army combat command in Vietnam. It exercised operational control over all U.S. and allied forces in the South Vietnamese Army's III Corps Tactical Zone, which meant the dozen or so provinces immediately surrounding Saigon.

I Field Force was activated at the same time in Nha Trang, but it emerged from Task Force Alpha (Provisional), which had been established in the I Vietnamese Corps area in August 1965. The I Corps Tactical Zone was composed of the five northernmost provinces of South Vietnam.

The field forces were equivalent to Army corps, but we called them field forces because otherwise it would have been confusing, operating as they were within the existing Army of Vietnam corps zones I, II (the dozen provinces of south-central Vietnam and including the cities of Da Lat, Cam Ranh, Nha Trang, Tuy Hoa, Pleiku, and Kontum), III, and IV (the area to the south of Saigon). Also, the field force was more flexible than a regular U.S. Army corps formation in that it permitted adding subordinate units and additional responsibilities not normally a part of a corps' tactical mission and peculiar to Vietnam, such as pacification and advisory roles to the Vietnamese Army.

General Seaman asked Sergeant Major Wooldridge to go with him to IIFFV, but Bill did not want to leave the division. Nevertheless, General Seaman was determined to pick his sergeant major from some unit in the 1st Division. Bill Wooldridge, so I am told, suggested he take a look at me for the job, and General Seaman said, "I don't have to. He's the only battalion sergeant major who's always where the battalion is. I've never found the battalion in the field and him in the base camp."

I did not know any of this was taking place when I got a call from brigade headquarters that Danger 6—the division commander's call sign—was on the way to our location and wanted me to meet him. I told Colonel Haldane that Danger 6 was on his way and wanted me to meet him. "I'm sure the transmission was garbled," I said. "He probably means you're to meet him." Colonel Haldane said no, he really wanted to see me.

I met General Seaman at brigade headquarters. He had with him a captain by the name of William Dorris Merritt—I always asked him if anybody else ever knew what his middle name was—who retired as a colonel at the Pentagon about the same time I did. It was when General Seaman announced that he wanted me as his sergeant major that Colonel Haldane told him he'd have to replace me with a guy who could do all the things I had done while I was with the battalion.

I told General Seaman that I was getting ready to go on leave, and he said that was okay, I should go to Hong Kong first and then report to II Field Force when I got back.

Then Captain Merritt informed me that the general wanted to take a driver out of the battalion in addition to me and he'd like me to pick the man. I agreed, and I knew just who it was going to be—Specialist Fifth Class George Johnson out of the motor pool. I told Colonel Haldane about the general's requirement, and he said, "Yes, and I bet it's going to be Johnson out of the motor pool." He admitted that he didn't want to lose either of us but said that he'd rather he lose us that way than have the general come down and levy someone at random who might not work out. "I know this way he's getting good men, and I'd rather have my motor officers pissed off at me, Top, than the corps commander."

Warrant Officer Thurston, the battalion motor officer, was hacked off at me and the battalion commander. When I told Johnson about the decision, he didn't want to go. He said he liked it in the battalion and they needed him there. I told him the general needed him too. "Pack your foot locker. You're going. When I get back from Hong Kong I'm coming to get you, and you just be ready to go." He hemmed and hawed, but when I got back he was ready. As it turned out, he was very happy he did go, because it gave him a chance to head up the line. He was a master sergeant driving out of the White House motor pool when I came to town as the Sergeant Major of the Army.

* * *

But back to Hong Kong.

The just-married Captain Goodrich was a good battalion surgeon, a young doctor out of New York. We flew Air Vietnam into
Hong Kong, out of the clouds and into Kai Tak Airport. It's just
a finger of land sticking out into Hong Kong Bay, and when you
first see it, coming in between the mountains, you wonder how in
the hell a plane can land on *that* little thing.

As soon as we got into the airport, we checked on the flight for
Hazel and Diane, Captain Goodrich's wife. Diane was coming
from New York and Hazel from Kansas and they were going to
meet us in Hong Kong, and we got there within two and a half
hours of one another. Pretty good connections for flying halfway
around the world. Hazel and Diane had not met before the trip,
but they met by chance in San Francisco and flew over on the
same airplane together and through casual conversation discovered who it was they were going to meet and where.

While we were waiting, Captain Goodrich kept asking me what
time it was. This went on for quite a while. He must have asked
me thirty times in thirty minutes, and I finally had to tell him,
"They're gonna be here, Doc. Why don't you go into the rest
room and shave. It'll give you something to do." He came out
about twenty minutes later, having cut himself twice. As I said
earlier, he and Diane had been married only about four days before he left to go to Vietnam.

When the girls finally arrived, we all went to the hotel together,
but after that we went our separate ways. I decided to check out
the Carleton, so we took the ferry across the bay for a Hong Kong
dollar—five cents U.S. in those days—and then took a free shuttle
bus up to the hotel. The Carleton was way up on a mountainside,
and the view of the harbor and Hong Kong was absolutely beautiful. I told the management that I'd written for reservations but
had never heard anything back. "We've been holding a room for
you, Sergeant Major!" the manager told me. They showed me a
copy of their reply, but somehow it had never reached me in Vietnam before I left.

That same day we checked out of the Holiday Inn and into the
Carleton. It was marvelous. We sat up there at night and had our
dinner while watching the lights out in the harbor, and it was
just beautiful. When we were in our room all we had to do was
rise up a little from the bed and we could look out the window
and there was another view of the bay. And it was all about a
third of the price of our room over on Hong Kong Island.

We traveled all over the colony. We went shopping in the duty-free shops every day—we didn't do a lot of buying, but we did a lot of looking. We visited Aberdeen on the south side of Hong Kong Island, where they have all the floating restaurants, and ate there. It was an experience that neither of us will ever forget.

Those first months in Vietnam I'd lost a lot of weight. I hadn't been sick, but life in the field, living off C rations, and the constant walking in the high heat and humidity had reduced me to my "fighting" weight. One night during a rainstorm I had taken refuge under a poncho propped up by a stick, and as I reached out to adjust it, the rainwater ran down my arm, and when I shook it off, my wedding ring flew off. I just managed to catch it at the last instant. I put it on my dog-tag chain. I had it with me in Hong Kong when we stopped in a jewelry store, and I was fiddling with it while I was looking over the displays.

The jeweler observed that my ring was too big for me, and I told him the story. He clapped his hands together, and a little guy came out of the back of the shop and took my ring. About forty-five minutes later he returned my ring with a piece out of it, and it fit me perfectly. The jeweler refused any payment, although the piece he'd cut out of it was probably well worth the effort.

The last night we were there, we had dinner with the Goodriches at the Peninsula Hotel, an old hotel built by the British over on the Kowloon side of the bay. The cost of the meal was exorbitant by the standards of the day, but we thought, What the hell? We didn't have too much to lose—we were going back to Vietnam.

We had spent ten days in Hong Kong. I left about three o'clock in the afternoon the last day, and Hazel flew out the following morning.

During our stay in Hong Kong we saw as much as we could of the sights and really enjoyed ourselves. While nothing was for sure in those days—I had another five or six months to go in Vietnam—I had the feeling that somehow everything was going to turn out okay and I'd make it back to Kansas. I think that feeling of optimism about the future, which I shared with Hazel, made our time together in Hong Kong all the more enjoyable. We did not take our meeting there as any kind of a farewell.

The final episode of that trip didn't occur until 1974, when we were stationed at Fort Bliss, Texas. Hazel was cleaning out a closet in our quarters and found an old purse. She decided to throw it away, but before she tossed it out she went through it, and inside she found $60 worth of traveler's checks left over from our Hong Kong trip. About a month or so later we were up in

Mesilla, New Mexico, near Las Cruces, and she saw a little painting of a yucca cactus that caught her fancy, and lo and behold it
was on sale for $60. We still have it. It's one of Hazel's favorites.

Well, back to Vietnam.

As I mentioned, II Field Force Vietnam was just setting up
when General Seaman tapped me to be his sergeant major, and we
were out at Long Binh, about fifteen miles north of Saigon. We
had no permanent facilities out there at the time, just tents; there
was no mess, no club for the troops. The CG and his staff and
most of the senior NCOs, including myself, stayed at Bien Hoa in
a little complex and flew back and forth to Long Binh until we
got established.

The rest of the time I was in Vietnam we were still getting that
headquarters squared away. In 1966 we had an authorized strength
of 284 officers and men. Eventually the IIFFV headquarters elements consisted of an artillery battery; the 303rd Army Security
Agency, 6th Psychological Operations, and 53rd Signal Battalions;
military police, civil affairs, and transportation companies; a
postal unit; and various detachments such as military history, intelligence, public information, etc.

The headquarters eventually controlled the operations of the 1st
Cavalry; 1st, 9th, and 25th Infantry Divisions; at least five separate or detached infantry brigades; aviation, artillery, and armored
units; and even a Special Forces company. As I mentioned, it became the biggest U.S. Army tactical headquarters in Vietnam.

But in March 1966, things were just getting organized. When
we first came to Vietnam, every position in our battalion was
filled, but as the pace of the war increased, we started getting promotion vacancies as a result of the casualties we were taking and
people rotating out of the combat zone when their tours were up.
In Vietnam the units did not rotate after a year, individuals did. So
as time went by, the units were filled and refilled with new men
from the States.

I once again established a promotion board, this time for the
IIFFV headquarters. I set this one up as I had the one back in the
battalion, using the G-1, G-2, G-3, and G-4 sergeants major and
the first sergeant from the headquarters detachment.

The G-4 sergeant major was a guy named Farley, and during
one of the boards he asked an off-the-wall question of a man who
was up for sergeant first class: "Tell me, what is Building No. 1
on all Army posts?" This staff sergeant didn't have a clue. Neither
did I, and I was president of the board. I didn't say anything while

the man was in the room, but after he had been dismissed, I asked Farley, "Number one, where did you *get* that question? And number two, what's the answer?" He said, well, *everybody* knows that Building No. 1 on an Army post is the flagpole. Wrong, I informed him. "But where did you get that question?" I asked again. Farley admitted he'd just made it up, because at every post he'd ever been on, Building No. 1 had been the flagpole. Well, I just happened to know that the flagpole at Camp Forsythe at Fort Riley happened to be Building No. 460, so how in the hell could it *always* be Building No. 1?

"Strike that question," I told Farley, "and don't hold it against that guy or ask it anymore." I'd been in charge of the flagpole at Camp Forsythe, and had had to put the flag up and take it down many times. I knew old Farley was way off on that one.

While I was sergeant major of IIFFV we had a commanders' conference at Nha Trang, in central Vietnam, where IFFV was located. The sergeants major also had a meeting, and then afterward General Westmoreland spoke to us and asked us if we had any problems in the field. One of the problems we'd been experiencing down at the division level was that we, couldn't get promotions down to the troops. We felt that brigades ought to be able to promote their own people, at least at the lower enlisted grades. Why should they have to wait for allocations? If promotions were made based on the Army strength worldwide, why couldn't a combat unit in Vietnam promote to fill its own combat vacancies? About four months later we received that authority.

Keeping the exchanges stocked was another problem, but often correcting it was a matter of getting the word to the right people. I learned down in the battalion that when people told us we couldn't get this or that, you could send someone up the line to talk to the right people and get what you wanted down to the troops.

In those days there were a lot of secret, covert operations going on. I remember one day we were coming back from a trip and as our C-47 came in to land at Bien Hoa, down on the runway getting ready to take off was a U-2. There was a lieutenant on the aircraft with us, and he shouted out, "Lookee there! There's a U-2!" I asked where. "Right down there, Sergeant Major," and he pointed to the runway.

"I don't see any U-2," I told him.

He thought about that for a second and then said, "Oh, that's right. There aren't supposed to be any over here, are there?"

I spent a lot of time out in the field with the units. General Weyand, the commander of the 25th Division, was one of General Seaman's favorite commanders. General Weyand was a very tall man. He had a little Hawaiian lieutenant colonel as his inspector general, and when they opened up the officers' mess for the 25th Division, they invited us over to eat a meal. This little lieutenant colonel said he knew General Weyand was "against" him because—he turned to the bar—look how he'd had this bar built. This colonel was about the same height as I am, and our noses just about reached over the top of the bar, but it was just fine for General Weyand. "See, he's against us short people," the colonel insisted.

Weyand said, with an IG like this colonel, how could he ever go wrong? "If there's no problem out there, he goes out and makes one and then he fixes it."

Some of the division chiefs, the G-1, G-2, and so on, were sending out messages to the field commanders that they "will" do this or they "will" do that. We had a briefing every morning at around half-past seven, and after about maybe six weeks of this, General Seaman told his staff he'd been watching the message traffic between the staff and the field and he was concerned about the dictatorial attitude some of them had when passing on guidance. "It seems to me those commanders out there have been here awhile and they know what they're doing. In the future you might make 'suggestions,' but I want you to tone down your messages a little bit."

About three weeks later, one morning after the normal briefing, General Seaman told us, "I noted the message traffic this morning before I came to the briefing, and in it there were three messages *telling* field commanders what they should be doing in certain instances. I have noted who sent them. Now unless we can get those messages retracted and reworded, there will either be some field-grade Article 15s here or some healthy contributions to the Dong Nai Orphanage." The briefing ended with a mad scramble, and there were some "healthy contributions" to the orphanage.

The offensive messages came out of the G-2/G-3 shop and concerned tactical matters. General Seaman was of the opinion that those field commanders were doing a good job and didn't need advice from headquarters in the tone the staff was using. Providing advice is what the headquarters was all about, but General Seaman thought they were going about it the wrong way, with too much "direction."

As I mentioned earlier, during my time there I traveled a lot to the field with General Seaman. We traveled from the Mekong Delta region to up north of Saigon, into War Zones C and D. At that time we didn't have a lot of troops in the Delta. I got down into that region more often after I became U.S. Army Pacific sergeant major than I did while I was with IIFFV. More on that later.

I remember one trip when the commander of the aviation command out of St. Louis came over and we were flying out to visit some of the units. The general from St. Louis, a rated officer—that is, a pilot—insisted on flying his own helicopter. He was a terrible pilot. Most generals who fly helicopters aren't very good at it, in my experience, because they have too many other things to do and therefore never get the stick time they need to keep their hand in. There are exceptions, one of whom I'll mention later on.

During this particular trip, we had an escort or chase ship. At our first stop I told General Seaman that I would ride the chase ship from there on in. "I don't blame you, Sergeant Major," he said. "I would too if I could!"

Even a rough flight was worth it, because I was able to get a lot of things done on those visits. I could get the word to and take it back from the soldiers in the field units. I used to travel on my own, too, but when I traveled with General Seaman I'd always break off from his itinerary after our initial introductions and briefings. For instance, we'd go in to a division headquarters and get an overview briefing and then visit a battalion base camp, where General Seaman would receive another briefing. I wouldn't catch that second briefing, but with some knowledge of what the units were doing from what we'd learned at division, I'd go down with the battalion or brigade sergeant major and talk to the soldiers and noncommissioned officers and find out what was going on in the units, what they needed in their foxholes, in their base camps, and so on.

I'd talk to the first sergeants and platoon sergeants, and go right down into the line. If it was a base camp I'd ask them to show me their perimeter defenses. Not that the commander wasn't looking at that, too, but he looked at it from a different viewpoint from mine. I wanted to find out such things as whether or not everybody had an air mattress. You have to have those comforts in the field. It takes no practice to be miserable, and I believe if you can help a soldier improve his quality of life at whatever level he is in the Army, then you ought to do that. I think that's what "noncommissioned officer business" is all about, taking care of soldiers. As Gen. Bill Rosson used to say, you spend half your life taking care of soldiers and all of a sudden you turn around and find out that all along *they've* been taking care of *you*.

That assignment taught me the importance of having senior noncommissioned officers at that level, to provide input to the commander that he might not otherwise get. Not that subordinate commanders don't take care of their soldiers, but they have so many other things on their minds, especially in combat, that some things slip through the cracks. My job was to pick up those things.

For instance, you might think the post exchange is rather unimportant in the context of combat operations, but it can be very important to soldiers, providing cigarettes, chewing tobacco, writing paper, cigarette lighters—the things that one takes for granted during normal times but that take on great significance to soldiers when they aren't available out in the field. Also, the mail has got to get through. One of the most important things to the morale of a soldier in a combat zone is his mail. When such things were neglected, I could get the word to people who could fix them. Soldiers operate better if their morale is high.

Having been on the other end of things, I knew firsthand what some of the problems in the field were, and I think that was my greatest contribution while I was sergeant major of IIFFV. General Seaman was a great commander—he's dead now—but he also believed in taking care of his soldiers, and I had a hand in that. That was my first experience at corps level of being responsible for giving the commander advice.

One trip I'll never forget, because it brought the war home to me personally.

During that time one brigade of the 101st Airborne Division was attached to IIFFV. We visited the division when it was on an operation up in the II Corps Tactical Zone and went into a site just after it had had a firefight with some VC/NVA units. They had twelve or fifteen enemy bodies laid out, and on one of them they found a U.S. government check and a personal copy of an order for a new car and a photograph of a Capt. Jake C. Holland, who had been killed about a year before, when the enemy overran his position.

Holland had been A Company commander in the 1/28th Infantry at Fort Riley. He'd gone to Vietnam as an individual replacement, not with us when the whole unit deployed. That was hard to swallow. Here was an officer I'd known well, and evidently this dead enemy soldier had been in the action when Holland had been killed and had taken those personal items off his body.

When the notification that Captain Holland had been killed came back to the battalion, we hadn't gotten ready to go to Vietnam yet. His wife was still in the Junction City area. Colonel Fleeson, my battalion commander, and I went out to her quarters and presented her with the Purple Heart Medal that had been awarded to Captain Holland posthumously. This all came back to me then, a year later, and what made it all so poignant is that the guy who probably was responsible for Jake Holland's death had now been paid back in full.

I had little contact with the South Vietnamese Army (ARVN) in that job. On one occasion, when we visited the An Loc area, the Vietnamese had a whole bunch of jeeps lined up to meet us at the airstrip to take us to the local ARVN headquarters for a briefing. In a situation where we'd have had one corporal in charge of the transportation, there was an ARVN lieutenant or a captain at every vehicle, to make sure the general and his party were taken care of. That just proved to my mind how superior our Army's organization is to that of a lot of other armies around the world, in which for all practical purposes noncommissioned officers don't even exist.

We had other contacts with the local people, of course. There was this little village just outside the headquarters, a typical Vietnamese village with typical American soldiers riding around in these little three-wheeled Lambretta jitney buses that could carry a dozen Vietnamese or three Americans. We had a chaplain by the name of Holland C. Hope who was more of a jock and pistoleer than he was a chaplain, but once in a while he'd do a little preaching. Last time I heard of him he was down in El Paso, ministering in a parish.

On this one occasion, Chaplain Hope was headed downtown in one of those little taxis. He was in civvies. Another Lambretta with five or six GIs in it passed him. Evidently these soldiers had seen some Vietnamese gals by the roadside and had showered them with wolf calls and language the chaplain considered inappropriate for mixed company in public places.

Chaplain Hope told me later he stopped the jitney and asked the GIs to show him their IDs. He said they were shocked and didn't know if they should comply or not. He was a pretty good-sized fellow and he told them, "C'mon. I'm bigger than most of you guys. Just show me your cards. I want to compare IDs with you." They took their cards out, and Hope said, "Well, let's see now. Nobody else here is a colonel, and I am a colonel, so that puts me in charge." He then proceeded to tell them how they should conduct themselves in public and promised to give every man's name to me! He confessed he had no intention of doing that, because he didn't think it was really necessary, but he wanted me to know that they were concerned that I would find out about the incident.

Chaplain Hope was quite a guy in other ways too. One day General Seaman and I were visiting some wounded troops at the 93rd Evacuation Hospital and there, sitting on one of the bunks, was Chaplain Hope with a big bandage on the side of his head.

General Seaman said, "Holland, what are you doing here? I didn't know you'd been wounded!"

"Well, I really haven't been wounded, sir. I went to make a save on the volleyball court and hit my head on a jeep bumper and tore an ear off."

He never mentioned to anybody on the staff that he'd been hurt, much less stuck in the hospital.

That's another thing I was able to do in that job—visit the wounded and help bolster their spirits a little. Those field hospitals in Vietnam weren't the nicest places in the world. They were adequate, much better than anything the enemy had, but lying about in a field hospital is not the best way to spend your time. I made it a part of my business to get some messages to those guys and up their morale.

I also learned to eat water buffalo steak in that job. We'd have a little sergeant major get-together about once a month at some restaurant where we'd provide the meat. I'm sure the owners switched it on us as soon as we got to enjoying ourselves, but the dinner was a way to organize the sergeants major in the corps and make us into a team.

We were also able to organize a little villa for the senior noncommissioned officers in Bien Hoa that really contributed to the morale of those folks. We had our own generator and could get a cold beer in the evening. We never abused the privilege. We weren't a going-to-town bunch, and going to town at night wasn't the smartest thing to do anyway. I just didn't permit nighttime partying with those guys, because we had to be ready for duty at any time. We had plenty of chances to be in trouble in the daytime without looking for it at night.

Going from battalion to the IIFFV changed my perspective on the war completely. At IIFFV I was removed from the bang-bang part of the war—not that you couldn't get hurt at Long Binh, but you weren't right across the little Suoi Gai from the VC. But having spent time as a battalion sergeant major, I knew what the men in the field were going through. As far as I can remember now, I was the only enlisted man in the headquarters who had that kind of perspective, and the rest of them benefited from it. We had some good men on that team. There was no question in anybody's mind what he was there for.

I've run into some of them over the years. Once, when I was making a tour of the northwest as Sergeant Major of the Army, I saw the old IIFFV IG sergeant major in a hotel out in Seattle. He was still in the Army, and our paths just happened to cross in that hotel on that day. I'd just been told by the Chief of Staff that he was going to extend me in the job. We were sitting there talking, going over old times, and I confided in him, knowing that the news would go no further. It was just one of those old-soldier get-togethers. We'd been through some experiences together out in Vietnam.

We got a little NCO club started at Long Binh. Some of the people associated with that club ended up testifying before the Senate later in the infamous "khaki Mafia" NCO club scandal—but not because of that little club at II Field Forces! We took on Sergeant Higdon as the club manager about the time I was getting ready to leave. The guy had a great background and he was a good club manager. We didn't have a mess at IIFFV, so we put up a tent that served as an NCO club and kitchen. Higdon ran it as an NCO club in the evening for the troops at the headquarters, and from ten o'clock in the morning until one in the afternoon it was a mess hall. Meals were prepared in an outside kitchen and served in the club.

I was told we couldn't have a club, that we were in a war zone and we shouldn't have one. The G-1 did not want us to have it. I told him I didn't understand why. He explained that it just didn't seem "proper" to him to have one under wartime conditions. I told him I'd already gotten everything all set up.

"Well, I'm telling you, you can't have it," he told me.

"I'm going to have to inform you, sir," I responded, "that the chief of staff said we could."

"You mean to tell me you've got the Chief of Staff in this already?"

"Hell, yes," I said. "You know I work for the general, and the

Chief of Staff is his right-hand guy. We talked about this project, and there isn't any reason why we can't have our own club."

We set up the club.

The Chief of Staff was Brig. Gen. William C. Knowles, the only general officer pilot I ever knew who could really fly. He came to us from the 1st Cavalry Division and he brought with him his aide, Capt. Wayne Knutson. Knutson ended up with two stars, but he was also an instructor pilot, and he taught General Knowles the right way to fly. He was a younger fellow, had just made brigadier, and was serving as the assistant division commander with the 1st Cav.

What a hell of a pilot that Knutson was. One morning he took General Seaman to the headquarters. For some reason, I didn't go with him that morning. I had something to attend to back in the billet area. Anyway, Captain Knutson came back for me about ten o'clock, and as he was coming to land on our little helicopter pad the tail-rotor driveshaft on his bird broke. Well, I'd never seen a helicopter do so many gyrations in my life! But Captain Knutson landed that helicopter safely. It was a hard landing, but there was no damage to the ship.

I said, "Goddamn! That was a hell of a good piece of flying! Been a hell of a note if that had happened when you were a thousand feet up."

He said he wished he had been at a thousand feet, because if he'd had that much altitude he could have autorotated the helicopter in. As it was, he had to "fly" that machine to the ground. That's when I learned that a helicopter in autorotation is aerodynamically more stable than it is in flight, because there's no torque from the engine. But that morning I rode a jeep into Long Binh.

The road from Bien Hoa to Long Binh was a narrow, twisting section of Highway 15 about five miles long that came out near a small village.

Although Long Binh was only about fifteen miles north of Saigon, I got to Saigon only twice while I was there, both times to pick up equipment with my boss. I also made it down there when I caught my flight out of Tan Son Nhut, to go home, and we went through there on our way to Hong Kong. I was in Tan Son Nhut probably thirty or forty times. I had no business downtown. The Military Assistance Command, Vietnam (MACV) sergeant major while I was with IIFFV was Lew Coleman. He's in Audie Murphy Hospital in San Antonio now, suffering from Alzheimer's.

* * *

In July 1966, Bill Wooldridge was selected out of the 1st Division to be the first Sergeant Major of the Army. He was nominated by General Depuy, the division commander, and the nomination was endorsed by General Seaman, my boss. General Seaman showed me the nomination and told me he was going to endorse it. I told him I thought that was great. I said, "You ought to have somebody in there to start this thing out and start it out right, so that if I ever get the chance to be the Sergeant Major of the Army, at least the base will be right." I was serious, in that I thought Bill Wooldridge was a good choice to be the first SMA because he was a good soldier.

Bill Wooldridge was subsequently accused of a lot of things in connection with the NCO-club scandal, but to this day I don't think he has ever been found guilty of anything. Despite this, he and his family suffered for it. Whatever he did do that might have been wrong, it didn't happen during the time he was SMA. He acquitted himself well in that assignment and established a good precedent as SMA for the rest of us to shoot at. He deserves credit for establishing the office of the SMA on a solid footing. I'd also like to point out that several general officers went down the tubes over that scandal, most notably a major general who was Army Provost Marshal General.

I thought the new office of the SMA was a good idea. There was no doubt in my mind that the Chief of Staff of the Army had the soldiers' welfare in his mind. Yet he's got so many things to do, as does the rest of the Army General Staff. This new position provided an enlisted voice at the top level in the Army, to let the Chief of Staff know about the same kinds of problems I was trying to solve at the division and brigade and battalion level, only he could do it Army-wide.

A lot of things happen in the noncommissioned officer channel of communications that really pay off for the soldier while usurping no officer's command. It's a channel that provides information not obtainable any other way. You just think differently and act differently when you come from the grunt side of the Army than you do if you come from the officers' side. Anybody who fails to realize that is just not thinking straight.

General Seaman's stenographer, SP6 Mike Mays, had the only electric typewriter in the headquarters. Everybody else made do with an old manual. One morning he came in and started to type up a memorandum for the boss and his typewriter stopped. It squeaked. We raised up the top, and there, its hind leg caught in the drive, was a mouse. I'll never forget that little mouse tugging away, his hind leg caught in that motor belt. After that we called Mike the Great White Hunter. Mike went on to get a direct commission, and last I heard he was a major. We served together again in U.S. Army Pacific headquarters a few years later. What a ladies' man that guy was in those days. When we traveled around he'd disappear every chance he got.

When my time came to go back to the States, we began looking for a replacement. General Seaman was not going back himself, and he said he wanted someone from one of the field units. I knew a couple of people in the 1st Division who might fill the bill, but he decided we should look somewhere else, one of the other divisions, just to spread the honor around a little bit—not that they didn't have fully capable men in the 1st Division. He asked me to scout around and make some recommendations. Finally he picked Sgt. Maj. Jerome Syfranski out of the 25th Division to replace me.

About halfway through my tour at IIFFV, I got a set of orders alerting me to go to Minneapolis, Minnesota, as an adviser to the Minnesota National Guard. General Seaman got the orders before I saw them and said to me, "Sergeant Major, I just got this set of orders for this assignment, and I don't think the Army ought to waste your talents there. What do you think?" I told him I wanted to stay with troops if it was at all possible. He said he would send a message to Gen. William Beverley, who was the deputy chief of staff for personnel, to see if he could get those orders changed. I didn't think anything more about it.

Two or three weeks later, a message came back canceling those original orders and assigning me to the committee group at Fort Benning, Georgia. That organization conducted certain aspects of the basic training program at the Army Infantry Training Center at Fort Benning.

When I got back to Fort Riley, where I'd left Hazel and the girls, I got a message from the Sergeant Major of the Army's Office asking me to be the sergeant major of the Inspector General's Office at Department of the Army. I wasn't too keen on that and told them so. In the meantime, it developed that the sergeant major of the training center at Fort Benning, Clifton Benefield, was getting ready to retire. Gen. Charlie Mount, who had been our assistant division commander when we went to Vietnam, was now commanding the training center, and he asked that I be his sergeant major. So no Fort Snelling, Minnesota, no Pentagon—which pleased the hell out of me. I was still going to Fort Benning, but now I'd be the training center sergeant major as opposed to being an instructor with the training committee group.

I was scheduled to go back to the States on Continental Airways. I got down to Tan Son Nhut, all ready to go, and they called me over the public address system to report to the flight desk. My flight had been canceled and they were going to send me back on a C-141. I told them they could send me back on a Piper Cub if they wanted to—I was ready to go and didn't care how I got there!

We had to wait another day for the C-141 to come in. We flew into Clark Air Base in the Philippines, where we were supposed to change to another C-141. At that point, Murphy's Law took over. It turned out that the plane we were supposed to catch for the last leg of our flight to Travis Air Force Base was a medical evacuation aircraft. We had to sit around Clark for about thirty-six hours while they reconfigured that airplane for passengers instead of patients.

I spent that time tanking up on milk shakes and hamburgers. I want to gain weight after every war, it seems. I expect I put on four pounds in the snack bar while I was waiting. The shakes weren't made with fresh milk, but that didn't make any difference, they had ice cream in them and the hamburgers had catsup on them.

Hazel, Mary, and Kathy and son-in-law Steve picked me up at Kansas City. That was quite a homecoming. Most of the antiwar sentiment in this country at that time was from Las Vegas west and Pittsburgh east—the Midwest really didn't play host to most of that stuff. There certainly wasn't any in Ogden, Kansas. Those people welcomed me back as if I'd lived among them all my life. Damn near had, eight years on one assignment and three more before I went to Vietnam.

What are we to make of Vietnam? I saw a coffee mug the other day that had on it:

VIETNAM VETERAN
We Were Winning When I Left

Whoever thought that up was right. We were winning when I left. The reason I agree is based on what we did in the 1st Battalion of the 28th Infantry when I was there.

As the battalion sergeant major, I saw war again as the infantry-man sees it, at first hand, and it is not a pretty thing. It only takes minutes and you've got all the combat experience you'll need—ever. But it is something a soldier must do and is trained to do.

Going back to my World War II training experience, while it was not good, it was not all the fault of the trainers. Part of it was the system and part of it was that we didn't have time to train properly for war. Going into Vietnam, we'd had a bit longer to prepare, but we were still committing a terrible error with the on-the-job-training program. We taught well the things we knew well, but we did a terrible job teaching those things we didn't know well. That's the problem with OJT.

Our battalion in Vietnam was a good outfit. We had good soldiers and they acquitted themselves well in the field. There wasn't any doubt in their minds that they were in fact better soldiers than our enemy. We didn't always know what we were facing, but those men knew they had good equipment, good noncommissioned officers, good commissioned officers. The problem was with the orders from on high. We weren't permitted to conduct the war the way we knew how to fight it. It was a hit-or-miss thing, and we spent too much of our time trying to Americanize the Vietnamese. We wasted our time on civic action programs, the "pacification program," for which we were never trained—sending squads out into the villages. Those men became rusty as soldiers because they weren't doing what they were trained for.

I think the Army should have been turned loose to do what had to be done. We had all the artificial barriers: we couldn't cross the Demilitarized Zone, we couldn't go into Cambodia, we couldn't go into this area or that one. We were hampered by too many "couldn'ts." When I was there, we couldn't fire artillery into certain areas. You will remember the little village outside Phuoc Vinh from which we'd get mortars—we couldn't return fire, because there was a church located there and we weren't permitted to shoot at it. But the VC had no restrictions on firing at us from behind that church.

I understand that politics is what determines wars. During the Gulf War, a reporter asked Gen. Norman Schwarzkopf when the cease-fire would take effect and he answered that that was for the decision-makers to determine. Here's a four-star general, running the war, and he's not the ultimate decision-maker. Everybody's got a boss. But what went wrong in Vietnam was that we had too many bosses telling us what to do in the field.

We put a large force in Vietnam equipped to win, and then we decided to turn things over to the Vietnamese and let them win it. Well, they didn't win their war, because they weren't ready to win it. The people on the other side had more resolve, and they overwhelmed the southerners. I think it could have been won if our soldiers had been permitted to do what they were trained for. Our leaders kept demanding more men and telling us they could see the "light at the end of the tunnel." It turned out that light was an oncoming freight train.

Now, I do not think that any serviceman, any soldier who came out of Vietnam, has to feel ashamed for that war. In my battalion, when we kicked hell out of the VC, we felt proud. We felt we'd won that one. We lost some people and that was hard, but we did our job.

To contrast Desert Storm with Vietnam—and all I know about Desert Storm is what I saw on CNN—the commanders there were permitted to do what they knew was right. They got all the forces they asked for, and they were permitted to hold off the attack until they were ready for it. Thus they were able to put things together so they could fight the war on their own terms. Our commanders in the Persian Gulf were able to fight by the rules of war—to destroy the enemy as quickly as possible with the least amount of damage to their own forces. We sure as hell didn't do that in Vietnam. It was peck, peck, peck, draw back; peck, peck, peck, draw back. If we are going to have a war, we shouldn't tie our commander's arm behind his back.

Also, the war in Vietnam continued to go on for so long, because of this peck-and-draw-back approach, that the people back home got fed up with it. I don't care how much "resolve" a nation has, when you're in a conflict for that long and the body bags keep coming back day after day, it's going to wear on your people, particularly when your forces aren't allowed to really fight the enemy. That didn't happen in Desert Storm. When General Schwarzkopf got the word to go, he knew that meant go all out. One of his commanders said he'd been training for that battle all his life. That tells you something about how far we've come since World War II. We now have a graduated training system that has provided us with the best fighting force we've ever had.

And this time we had a President who made up his mind early on that he was not going to take a backseat to anybody. He insisted that the war would be fought on our terms and not on the other guy's. That's got to concern you, if you're the "other guy." The public felt that here was a President who didn't want to go to war in the first place, but now that he was committed, he was going to do it *right*. That didn't happen in Vietnam.

When President Bush talked about his commanders in Saudi Arabia, he glowed with confidence in them. How do you think that made them feel about his leadership? He knew he had some great people over there, and he relied on them. The *Washington Post* said just after Desert Storm that Bush's overall popularity according to a poll they commissioned was at 91 percent. That's unheard-of. I'm no big George Bush fan, but I have to give the man his due. He flat put that thing together, and he put it together right. Again, he let his commanders do what they knew they could do. He told them to tell him when they were ready, and then he gave them the order to execute the attack. You can't beat a deal like that.

Gen. Bill Rosson, who was my U.S. Army Pacific commander, didn't like staff work at all. When we got on his aircraft to head out to Vietnam or to Korea, anyplace where there were soldiers, General Rosson took on an entirely different demeanor. You could just see the glow. Well, that's almost the same relationship I saw the senior military command having with President Bush. It's like the relationship a good commander has with his command sergeant major. There's no way to describe that kind of rapport unless you've been there, and I think Bush had it with his senior military commanders. The sergeant major asks his commander to give him his guidelines and then backs off and lets him do the job.

That's not how we did it in Vietnam. But that's all behind us now. On to Fort Benning.

≡ 7 ≡

STIRRING THINGS UP AT BENNING

At the time I was assigned duty at Fort Benning, Georgia, in September 1966, I was better than midway through my Army career. That was my first visit to Fort Benning, which is unusual for a Regular Army infantryman. Known as the Home of the Infantry, Benning is also home to the Army's airborne and Ranger training courses. Had I gotten there earlier in my career I might have become a paratrooper or a Ranger, but I never did see the reason why I had to be a jumper or a Ranger to be a good noncommissioned officer.

In those days the "elite" thing to do was to be airborne or Ranger, but my philosophy has always been that regardless of the kind of unit you're in, it ought to be an "elite" outfit, because its NCOs can make it one by ensuring that every soldier understands his job and how to do it right. Everybody doesn't need special qualifications to make that work. I think that's one reason I never became jump-qualified or went to the Ranger course, and by the time I got to Benning it was a little too late for that stuff anyway. I'd already done fairly well as a noncommissioned officer without being three things: I wasn't airborne, I wasn't a Ranger, and I wasn't a Mason.

Masonry used to be a big "in" thing in the Army. I never was one. I was an Odd Fellow at Fort Riley for a short period of time. That was because some friends of mine decided that I would be a good member of their lodge. I went from being a member to being the senior guy in the quickest time it'd ever been done in that lodge. Several times while I was Director of Member Services at the Soldiers' and Airmen's Home, residents mistook me for a Mason and gave me a sign and when they drew a blank said, "Oh, I thought you were a Mason!"

I always used to joke when I first came into the Army that I wouldn't have made a good paratrooper anyway because I'd probably go *up* instead of *down*, being as light as I was. I know being a paratrooper or a Ranger is a glamorous thing, and I think there's a definite requirement for the skills, but it's a small and very specialized one. The intensive individual training those men get certainly adds to what they can do in other types of units, but it sometimes works the other way, too, by making them shortsighted in some other important ways when it comes to soldiering.

Fort Benning is named after Confederate States Army Brig. Gen. Henry Lewis Benning (1814–1875), a Georgian and a former member of the state supreme court. The old boy served throughout the entire Civil War, from August 1861 to Appomattox. Fort Benning was established in 1918 and today comprises over 180,000 acres of maneuver and training areas.

Fort Benning is on the south side of Columbus, Georgia, population 170,000. It sits on the east bank of the Chattahoochee River. In 1966 the area reeked of the paper mills along that stretch of the river. You have to smell them to believe them, but the human nose can get used to anything.

We drove from Fort Riley to Benning. We sold our trailer before we left. We'd bought it in 1954 at Manhattan, Kansas, for around $7,500, an exorbitant amount then. We sold it now for about $2,500. That trailer paid for our household furniture when we got to Fort Benning.

We had a 1962 Buick, and our youngest, Mary, took that car to Manhattan, Kansas, without permission while we were waiting to go to Fort Benning and she wrecked it. I don't recall anymore if it was her fault or the other driver's, but I do remember the car was damaged to the point we couldn't drive it to Fort Benning. Luckily, Mary wasn't hurt in the accident, but her feelings were sure hurt after the talking-to I gave her.

Well, our son-in-law, Steve Koop, insisted we take his car, a two-door Ford. We did and put our car in the garage. Later we drove Steve's Ford back and picked up the Buick. Mary traveled down to Benning with us, of course.

There were no quarters for us when we got to Benning. We were given a cabin out in the Sand Hill area of Fort Benning, which was six miles from my office as the training center sergeant major. Sand Hill was the old World War II cantonment area and the basic training center for Fort Benning.

When we got permanent quarters they were at 225 Bryant Avenue, up on the Main Post. They were duplex quarters, and our apartment had three bedrooms. We furnished it with the money from the sale of our trailer. We took that money and went to the Sears, Roebuck in Columbus, Georgia, and bought a trailer's worth of furniture.

We bought a washer and a dryer, a couple of beds, a davenport, some other things. We still have the dryer and it's still working. We still have the beds and the davenport too. Not having a big bankroll in those days, we decided to put a little of that trailer money in a savings account and pay off the Sears balance on time.

That store had a policy that if you paid off a credit account within ninety days there'd be no interest charged on it. We went about six months and then decided that the 18 percent interest we were paying Sears and the 6 percent interest our money was earning in the bank didn't hardly match up, so we went back down to Sears one Saturday and told them we wanted to pay our account off. We compared our figures with Sears's and there was about an $8 difference—in favor of Sears.

The credit manager, the dependent wife of a soldier at Fort Benning, went to get the store manager. After about fifteen minutes he came out and informed us he'd let us pay off the account and the store wouldn't charge us *any* interest. We saved that six months' interest and I've been a Sears customer ever since.

The quarters themselves were great. We had a driveway off the street, no carport or garage, but off-street parking. We had a yard and a small patio out back. There were probably two hundred other sets of quarters like ours in that housing area, all built in the late 1950s. They were of brick-and-frame construction with central heating and also central air, something we'd *never* had. Before, in those hot summers at places like Fort Riley, we'd survived by opening all the windows. At Benning for the first time we had air conditioning.

Mary went to school at Columbus High. The city of Columbus, Georgia, abuts Fort Benning, and Phenix City, Alabama, is just to the west of Columbus, across the Chattahoochee. At times, Phenix City had been off-limits to the troops from Fort Benning, but not while we were there. I don't recall ever going over there anyway, unless I drove through it a few times going home on leave to Illinois.

The Infantry Training Center consisted of three basic training brigades, the committee group—instructors who taught phases of the basic infantry training courses—and the training center headquarters, a general staff commanded by Brig. Gen. Charlie Mount. At any given time while I was there, the Infantry Training Center had about fifteen thousand men in the various stages of its basic training program from Zero Week to graduation.

That was where I ran into Jim Runyon and Russ Keene, two of my brigade sergeants major. Russ is dead now. I don't know what became of Jim. Later on, Jim took my position as Infantry Training Center sergeant major when I went to Fort Meade, Maryland, as First Army sergeant major.

One of the first things I found out I had to do when I got to my new job was attend the annual Association of the United States Army (AUSA) convention in Washington, D.C., in October.* I was told I needed a set of dress blues for the occasion. I never had had a requirement for them before. I shelled out about $180 for a set, a pretty good pinch in 1966 even for a sergeant major.

In those days the AUSA was not as well publicized as it should have been. I certainly didn't know much about it. I'd been a member at Fort Riley early on, back in the 1950s, when it was first formed, but I really had no idea what the organization was all about. That is why today I try to tell soldiers what it stands for, what it can do for them, and what it's been doing for them for years.

Benning had one of the biggest chapters, and one reason for that was that going through officer candidate school required becoming an AUSA member. Joining was part of your processing. It was also part of your processing at the NCO academies.

The requirement to go to the convention came at a bad time, because we were trying to get organized, living in temporary quarters, and getting my daughter into school, although the trip turned out to be nice. Registration was on Sunday and the official meetings commenced on Monday. Tuesday was the "hospitality rooms," and in those days it was one big bash. Lots of people got into trouble—not big trouble but plenty of little trouble, swinging

*The Association of the U.S. Army is a not-for-profit professional organization composed of active-duty and Reserve Components officers and enlisted soldiers, retired personnel, and civilians, formed, according to its charter, "for the purpose of exchanging ideas and information on military matters and to foster, support and advocate the legitimate and proper role of the Army of the United States and all of its branches and components in providing for and assuring the nation's military security." The association is administered by officers and a council of trustees and various advisory committees supported by a small administrative staff with headquarters in Arlington, Virginia. The association publishes a monthly professional journal, *Army* magazine.

out of hotel-room windows on ropes, that sort of thing. That's one reason I'm glad I wasn't a Ranger, because I would have been no good at rappelling. I remember a guy who rappelled out a window and scraped himself all the way down the side of the building and into some vines. That's the story, anyway. Maybe he just got into a fight he couldn't finish.

The Army flew us up to Washington for the convention on a C-130, which landed at Andrews Air Force Base, in Maryland. Buses met us there and took us right down to the hotel. All we had to pay for was our hotel rooms and what we ate. Today if the Army were to run a C-130 load of soldiers out of Fort Benning up to Andrews just to go to the AUSA conference, somebody would probably wind up in jail.

But on the other hand, what used to be a three-day party at those annual conventions is now a much more serious affair, a three-day learning experience. Attendance at the conventions these days is just like another training exercise. The soldiers who go learn a hell of a lot—they rub elbows with people they'd never see under normal circumstances, senior officers and NCOs and important people in the defense industry who supply the equipment soldiers must train with and use in combat, the equipment that makes ours the finest army in the world today. I think Saddam Hussein would back me up on that statement.

At Fort Benning there was the Main Post and the training center. On Main Post was the Ranger course, the OCS, the airborne school, and other schools like the operations sergeant course, the weapons course, and so on. The chain of command ran from the post commander through the school commandant to the training center commander. The post commander was the big wheel, the commandant took care of all the schools, and my boss took care of basic training.

At that time they had a Zero Week at the training center. During Zero Week the basic trainee was processed into the Army— was issued his uniforms, got his immunizations, and so on, before his formal training actually began. Zero Week was really a detail week. As the training center sergeant major, every morning I had to make sure that a certain number of people from the Zero Week battalion or company were furnished for details at different places around the post.

After I'd been there about a month, I was able to start recommending some changes. I observed that the Sand Hill Chapel got four men a day. The post sergeant major got a hundred. First I took care of the chapel. I called the chaplain and told him henceforth he'd only get one man one day a week. He fell apart. I told him those four men were doing all the stuff his chaplain's assistant was getting paid to do. After some negotiation we settled on two men one day a week. That worked out fine.

Then I started a surveillance of what the one hundred detail men were doing up on Main Post. We had to have them up there at seven o'clock in the morning, but I discovered that most days they weren't doing anything until about nine-thirty or ten, just sitting around waiting for somebody to decide what they should do. I called the post sergeant major, Pete Jones, and told him he was only going to get fifty people starting the next week. All hell broke loose. I told him he didn't need even fifty men, the way I saw it, but I'd give him the fifty anyway. I told him what I had observed. After a while, John agreed to try it. We left it that way for about a month and then cut the number down to forty men. By the time I left there to go to First Army less than a year later, we had it down to twenty-five men.

Make-work for soldiers, especially soldiers who are just learning to be soldiers, doesn't make sense to me, and my commander appreciated what I did.

I knew what we were supposed to be doing at Benning, what our charter was. I went around first with General Mount and got acquainted with everybody, but once I got on board with all those noncommissioned officers, I didn't have any problems. I started having NCO calls* at least once a month. We'd get together at the club just to relax—no big party—at the end of the duty day, from five-thirty or six to maybe seven-thirty or eight, and we'd enjoy a sandwich and a beer and iron out some of our problems. These NCO calls were great for exchanging ideas—on training procedures, on how to improve communication between noncommissioned officers, on how to get the most out of each training day—and they also helped us strengthen our sense of community. I was told they'd never had much of that type of activity at the training center before I got there.

I spent most of my time at Benning out where the training was being conducted. I estimate I spent maybe 20 percent of my time in the office. The rest of the time I was out looking around on my own.

---

*An NCO call is a semiformal meeting of a unit's noncommissioned officers, usually presided over by the unit first sergeant or sergeant major, designed to exchange news and views and discuss problems and items of common interest.

The training day at Benning began at four o'clock in the morning. I was usually at work by five-thirty. By then the troops would already be out doing physical training. I liked to hit a battalion or a company not just at one o'clock in the afternoon but also at four-thirty or five or even after dark, to get a feel for what they were doing.

I've often told NCOs I've met in my travels that it's always good when you're at a training center to get up when the troops get up, go out and stand on the street and *listen* to the sounds of basic training. They are different at four o'clock in the morning from what they are at three in the afternoon. In the mornings the day is crisp and the rest of the world hasn't even thought about getting up yet, but here the Army is, full-bore into a day's training. That day doesn't end until eight o'clock at night. I tell them, "Don't forget where you come from. Don't forget how you got where you're at now." It all starts down in the basic training units, and NCOs shouldn't forget, when they're in the catbird seat, making decisions and running their own training programs, that they were once down there on the receiving end.

When I got to the office I'd work on the detail list and then have a staff conference at eight o'clock, visit with the commander at his desk around eight-thirty; I might go over to the G-1 (personnel) to check on orders for the men leaving or on the status of the men being held over. I never liked to have men hanging around for some silly little thing. Maybe I'd be over at the post office, asking why the mail wasn't being delivered to our units on time.

After lunch I might visit a post exchange down in one of the brigades, trying to find out why the men couldn't get the right kind of collar brass insignia. Those insignia only came in sets—two "U.S." and two insignia of branch. This was a holdover from earlier times when soldiers were required to wear insignia on each lapel of the uniform dress jacket. But you needed only one of each, because the uniform regulations then required a "U.S." insignia on the right collar and the branch on the left. So why continue making soldiers buy *four* to get the two they needed? Eventually I got that fixed.

Then maybe I'd visit a company and find it had seven people excused from training. Why? Because their feet hurt. Why? I might find that four of those seven hadn't been issued boots yet. Why not? Because the quartermaster hadn't had their size when they came through for initial issue. Why not? Somebody had screwed up. So I'd find out the who and why and straighten the situation out.

My day usually ended around six or six-thirty.

That was a typical day, attending to a hundred different things, and with luck I wouldn't have to go to the general to get any of them fixed—some noncommissioned officer along the way could fix all those things, and my job was to find out who he was. It was the usual stuff, taking care of soldiers.

But it wasn't all work and no play. We had unit picnics. I learned how to play golf at Fort Benning. They had a terrible nine-hole course. Naturally, I didn't know a good course from a bad one in those days, but I got to playing with some of the guys there. I think I spent a fortune on balls, many of which seemed to wind up in a little pond on the ninth hole.

General Mount's driver was an enterprising young guy from Albany, New York. He and his wife lived in quarters at Benning. About twice a week he'd wade into that pond and recover the balls and sell them. I don't know why nobody had ever thought of that before, but the first time he went in there he got two thousand balls out of the water. He took them home and put them in the washing machine, on a slow cycle, got all the algae washed off, ran them through clean water with a little bleach, and sold the good ones for fifty cents apiece. He made a lot of money. But I'm sure, after so long under the water, some of those balls he sold to golfers didn't go very far when they were hit.

I think we did a fairly good job preparing young men for Vietnam. By then we were getting some Vietnam feedback experience, and we were able to take advantage of it. I mentioned earlier that I went into World War II very poorly trained, compared to what we gave to the new soldier at Fort Benning in 1966. The big difference was that at Benning we had "trained trainers," NCOs who had been schooled on how to handle new soldiers, whereas most World War II trainers were cadre from other units, and much of their own training had been on-the-job. Training soldiers by OJT does not provide the checks and balances built into a formal system run by NCOs—drill sergeants—adept at administering it.

One of the problems we encountered during Vietnam, and it was beginning to make itself felt about this time, was that we were running out of noncommissioned officers in the combat MOS's. Because of that we set up the first infantry Noncommissioned Officer Candidate Course (NCOC) at Fort Benning, an offshoot of the old NCO academy system. Our NCOC was different because we taught junior NCOs how to survive in combat. The traditional NCO academies, on the other hand, taught leadership skills that were not specific to any branch of the Army, such as how to drill troops, conduct inspections, teach classes, and so on. Our NCOC was the forerunner of the NCO courses in all the other branches of the Army.

We took 5 percent of the best of each NCO course and promoted them to staff sergeant (E-6), and we promoted another 10 percent to sergeant (E-5).* These men were derisively called "Shake 'n Bakes," after the commercial product of that name. In my view that nickname was not fair to those soldiers. They were trained to do one thing in one branch in one place in the world, and that was to be an infantry fire team leader in Vietnam. The course taught them *nothing* about how to inspect a barracks, how to check a chow line, how to conduct a police call. It was all focused on being a combat leader in Vietnam.

The sergeants were promoted after finishing their advanced individual training, while those 5 percent promoted to staff sergeant went through a cycle as assistant drill sergeants at Fort Benning and then went to Vietnam. Critics said these men didn't know much about traditional NCO duties because they had earned their stripes so quickly. But Benning was not the time or the place to teach them noncombat duties.

Generally those men did well—not all of them, of course, but they did a heck of a lot better than they would have if they had not had that additional instruction. That early NCOC was patterned after OCS in some respects. We were running out of fire team leaders, squad leaders, platoon sergeants. We had a one-year rotation cycle going in Vietnam and we'd had large units over there since early 1965—this was almost 1967—so we had been losing a lot of experienced NCOs in those frontline units. You have to "grow" good noncommissioned officers, and when you don't have time to do that, then you've got to "manufacture" them.

The critics of the program had forgotten or never learned the lessons of World War II. The difference between the Shake 'n Bakes and us at the Bulge was like night and day. In the Bulge we had men who became fire team and squad leaders from pri-

*The remainder of the graduates went to their units with the rank they'd held when they entered the course.

vates without any special training, and some of our sergeants didn't have the training the NCOC guy got.

That NCOC provided something the Army had never had before, except for second lieutenants out of OCS. The principle is the same, to me. You take a private soldier and run him through basic training and advanced individual training, and if he's a smart cookie he fills out a form, goes before a board, goes to OCS, and goes to a basic officer's course, and then he's off to fight. There is no difference between that and the NCOC. You take a man off the street, make him a private, run him through basic and AIT, make him a sergeant, run him through an NCOC, and you've taught him what you've taught that lieutenant—how to run a platoon. The difference was it took sixteen weeks to qualify that private for staff sergeant duty in Vietnam.

Does anybody know everything about what he'll do when that first rifle bullet cracks by his ear? I don't care whether you're a private or a general, that's not a good experience, and it can't all be taught. You've got to learn on the job—the only form of OJT I respect—by doing it and praying to God you last long enough to do it well. The important thing to learn is what you need to survive and to help your troops survive. That way you know it's going to be you, not the other guy, who marches in the victory parade.

I'll illustrate what I mean with a story. Maj. Gen. Charles Brown, an old artilleryman, who had been the training center commander at Fort Sill, was visiting a firebase in Vietnam when he was at I Field Forces Headquarters. There he met a young artilleryman who had trained at Fort Sill when he was the commander there.

"What do you think about the training at Fort Sill?"

"It really didn't bother me too much. It was kinda easy. I didn't have to work at it too hard. I'm a fairly bright guy, so I kind of goofed off a bit."

General Brown asked him, "What about up here?"

"Oh, up here, General, I listen to everything my sergeants tell me, I listen to everything my commander tells me. I think it out. I'm concerned."

"What's the difference between here and Fort Sill?"

"General, up here your ass is in jeopardy."

Now, a lot of old sergeants said guys like him weren't dry behind the ears yet. Of course they weren't. But they were over there doing the job that those old sergeants would have been doing had it not been for those lads not yet dry behind the ears.

And those old sergeants might not even have been as professional anymore in what the younger sergeants were doing in that place and at that time.

The NCOC was a part of the infantry school, and Sgt. Maj. Don Wright was the first commandant.

While I was at Benning we got in some of "McNamara's 100,000." These were men brought into the military service under a program known as Project 100,000, sponsored by Defense Secretary Robert Strange McNamara. The program was designed to give men who would not normally be eligible for military service a chance to become soldiers. The usual reason these men were disqualified was their below-average scoring on the Armed Forces Qualification Test.*

Training these men really posed a challenge to our cadre. However, the experience we had was that while it took a little bit longer to train them in the art of soldiering, once you were able to show them how to do something they could do it from then on, possibly only by rote, but by golly you could count on them not forgetting.

These men generally accepted discipline pretty well, and most of them were in better shape physically than one might have expected. Seldom did any of them have to be recycled because of physical training difficulties. As a matter of fact, we had one company composed only of these men that set some physical training scores that probably have never been broken.

General Mount was a great people person, and through his brigade commanders he made some good soldiers out of these Project 100,000 men. Personally, I think the program probably did worlds of good for those who made it through. There is no doubt in my mind that it did some great things for individuals. It provided a "first" for many of them in that they were given a chance to complete something successfully. That's a big plus. If you've been dragging behind everybody else all your life and someone can teach you how to do something right for a change, it really does something for your psyche and helps you to be a better per-

*Placing them in mental category IV, between the 10th and 30th percentile. Eventually this program brought a total of 354,000 men into the military service, of which some 243,000 were taken into the Army and the Marine Corps. The men with physical disqualifications accepted into this program generally were all under- or overweight.

son. But the program probably taxed the training base more than it was worth overall.

Life in a training center is tough. In those days we had very few new-blood drill sergeants. It seemed that the Main Post was knee-deep in assistant instructors—they had assistants to the assistants—but in the training center we were running whole companies with only one or two drill sergeants.

One day I suggested to General Mount that we try to get some of those instructors up on Main Post to go to drill sergeant school at Fort Jackson, South Carolina, to improve the quality of our cadre. Being a drill sergeant is tough work. The drill sergeants we had at that point had been drill sergeants forever. They'd transferred from Knox to Benning to Sill, to wherever they were needed. The problem with that system was that the men were becoming burned out. And some of them were becoming "entrepreneurs"—collecting money from the trainees for the purchase of "cleaning supplies" and running other kinds of scams. They were in trouble if we caught them at it, but they had been in the system so long they were finding ways to make life easier for themselves. We were trying to train troops and give them an idea of what the Army was all about, and these drill sergeants weren't giving them the right idea. We needed change in that system.

We didn't fully turn the system around until I got up to the Pentagon, but while I was at Benning we did get some reluctant volunteers to go to drill sergeant school so we could transfer out some of the men who'd been around too long. You can't train soldiers well with soldiers who are just showing up for work. The drill sergeant's job is a twenty-four-hour-a-day job, and it's just not the kind of work you can stay in for very long. Helping to improve this system was one of the most important impacts I had on the Army.

Benning was really my first close, objective look at how initial Army training was conducted—my own World War II experience was hardly "objective." It was also the first chance I had to put some of my ideas about troop training into practice. I tried to humanize the process a bit. I've said it before—it doesn't take any practice to be miserable. Sometimes being miserable does help make a man into a better soldier if the experience is used as a training tool, but just heaping misery on a soldier for its own sake doesn't make him a good soldier.

Gen. Robert York, the post commander, went someplace one day and left General Mount to act in his capacity. General Mount and

I went over to Martin Army Hospital to award an "E Flag," a tro-
phy given to units that had signed up a certain percentage of soldiers to purchase U.S. savings bonds. After presentation of the
flag, we went inside for refreshments, and the hospital commander, Col. Hal C. Jennings, began introducing General Mount
to some of his senior noncommissioned officers.

He came by me and said, "General Mount, I'd like to have you
meet another one of our senior NCOs"—he looked at my name
tag—"Sergeant Major Bainbridge."

"Oh? And what does he do, Hal?" General Mount asked, shaking my hand.

"Well, um, ah, what *do* you do, Sergeant Major?" Jennings
asked me.

I told him I was General Mount's sergeant major.

Colonel Jennings never missed a beat—he reached out and
shook my hand and said, "Well, I guess I haven't met you before,
Sergeant Major." Hal Jennings went on to become the Surgeon
General of the Army.

We had a lot of people who liked to speed on post at Fort
Benning, so the provost sergeant major went to the post commander and asked if he could deputize all the sergeants major on
post to issue tickets to these speeders. He got that authority. About
that time I'd bought a 1957 Volkswagen from the training center
deputy commander. It was a ratty-looking old thing, but I needed
a second car to drive to and from work, so Hazel could have
transportation during the day.

I took it to the garage and had the speedometer calibrated to
make sure it gave accurate readings. When I bore down on a
speeder, he'd never give that old Volkswagen a second thought.
Driving back and forth to work, I probably got more speeders
than anybody else on the post. I would just clock the speeder for
a quarter of a mile or so and then pull around him and cut him
off, show him my ID card, and write the ticket. At times an offender would argue with me, particularly if he happened to be a
senior officer, but it didn't do him any good. If the guy outranked
me and tried to use his rank on me I just told him, "I understand
that you outrank me, sir. However, you also understand that in
your position you're the last one we ought to be catching out here
speeding. Here's your ticket."

Old Pete Jones, the post sergeant major, was a good man, but he
had a mindset that was common among Army people in those

days. Jones lived within thirty or forty miles of Fort Benning while he was growing up, went into the Army during World War II, served in the Pacific, spent nine months at Fort Lee, Virginia, came to Benning, and never left it again. He was behind the times so far as the rest of the Army went, but he was the post sergeant major, the senior enlisted man at Benning, and he had a little fiefdom there.

My boss, the number three guy on post, had a No. 3 identification tag on his car—the post commander was No. 1, the school commandant was No. 2, and so on. But down in the NCO ranks, Pete Jones was No. 1, the school sergeant major was No. 2, and the provost sergeant was No. 3. Now, this was a small thing, but in those days people took such formalities seriously.

One day I was up in Pete's office and I decided to ask him who decided who got which post tag number for his car. "Well, I do," he said. I asked him then to explain to me why the provost sergeant major had tag No. 3. Pete told me, "He controls the tags."

"But you just told me you're the guy who decides among the NCOs who gets which tag. How come I don't have No. 3? Why don't you do it by seniority and give me No. 3, the way you do with the officers? Why don't you give Jim Runyon in my third brigade No. 4? He's next-ranking enlisted man on this post."

"Oh, we couldn't do that!" Pete protested. I asked him why not. "Well, that's just not the way the Army operates."

"Pete, tell me, how does the Army operate? What do you base that on? Give me your experience factor."

"Well, that's the way we do it here at Benning."

"That's your goddamn problem," I replied. "You've never been anyplace else but Benning! I think you ought to take a look at this system."

After about a month, the tags of all the post sergeants major were reshuffled. That way the troops could tell by the post tag who was driving by. It was a little thing, but changing that system helped break up one aspect of the little old clique they had at Fort Benning. Nothing wrong with having a clique, so long as everybody's in it.

Hazel made an impact there, too. She had a coffee party for the other NCOs' wives, after we got moved into quarters up on the Main Post. She invited the wives of all the brigade sergeants major, the post sergeant major, and so on. Well, she asked the senior sergeant major's wife to pour. She did the pouring, but afterward word got back to Hazel that this lady was not going to go to any more coffee parties hosted by Hazel Bainbridge. "It was the first time I'd been in that woman's house," she said, "and she put me to work, pouring the coffee!" The poor woman had no idea that it's an *honor* to be asked to pour. That taught both of us that we had people in the Army who didn't know the social protocols of the community. A lot of folks in the Army in those days wanted to keep it that way, but I thought that if the Army wanted smart sergeants we ought to have smart wives to help carry on the traditions.

So I think between the two of us, Hazel and me, we stirred up some things at Benning that needed stirring up. All of this, I felt, had to do with things that would make life better for soldiers, particularly in the basic training area. One of the things I never forgot about my early training was my six solid weeks of KP at Lowry Field, Colorado, which sure as hell didn't make me feel I wanted to be a soldier. Ever afterward, when I got a chance to do something about it, I tried to change things like that, as you will see as my story continues.

We all have our little idiosyncrasies, and General Mount had his. I always had free access to his office. He had a south-facing window, and sometimes he'd pull out the writing leaf on his desk, put his feet upon it, rear back in his chair, and look out the window. I don't know why, but whenever I saw him that way I never interrupted him. I could see his feet through his office door before I could see him, and whenever I saw his feet up like that I just stayed out. That was his quiet time, when he got his thinking done.

One day he told me, "Sergeant Major, I've seen you several times coming in and then turning around and leaving when you saw me sitting here with my feet up."

"I didn't know you saw me, but it appeared to me that you were doing some serious thinking that might make things better for those troops out there."

He said, "You're exactly right. I appreciate your not disturbing me."

Then one day I got a call from General Seaman, First Army commander at Fort Meade, Maryland. He'd commanded the 1st Infantry Division at Fort Riley and later had been my boss at II Field Force Vietnam. He was back from Vietnam and was commanding First Army.

When I was on leave at Riley, just after I'd come back from Vietnam and before I went on to Benning, he was home on leave, and I dropped by to visit with him. He showed me some pictures of an attack on IIFFV Headquarters. In one, the fluorescent light that had hung over my desk had fallen when they blew up the local ammunition dump, and General Seaman said, "Of course, that wouldn't have bothered you at all, Top, because you were never in your office anyway—you were out checking around all the time."

Well, about nine-thirty one morning—this was in August 1967—I got a call from him. We exchanged pleasantries and then he said, "What would you think if I asked you to come up and be the First Army sergeant major?"

"Well," I said, "I'll need about thirty minutes to pack." I wasn't unhappy at Benning, but I really wanted to work for General Seaman. I reminded him that I'd only been there a short while and I'd come to Benning at General Mount's request, but I was sure he'd understand.

"No-o-o-o-o, he won't," General Seaman said. "And I'm not going to tell Charlie. *You've* got to tell him. He'll chew me out if I call him."

I agreed to ask General Mount to let me go. General Seaman had told me there was no rush. The quarters he wanted me to occupy were not available at that time and wouldn't be ready until after Labor Day.

About two o'clock, I went into General Mount's office and talked to him a while and then said, "By the way, sir, I got a call from First Army today."

"Oh-h-h, Christ," he said. "When are you leaving?" I told him the situation. "Sergeant Major," he said, "I don't want to lose you, you understand that, but I'd be the last guy to keep you from going back to work for General Seaman. You know what I think of him."

As it turned out, General Mount followed me to First Army as chief of staff that November. As the old song had it, we were together again.

As much as any tour I ever had in the Army, that time at Benning helped me to realize that you have to start the soldier out right. You've got to *listen* to those young folks, because they may have ideas you've never considered. I think most people realize too late in life that you learn a hell of a lot more by being a good listener than you do by talking. It's particularly hard for senior people to listen to people who aren't even soldiers yet themselves, but you find that there is no corner on the good-idea market.

Training has to be humanized. Harassing troops all the time just because they're new to the Army and don't know anything is the wrong approach. When you do that, the soldier has got to ask, "Why is this happening to me?" When that kind of treatment is eliminated, I think you have a better soldier.

Two things I was able to do at Fort Benning were to make it better for the basic trainee, and to put into effect some of my ideas on how soldiers should be treated and trained. And this re-affirmed my belief that noncommissioned officers have to work as a team. When you get all that experience together and get it to gel—Runyon helps Keene and Keene helps Bainbridge—everything works a hell of a lot better. Too often you have brigades and battalions and companies instead of having a division.

It all boils down to this: You can make a soldier out of anybody. If you treat him like a human being to begin with, let him retain his dignity, the soldier will do anything you ask of him.

≡ 8 ≡

MY SIX-STAR GENERAL

We left Fort Benning for Fort Meade, Maryland, in August 1967. We made the trip up Interstate 95 in two cars, me in the Volkswagen that I'd bought from Colonel Edwards at Benning, Mary and Hazel following along in the 1962 Buick that Mary had wrecked before we left Fort Riley.

We stopped for lunch somewhere in North Carolina. About one-thirty in the afternoon we resumed the trip north. The traffic was a little heavy. I was leading, and Hazel was driving the Buick behind me. A truck, hauling probably ten tons of sand or gravel, was doing a lot of weaving in and out of traffic, making fifty-five or sixty miles per hour. I looked in the rearview mirror and saw him cut in front of Hazel and hook the left rear fender of our car with his bumper, which threw Hazel into a spin among all the northward-bound traffic. I pulled the Volkswagen off onto the shoulder and ran back to the Buick, which had come to a stop headed back south, in the ditch, the horn blowing and Mary under the dashboard.

Luckily neither she nor Hazel was hurt badly. All morning long, both Hazel and Mary had been wearing their seat belts. When they got back in the car after lunch, they neglected to put them back on again, and that's why Mary ended up under the dash. That just goes to show you that you should always wear those seat belts.

The horn was still blowing, and I pulled up the hood and shut it off. The car was not too badly damaged but it did need some body work and a front-end alignment, as we found out later. The truck driver had stopped and the state police arrived and we got everything squared away. Mary and Hazel had to go to the hospital to get checked out, and we spent the night in a motel by the roadside. The car was towed to a garage. All our stuff in the trunk came through okay.

Not two months before we left Benning, I had bought a new set of tires for the Buick. They were Atlas tires from Standard Oil. I believe that had I not bought them the outcome of that accident might have been much more serious, because the rubber stayed on the car. Never since have I had a bad set of tires on any car I owned. Even when I couldn't really afford them, I never bought anything but the best damn tires available. And we wear our seat belts religiously!

The old Volkswagen had an emergency brake that set the rear wheels. Despite my setting the brake, the vehicle slid a considerable distance from where I'd bailed out of it. Evidently I'd left it on the move; the state patrolman said my footprints were clearly visible beginning sixteen feet from where the car finally came to a halt. To this day I couldn't tell you how I managed to do that.

We continued on to Fort Meade in the Volkswagen, and I went back later on and recovered the Buick.

Fort Meade is named after Union Maj. Gen. George Gordon Meade, the victor of the Battle of Gettysburg and commander of the Army of the Potomac during the last two years of the Civil War. Fort Meade was established in 1917. It sits on about thirteen thousand acres between Baltimore and Washington, D.C., just south of the Baltimore–Washington International Airport and just outside the little town of Odenton, Maryland.

Originally, Second Army headquarters had been situated at Fort Meade. During an Army reorganization in the late 1950s or early 1960s, when the armies were shifted around, First and Second Armies were combined and Fort Meade became the headquarters. Besides being home to Headquarters First Army, Meade also hosted the 6th Cavalry Squadron, the National Security Agency, and Reserve Components training. Compared to Fort Riley or Fort Benning, Meade is a very small post.

The mission of First Army was a training mission. First Army was part of the Continental Army Command, CONARC.* While CONARC was responsible for the mission of the tactical units within the First Army area, First Army trained and administered them. We did not get involved in the business of the formal army schools within our geographical area. However, we controlled the

*CONARC was created on February 1, 1955, to direct the activities of the forces within the United States. It also was responsible for command of the (at that time) six field armies within the continental United States (Second Army had been eliminated by the time I arrived at First Army).

installations at Carlisle and West Point and administered some of the garrison personnel assigned there. We were also responsible for National Guard and Army Reserve training in the First Army area, which comprised all the states from Maine to the Carolinas, Puerto Rico, Kentucky, etc., a total of thirteen states in the mid-Atlantic and northeastern portions of the country. Our mission was somewhat akin to what a corps does within an army's structure.

At that time there were five field armies within the continental United States: First, of course, and Third, Fourth, Fifth, and Sixth. Seventh Army and Eighth Army were overseas, in Germany and Korea respectively.

We reported in on Labor Day 1967, and I became General Seaman's liaison for enlisted matters throughout the First Army area.

Now for the first time in my Army career we were assigned a detached set of quarters, a three-bedroom, full-basement house. The midpart of the week after our household goods arrived, I was up on the second floor getting some furniture squared away when I heard a voice from downstairs: "The water is only waist-deep!"

I hollered back, "Come on up, Major Wooley!"

Maj. John Wooley had commanded A Company in the 1st Battalion of the 28th Infantry back in Vietnam when he was a captain. He's one of those tall fellows, about six feet nineteen, and on one operation he had the lead company and we were getting ready to cross a stream. He radioed back to the command post that he'd found a crossing "just about waist-deep." When we crossed, I discovered the water came up under my armpits, and after we'd regrouped on the other side I told him that when he said something was only waist-deep, he'd better specify *whose* waist. "Next time, Top, I'll be sure to give it to you in feet and inches!" he said.

But here he was, downstairs in our new quarters. He was assigned to the Pentagon at that time with the duty of traveling around the country lecturing people on the Vietnam War. He'd discovered that I'd just been assigned to Fort Meade and he'd popped in to spend an hour or so shooting the breeze. It was just one of those little courtesies you remember.

These quarters were situated on Washington Avenue along with twelve or fifteen other units for senior noncommissioned officers—that is, sergeants in the pay grades of E-7, E-8, and E-9.

One of the first things General Seaman had me do was look into the problem of "homesteaders" in the First Army area. Those are soldiers who somehow manage to remain in one assignment for years and years. In those days we had a lot of people going two and three times to Vietnam while there were others who'd never been yet.

We arranged to get rosters from various posts, camps, and stations telling us how long people had been at those places, what their jobs were, and so on. I learned a lesson I'll never forget about homesteaders in the Army. West Point, New York, the U.S. Military Academy, had an extensive roster of them. On a scale of one to ten it was a perfect ten. Some of them had been there since right after I'd come into the Army the first time, since the 1940s, certainly since the 1950s. That was one place I thought I'd really made a discovery.

I submitted these rosters to General Seaman. One day I got a call he wanted to see me, so I walked down to his office.

"Sergeant Major," he said, "I've been looking over these rosters, and you're doing a beautiful job. I see we'll have to get a lot of these names down to the Office of Personnel Operations at the Pentagon, get some of these people on the road.

"But let me tell you one thing. This one roster you've given me is off-limits." He handed it to me, and it was the one for West Point. "There's a lot of tradition there," he told me, "and the people who've been there the longest are members of the band. Once they get in that band, they don't go *anywhere* unless they mess up."

That made sense to me after I thought about it a little bit. There are other soldiers who fit into this category, such as enlisted aides to general officers. When a soldier gets into that program, there aren't too many places you can ship him, so once he fits into a place, leave him there. Moving a soldier just because he hasn't been anyplace else just doesn't make sense for men in these highly special jobs. If there was a requirement for bandsmen or general's aides overseas, that would be different. I learned that there are people in the Army who ought to be homesteaders because it isn't to the Army's advantage to move them.

I put together the first conference of sergeants major ever held in the First Army area. In discussing my plans with General Seaman, I told him I wanted to bring in all these folks from installations and commands for a conference to discuss things affecting all the enlisted personnel in the First Army.

I planned a conference of about three days: one day to get them checked in, a day and a half of talks, and half a day to get them checked out. At the meetings I learned that when you assemble a group of people like that, there are lots of problems that can be solved once they begin sharing experience and knowledge. For instance, a sergeant major at Fort Knox might have figured out the solution to something that's been bothering another sergeant major at Fort Devens, and when you get the two together, bingo!

General Seaman asked me what I planned to do with the conferees socially. I had about thirty people coming in, and I'd planned one luncheon and a dinner, a no-host thing at the NCO club. I told him we were going to ask him to come over to the dinner and talk to us.

"I'll do more than that," he said. "I'll host the dinner myself." Up to that time, I'd been down in the trenches, so to speak, and didn't know that general officers were allocated special funds for this sort of activity. General Seaman believed in sharing the wealth. That was a revelation to that group of NCOs also. The commanding general of the entire First Army was hosting a dinner for them. Something like that may have happened before, but I sure as hell had never heard about it. General Seaman was a commander who believed in his troops. Those sergeants major at my conference went away with a good feeling because they knew the army commander was behind them.

This assignment also marked my first foray into watching over soldiers' quarters assignments. I never forgot my experience at VII Corps, when I was No. 2 on the list and somebody bumped me back to No. 21. I vowed then that if I was ever in a position to do something about that kind of practice I'd remember what it was like to be screwed.

All those quarters on Washington Avenue where we lived had been designated for senior noncommissioned officers. There were another twenty-odd sets down by the commissary that had not been so designated, but we had enough NCOs eligible to fill them. I spoke to General Seaman about that and told him I'd like to expand the Washington Avenue group over into the commissary housing area. Those were also detached houses, three- and four-bedroom quarters, and it seemed to me that those NCOs should have them.

He agreed, but he asked how I planned to overcome the standard policy. In those days they assigned housing by the size of the family. If you had three children, depending on their gender, you got quarters with three bedrooms; if you had no children, you got quarters with only one bedroom. That policy was set in stone, and quarters on post were assigned accordingly by the post engineer.

My problem with the system was that we had NCOs with many years of service whose families were grown and out on their own, but they still had a houseful of furniture and other personal possessions. What do you do with it all? Sell it? Store it? Why should the Army pay that family to store excess furnishings? That didn't make any sense to me. Here's a senior noncommissioned officer who ought to have some space. He's expected to do some official entertaining of his own, like bring in all his NCOs at Christmastime and host a party in his home, and he can't do that in a one-bedroom set of quarters.

I thought the regulation should be changed so that local commanders could assign quarters based on their needs and their understanding of the local situation. General Seaman said that made sense to him, and since I'd stirred the issue up, he would have a meeting that next week. The First Army engineer, who set quarters policy, would be there, and he wanted me to present my case.

The engineer was a colonel who lived in a two-story, four-bedroom house with a full basement and a big sunporch, just he and his wife. We had sergeants major with as much service as the colonel or more who were living in one-bedroom apartments because their children had grown up. I explained that was the sort of thing we needed to look into.

"We have to go by the regulation," the engineer stated. "When the family gets smaller we have to assign the sponsor a smaller set of quarters."

"Then you're telling me," General Seaman said, "that you and your wife, there in that big old house, just the two of you, should exchange quarters with my aide, who has five kids and is in a two-bedroom house. We'll just swap you guys."

"Oh, no, sir, my house was built for a colonel."

"I understand that," General Seaman replied, "but I also understand that I'm going to take those twenty sets of quarters down by the commissary and convert them into quarters for sergeants major, and I don't care what size their families are."

That was a case where we defeated an unfair policy. But there was another side to the coin.

Art Carver was the 6th Cavalry Regiment sergeant major and a friend of mine. As a matter of fact, I'd recommended him as a good choice to be the top NCO in the 6th Cav to Col. Clay Gompf, when he took over as CO. Art was up at Old Pine Camp, now Fort Drum, New York, in training when on a Friday afternoon I saw a truck with 6th Cav markings on it hauling furniture into the house across the street from mine.

I knew that the next guy on the housing list was a Navy chief petty officer. We had all services at Fort Meade, because they were all represented at the National Security Agency. I checked

TOP SERGEANT

My grandfather, James Buchanan, is seated at center; my father, James Lyle, is standing just to my grandfather's left. Soperville, Illinois, 1903.

The Cameron, Illinois, District Rural School in 1936—all eight grades. The dapper young scholar with his hands in his pockets, front row, far right, is yours truly.

(left)
"Yep, that's me," I wrote to my mother on the back of this photo taken at the Jolly Flying School, Grand Forks, North Dakota, November 1943.

(right)
On the wrong side of the wire at Stalag 9A, Good Friday, 1945. The clothes I am wearing in this picture are the ones I was captured in at the Bulge, and I am down to eighty-five pounds.
(Photo by Phillip J. W. Glissner)

Col. Howard B. St. Clair, VII Corps G3, promotes me to
master sergeant, January 1962.

On the Siegfried Line, October 1962.

Left to right: Hazel, Mary, me, and Kathy. Fort Riley, Kansas, 1962.

Reading the names of the fallen at a memorial ceremony for the first combat deaths sustained by the 1st Bn, 28th Infantry, in Vietnam. Phuoc Vinh, Vietnam, November 1965.
(U.S. Army photo)

Reenlisting in War Zone "D" during Operation Jingle Bells.
Lt. Col. Haldane (right) is administering the oath. Note that
Col. Louis A. Williams, the aviation brigade commander
(center), also has *his* hand raised.
(Photographer unknown)

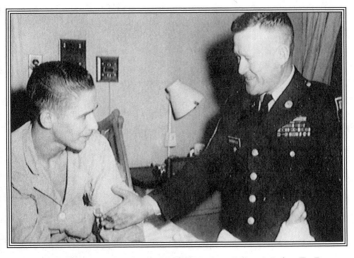

Presenting the Purple Heart Medal to Specialist 4 John E. Royer
for wounds he received in Vietnam. Ireland Army Hospital, Fort
Knox, Kentucky, March 1968.
(U.S. Army photo)

Lt. Gen. Jonathan O. Seamen passes me my new command
sergeant major chevrons as Hazel looks on. Fort Meade,
Maryland, March 1968.
(U.S. Army photo)

As the USARPAC
CSM, I was called
upon to go to some
unusual places and
do some unusual
things. Here I am
at Phu Nhon
District,
Vietnam, in February
1969.
(U.S. Army photo)

Welcoming Gen. William B. Rosson, incoming USARPAC
commander, 1971. Just behind Gen. Rosson's right shoulder is
Lt. Gen. William P. Yarborough, Deputy Commander and Chief
of Staff of USARPAC.
(U.S. Army photo)

Left to right: Me, outgoing SMA Leon Van Autreve, and
Chief of Staff of the Army Gen. Fred C. Weyand, June 1975.
(U.S. Army photo)

Maj. Gen. Verne L. Bowers, the Army Adjutant General, swears me in as the fifth Sergeant Major of the Army while Hazel and Gen. Weyand look on, July 1, 1975.
(U.S. Army photo)

Extending my enlistment through June 1979, so I can complete four full years as SMA. Gen. Bernard W. Rogers and Hazel look on, December 1977.
(U.S. Army photo)

with the truck driver and asked who was being moved in. When he told me it was Sgt. Maj. So-and-So from the 6th Cav, I told him who I was and not to unload another stick of furniture. I was going up to Fort Drum that Saturday and told the driver I'd get the situation squared away then.

When I got to Drum I contacted Art Carver. "You or somebody in your outfit tried to pull a shenanigan on me, moving that sergeant major into those quarters, and you did pull it with Mr. Brown down at post housing," I said. Mr. Brown was the civilian who ran the housing office. "It's not going to work," I went on. "We're moving that man's furniture out of there and that Navy chief is moving in."

Art said, "I understand, but it's sure going to be hard on that sergeant major."

"Art," I told him, "if it'd been *you* moving in there I'da made you move out, because it isn't right, you can't defend it. We set this system up where you didn't even have one before, and already you're trying to sidestep it."

About a week later I was in to see Mr. Brown. I told him I didn't know how he'd managed to switch the 6th Cav sergeant major for the Navy chief, but we *had* to go by the rules—the next guy up on the list for quarters had to get them.

He said, "All right, but I want you to tell General Seaman . . ."

I reached over and picked up his telephone and started dialing. "I'll get him on the phone, Mr. Brown, and you tell him yourself," I said.

He put his hand on the receiver. "No, no, I don't want to talk to *him!*"

"Well, then don't talk to me that way either, because that man put this thing together and told you how to run it and now you're trying to screw it all up. *Don't do that.*"

Never had any more problems with Mr. Brown.

You know, we got so hidebound in our thinking in the Army sometimes. This situation with the quarters illustrates what I mean: "It works well and that's the way we've always done it, so that's the way it should always be." When people think that way, it's a major effort to get them to change.

This reminds me of the pet cat we had when we were at Fort Meade. Her name was Kat. Mary brought her home in a shoe box from the NCO club, where she was a secretary in the office. That cat was trained to go in a box we'd put in the basement of the house. She was not an outdoor cat. Whenever she got her feet wet, she'd be beside herself. She went out one night and we couldn't find her. About ten o'clock I got tired of calling her and went to bed. The next morning at five o'clock I heard this "rowwrrr" at the back door. When I opened the door there was Kat, and like a shot she flew down into the basement and into her box. Here was a cat, out all night long, and she was so used to going in that box she wouldn't go outside. She was in misery out there until I let her in the house. I think she would've exploded if I hadn't opened the door for her.

Well, that's the way we were with that goddamn quarters business. We'd been out in the cold so long that we'd have exploded rather than make a change, until General Seaman came along and opened the door for us.

Today, not just because of what we did at Fort Meade, but maybe a little, senior noncommissioned officers in the Army have the housing in most places that they ought to have. That's because we fought for changes in the early days, and so the regulations were changed and today the commander on the scene has the authority to assign soldiers their quarters.

As I noted before, part of First Army's mission was to oversee the training of the Reserve Components units assigned within its area.

I should mention that one time when we were at Fort Drum the Pennsylvania National Guard was training there. A unit was doing some mortar firing out on the range, and they were showing General Seaman, who was an artilleryman—class of 1934 at West Point— how good they were. The state adjutant general, Maj. Gen. Harry Mier, Jr., wanted General Seaman to see his crack mortar crews in action.

The unit was firing 81mm mortars. The first round was about where it should have been, but the second was a grid square away. The third round was about a grid square the *other* way. I walked over to General Seaman and suggested he ask General Mier take him someplace else for a while so I could check out the problem with that mortar crew and he could come back in the afternoon to watch another demonstration.

I got with the crew and asked them if they had their manuals and determined if any one of them had ever set the base plate on a mortar before and so on. After a few minutes I asked them what their base plate was doing sitting on a half-buried log. They hadn't checked the ground before they set up their piece. The log wasn't evident at first glance, because it was about four inches below the ground, but I took a spade and dug a small hole and there it was. When they fired the mortar the base plate was shifting about four inches with each round. Four inches at the firing place causes one hell of a variation out in the intended impact area. When they fired again in the afternoon, they set up properly, got their aiming stakes right, and hit their target. The reason for the fiasco in the morning was simply that somebody in that mortar crew, some noncommissioned officer, had been in too much of a hurry to set up and fire.

That was the sort of thing I did when I traveled with General Seaman. Just as on those trips we made in Vietnam, once we were at the site we split up, because I could see more things if I looked around separately. I was really another set of eyes and ears for General Seaman on those trips in areas where he wouldn't have had them.

Another thing we accomplished on that particular trip was renovating the old World War II cantonment-type barracks that were common at Fort Drum. They'd deteriorated badly. We got some funds to restore them so that when the troops were in them they had hot water and were dry. If you've ever been there, you know Camp Drum is a cold, miserable place in the winter, and in the summer the chiggers and mosquitoes cross with turkeys, because they're big enough to tackle you.

On another occasion we learned that a unit was going to have a parade when it finished its training and was planning to use the local airstrip for it, tracked vehicles and all. When word got back to General Seaman through NCO channels, he put a stop to it, or we would have had to make extensive repairs to the surface of the airfield.

One of the Reserve units we checked was the 50th Armored Division of the New Jersey National Guard. Personnelwise, they were in pretty good shape—they had a lot of talent. But during one training cycle I got to talking to some of the men and discovered that in one little town in New Jersey the entire police force was in the Guard. In another town the mayor and a couple of his key staff were Guardsmen. In still another town the fire chief and seven or eight of his firemen were in the Guard.

I started putting this information together and asked myself what would happen if the Guard was called up for active duty. I didn't mean for training, because there were many ways to excuse key personnel from the training cycle, but for actual wartime deployment. What would happen to those towns? Would they have a police force? A firefighting force? Municipal government?

During Desert Storm, it was discovered that the 48th Brigade of

the Georgia National Guard, the "round-out"* brigade to the active
Army's 24th Infantry Division, was not ready to go to the Persian
Gulf, so the Army had to send the 197th out of Fort Benning in
its place. Not being trained is one thing, but not being combat-
effective because you don't have all your people is another.

I think if you were to go to any Guard unit anywhere in the
country, you would find the same thing still persisting—
municipalities being gutted because when the Guard is called
up, all these key personnel have to go. The same thing happens
in the Air National Guard, too, except it's different in the training aspect because a lot of its people do the same thing for a
living in civilian life as they do in the Guard—fly and maintain
modern aircraft—so their deployment from call-up to active
duty is much less than it is for the Army National Guard. Nobody drives a tank or carries a rifle for a living in civilian life,
and it's very difficult to keep those skills honed by going to
camp two weeks out of the year.

I was able to focus some attention on a potential problem un-
covered in my talks with NCOs in the 50th Armored Division.
Those NCOs were afraid that if their units were ever called up,
they wouldn't be able to go or to do the job they'd been trained
to do on active duty because some of their key unit personnel
would not be deployable.

This problem is not fixed yet, and today, when the active Army
is dependent upon the Reserve Components for so much of its
combat and combat support strength, these shortcomings are particularly dangerous to our national security. I think one very good
thing we've learned from the Desert Shield/Desert Storm experience in the Persian Gulf is that the active forces are going to have
to take a hard look at the Reserve Components and their wartime
mission. But we knew that in 1968.

Life at First Army wasn't all just inspecting things.

One time we went out to Columbus, Ohio, to visit Ohio
State's ROTC program. We flew on a special air mission aircraft out of Dobbins Air Force Base, Georgia, but coming back
there was bad weather, and since the military plane that took us
out had no radar, we had to return by commercial air. General
Seaman and his aide got the only two seats available on a

---

*When a unit from the Reserve or National Guard is assigned to an active-Army
organization for training and deployment for active service in an emergency, it is
said to be "rounding out" the active component.

United flight, and I prepared to stay over and catch a flight out the next day.

At the last minute, somebody didn't show up, so I got a seat on the airplane. Of course, I had to sit by myself. "I see you made it," General Seaman said as I walked down the aisle. I sat down about five or six rows behind him.

After we were airborne, the stewardess came back and asked me, "Who is that gentleman up there in uniform?"

"That's the First Army commander, Gen. Jonathan O. Seaman, the only six-star general in the First Army," I told her.

"Really?" she asked in awe.

"Yes. He's got three stars on each side—a six-star general."

"I've never seen a six-star general before!" she told me.

"Well, they're rare. He's the only one in the First Army. Just go up there and introduce yourself to him and tell him you've never met a six-star general before."

She did, and she talked to him for a few moments. Then he turned around and pointed back at me and said, "You've been talking to that fellow back there, haven't you?"

She came back and slapped me lightly on the arm and said, "You really set me up, didn't you?"

But General Seaman was the kind of person who enjoyed that sort of thing.

Another time we were catching a plane out of Baltimore when suddenly he said, "Sergeant Major, I understand you've got some property down in Florida."

"Yessir, we do. We bought some property down there back in the early fifties, a dollar down and a dollar when they caught up with us. But it's worked out okay. We got a letter the other day that stated they'd discovered land on it, so we're going to build a house."

Then there was the time we visited Camp A. P. Hill in Virginia and went deer hunting. It was the Commanding General's Hunt, as they called it. We stayed in a big lodge down there. I'd never been deer hunting before in my life. The hunt was organized into two groups, drivers and hunters. The drivers went out in the woods and made a lot of noise and drove the deer to the hunters, who, using shotguns, tried to bag their deer. You were allowed only one deer and after that you had to be a driver.

It was a three-day hunt and I got my deer before noon the first day, so I ended up being a driver for two and a half days. I learned never to get my deer the first day, because it's a lot easier to be on the hunting stand than run around in the woods. The worst part of it was that we couldn't eat the meat once we'd gotten it home anyway.

We took the meat back to First Army, but those deer had been feeding on acorns and pine cones and whatnot, and you couldn't stay in the house when they cooked the meat, the aroma was so bad. One of General Seaman's cooks cooked up the meat for dog food. I've eaten deer killed in Illinois, where they eat what the cattle eat, alfalfa, corn, and clover, and that's great-tasting meat.

Back at Fort Meade, the 6th Cav was planning to fire the Fourth of July salute for 1968. The First Army Headquarters building was situated at the east end of a long parade ground. The Cav set up about halfway between the headquarters building and the reviewing stands, to do a practice shoot for their July Fourth fifty-gun salute to the nation.

Their guns were pointed toward the headquarters. After the second practice round had been fired, I got a phone call from General Seaman. "Sergeant Major," he said, "any artilleryman worth his salt doesn't have to fire blanks at the army headquarters to get ready for a Fourth of July celebration."

Within five minutes I'd gotten Sgt. Maj. Art Carver on the phone and he'd reached his gun crews by radio, and we stopped the firing of those fifty rounds of blanks at the First Army headquarters. We had clerks jumping out of their chairs, particularly the civilians.

My office was about fifty feet from General Seaman's in the headquarters building. The deputy commander's secretary was Rose Cozaza. She was a great gal, but she was scared to death of the deputy commander. There was a double door to the deputy's office, and inside to the left was the deputy's desk. He was a stern officer but a decent man. There was also a peephole through the inner door so you could see if the deputy CG was busy before you burst in on him or disturbed him.

Rose was coming out of his office one morning, and as was her usual habit, she had picked up more than she could carry at one time, a real "lazy man's load." She had papers, the old man's coffee cup, all sorts of paraphernalia, and she was having a tough time getting the door open. I was on the other side, looking through the peephole, holding the door shut. She tried the knob and then looked back at the deputy, tried the knob again, looked back again. If you've ever seen pure panic on somebody's face, it sure was on Rose's at that instant. The old man never looked up, but Rose knew she was about to attract unwanted attention.

When she came out, I was laughing, and I admitted that I'd

been holding the door shut on her. The laugh was worth it, even though I really got chewed out. She said, "You SOB! You know how afraid I am of him!" I'll never forget the look of sheer panic on Rose's face.

As I mentioned earlier, Gen. Charlie Mount came up to Meade to be First Army chief of staff. I was tasked to find a driver. This was very reminiscent of what happened when General Seaman picked me to be his sergeant major at IIFFV. In fact, his senior aide at First Army was Maj. Bill Merritt, who was Capt. Bill Merritt in Vietnam, and once again he asked me to find a driver for him.

"Guess who happens to be down at Fort Knox, Kentucky, and would like to be a general's driver again?" I asked. You guessed it—George Johnson, now promoted to staff sergeant. General Mount said that if the man had been a driver once before for General Seaman he could be again, so we moved Sergeant Johnson to First Army Headquarters and the four of us—General Seaman, Merritt, Johnson, and I—were back together. I was to meet Johnson again in 1975, when, as a driver for the White House motor pool, he was to come to the airport and pick me up the day I arrived in Washington to become the fifth Sergeant Major of the Army.

General Seaman was a great humanitarian. I mentioned how he made his officers who'd screwed up donate to the Dong Nai Orphanage in Vietnam. At Fort Meade something like that happened in connection with the prisoners in the post stockade. He was concerned that the prisoners were not being processed for release rapidly enough. He had told the commander of the stockade it should take a certain amount of time to accomplish that, and on this particular occasion, maybe three months after he'd originally given the stockade officer those instructions, we were being briefed by him again.

He asked again how long it was taking to process the prisoners for release, and the answer was the same as he'd gotten three months before. That was the only time I ever saw him raise his voice and get emotional with anybody. He slammed his fist onto the desk and yelled, "By God, I gave you instructions on what ought to be done to take care of this problem *three months ago*, and you mean to tell me you haven't done anything yet? If it isn't fixed by the end of this week, you"—and he pointed his finger at the stockade commander—"are *gone*. You're history!"

Needless to say, the necessary reforms were effected. It didn't take long for that story to get around and embellished, and it took care of a lot of other things, making everyone more responsive to General Seaman's orders.

General Seaman is dead now. He was a great soldier's general. He believed in people.

In 1968, while I was at First Army, the position of command sergeant major (CSM) was introduced. Actually, the concept was proposed back in 1965, when we were getting ready to go to Vietnam. Originally the position was to be for color-bearing units—artillery, infantry, armor.* This was not to be a new pay grade but a new position, which would be authorized its own chevron, the star of the rank of sergeant major surrounded by a wreath. However, the idea was shelved then, because of "economics," we were told.

The board that made the first CSM selections met in Alexandria, Virginia, in 1968. It was understood that not everyone in the designated positions, all of whom were sergeants major to begin with, would be selected, but when they began, all units, not just color-bearing ones, were included, starting with the highest echelons. General Seaman recommended me, and in December 1968 I was selected on the first list. Subsequent lists included sergeants major down to the battalion level.

I believe the original decision to delay the process was not due as much to "economics" as to the fact that there was so much objection from the field that if only color-bearing units were to have CSMs, the Army would have senior noncommissioned officers at headquarters and staff units who would not be authorized the new title and chevron.

There has been a lot of controversy about the program since then, but in my opinion there is nothing wrong with it. There are commanders in the Army even today who do not believe in the program, but I think that is because they have erred by not telling their respective CSMs what it is they want them to do, and that is the commander's responsibility, nobody else's. I have maintained my entire career that all the commander has to do is let his NCOs know what his guidelines are and they'll do the job. When commanders do that and when they let their command sergeants major work within their own channels of communication, the program is very effective.

CSMs are not, as some disgruntled commentators have stated, commanders. They are the sergeants major of the command, and as

---

*A "color" is a distinctive flag given to a specific unit with heraldic devices symbolic of its history, including a motto, if one has been authorized. This is all embroidered against the unit's branch color—blue for infantry, red for artillery, yellow for cavalry.

such they command nothing, they do their commander's bidding. Nevertheless, twenty years after the program's inception, people were still carping about it. A case in point is an article that appeared in the June 1988 issue of *Parameters*, the quarterly journal of the U.S. Army War College, by Brig. Gen. John C. "Doc" Bahnsen and Col. James W. Bradin, entitled "The Army's Command Sergeant Major Problem."* The authors concluded that the CSM program had created "a legion of rarified and perfumed princes, fitter to carry a tale than a rifle or a wounded comrade."

In responding to this allegation, Lt. Gen. Crosbie E. Saint, who was commanding III Corps and Fort Hood, Texas, then, and Col. Richard C. Edwards, commandant of the U.S. Army Sergeants Major Academy at the time, pointed out that Bahnsen and Bradin were guilty of using hyperbole and exaggeration for effect while forming their analysis on a purely anecdotal basis.** Nevertheless, the story was picked up by the *Atlanta Journal and Constitution* in its edition of September 18, 1988; "critics" were quoted as saying the CSM program "is out of control and has produced a clique of powerful mid-level managers never envisioned when the rank was created."

Since I was a former SMA, my opinion on all this was solicited by the press, and I told a reporter what I thought. Right after all this came out, I was sitting at my table at the annual AUSA convention and who should come up to me but Doc Bahnsen. He talked for a few moments and then said, "I see where you gave some comments to some newsman on the CSM program." I said, of course, and I told the reporter exactly what the program was all about.

"Well, I wouldn't talk to the SOB," General Bahnsen said, implying, I suppose, that the reporter had asked him for a comment but he'd refused to give one.

"Well, nevertheless, you sure put out a lot of stuff about the program," I replied, "and it sure isn't right. You used a goddamn shotgun . . ."

"I wasn't talking about *you*, Sergeant Major."

". . . on the whole program, and I didn't appreciate it a damn bit, because your article is woefully off-base."

"I'm sorry you feel that way about it, Sergeant Major," he said.

"That's exactly the way I feel, because you screwed up, General Bahnsen."

*Vol. XVII, No. 2 (June 1988), pp. 9–17.
**Vol. XVII, No. 3 (September 1988), pp. 113–15.

He said, "Thanks. See ya." Well, we were both retired at the time.

That program *is* a success story. Those few commanders who might have let their CSM stray are at fault, and the CSM who might have been part of the problem is not a command sergeant major in my book, he's a stripe-wearer who has let his rank go to his head, and thank God there are just a few of them, I'd say damn few, in the whole Army.

It was during this tour that I ran into John Bull again, the man who'd been with me in the 28th Infantry, and who'd been busted in Berlin and sent back to the States. I met him again at Syracuse University. We had come from First Army Headquarters to look into the ROTC program there. He was NCOIC of the rifle team at Syracuse. Somehow he'd gotten that Article 15, which had reduced him from SFC to staff sergeant, thrown out, and with nothing derogatory in his record, he'd gotten two promotions since I'd last seen him. He'd won back his E-7 stripes and even made master sergeant (E-8).

John had always been a super noncommissioned officer. He knew his business, and at Syracuse he'd put together a good rifle team and was helping to produce potential officers in the ROTC there. He had done one heck of a job. There never was any question he had talent, it was just that his personality usually got him into trouble.

While talking to him on this occasion I discovered he'd mellowed and used that experience in Berlin as a learning tool and was probably a better NCO for it. That just shows you should never be too hasty to write off a soldier just because he screws up, not if there's any chance to rehabilitate him.

This assignment was the first time I'd ever had anything to do with ROTC or West Point. When Bob Hope received the Thayer Award* at West Point that year, General Seaman arranged for me to attend the ceremony. I ate in the cadet mess and toured the installation, including the Cadet Chapel, where I saw the stained-glass window General Seaman's class of 1934 had donated. To me, West Point is like Arlington Cemetery. I felt like taking my hat off when I entered its gates, and a chill ran down my spine. Those two places are an integral part of the history of our great nation.

*Named after Sylvanus Thayer, West Point Class of 1808, superintendent 1817–1833, known as the "father of the Military Academy," it is bestowed upon individuals who have rendered distinguished service to the country.

Now, having mentioned my feelings about West Point, I must say that the ROTC has its place too, providing a method to bring a cross-section of our citizens into the military services. The officers graduated from the ROTC are citizen-soldiers. I think they "temper" the Military Academy and OCS graduates so we don't have all West Pointers, or all OCS officers. ROTC has provided the Army some very distinguished officers—Gen. Bill Rosson, commissioned from the University of Oregon; Gen. Bill Depuy, ROTC, Minnesota; Gen. Colin Powell of CCNY.

During the Vietnam War, a lot of universities wouldn't have ROTC courses on their campuses. At one time I'd have said not to try to reinstate the courses if the universities didn't want them. But we need that program to round out the officer corps with people who have a different perspective from that of Military Academy graduates, and we would fail to develop some great leaders without it. The program works, and we should hang on to it. Sure, ROTC helps put young people through school, but I think we get out of it far more than it costs us.

That tour of duty at First Army was a career-broadening experience for me. It exposed me to a lot of things I'd never known about before. For instance, as a straight-leg infantryman,* it was my first brush with how armor really operates. Fort Knox, Kentucky, where the Armor Center is located, was within First Army's jurisdiction, and I visited there to observe the training. I knew what armor was supposed to do, but I didn't know how it got to where it is today. Fort Knox taught me that.

· The real eye-opener was what I learned about the Transportation Corps. Its headquarters was at Fort Eustis, Virginia. Before that experience, Army transportation to me was a greasy truck driver. But I found out that the people at the transportation school at Fort Eustis were some great professionals, and they taught me why that truck driver is greasy. They also train the helicopter mechanics, all the Army's boatmen—the Army's always had more boats than the Navy, numberwise—and all the other people who make up the Transportation Corps, which is so vital to the Army.

I think I made half a dozen trips to Eustis while I was First Army sergeant major, and I know I made a couple of them just

---

*"Straight leg" is a somewhat derogatory term used by paratroopers to describe any soldier who isn't airborne-qualified. On the other hand, nonairborne soldiers sometimes have great difficulty comprehending why anyone in his right mind would volunteer to leap out of perfectly good airplanes.

because I was eager to find out more about how the Transportation Corps worked.

Fort Lee, Virginia, also under First Army, is where the quartermaster school is situated, and I learned what that was all about. Before First Army I thought all the quartermaster did was issue sheets and pillowcases. The Quartermaster Corps feeds and clothes the Army and fuels its vehicles. Back at Fort Leonard Wood, I'd been going around inspecting food service courses, but that was just cooks and bakers. At Fort Lee they put together the entire quartermaster system, from stoves and rations to clothing. One time they made me a miniature parachute bag as a gift, to use as a toilet kit. That was in 1967, and I still have it. I've carried it all over the world with me. If you break a bottle of Vitalis inside it, that fluid stays in the bag and doesn't run out all over your luggage, that's how sturdy that little bag is, and to me it represents the quality of the work the quartermaster people do.

Incidentally, at Fort Lee is the A. Owen Seaman Petroleum Labs. That facility was named after General Seaman's father. A. Owen Seaman was a brigadier general, and at one time was the quartermaster of the Soldiers' and Airmen's Home. While I was employed at the Home, one day I discovered in the files a letter he had signed, and I sent it to his son, who at that time was retired down in Beaufort, South Carolina. Jonathan O. Seaman and his wife, Mary, were married at the Home. Funny how my Army service just seems to follow me around everywhere I go.

I should add here that Gen. Jonathan O. Seaman had a profound impact on my military career. Having served with him as a battalion sergeant major, a corps sergeant major, and an army sergeant major, I really got to know what kind of a person he was. Suffice it to say we knew and trusted each other.

The first time I met him was when he reported to Fort Riley from the old VI Corps at Battle Creek, Michigan, to become the 1st Division commander. All the sergeants major were lined up to meet him. He came down the row, shaking our hands. He paused when he got to me and said, "Sergeant Major Bainbridge, I have a message from an old friend of yours, Walt Irish. He says to tell you hello. He was my personnel chief at VI Corps."

Walt Irish had been my buddy when he was the G-2 sergeant major at VII Corps in Germany. But here was a two-star general taking command of the division who remembered to convey to a battalion sergeant major regards from another sergeant major. I knew this was one hell of a guy.

First Army rounded out Bill Bainbridge as a soldier. It taught me how the Army gets where it's going and who it is that gets it there. When I finished up at First Army I had the ability to talk to almost any type of soldier, and that served me well. I think that background was one of the reasons I was selected for my next assignment, as U.S. Army Pacific—USARPAC—sergeant major.

One day in September 1968, General Seaman called me into his office and asked me if I knew I'd been nominated to be the U.S. Army Pacific sergeant major. Hell, I hardly knew what USARPAC was or where it was. Next he told me that not only had I been nominated for the job, I'd been selected. I wanted to know what the hell I was supposed to do. Only the year before, he'd brought me up from Fort Benning, and now somebody else had tapped me when I didn't even know I was under consideration for a new assignment.

"Don't do anything at this point," he told me. "Just go home and talk to Hazel about it, mull it around for a couple of days, and then tell me what you think."

We talked about the new assignment at length, and Hazel and I finally decided that it would be another challenge, and since we'd always wanted to go to Hawaii, we ought to try it. We'd never asked to go there, and during our conversation speculated that maybe that's why I'd been selected, since the Army has a penchant for giving soldiers things they haven't asked for. There must have been thousands of other soldiers dying to get to Hawaii—but I had been selected without asking.

The selection process for that job was run from the sergeants major branch of the Office of Personnel Operations back at the Pentagon. I found out later that they'd sent several nomination packets to USARPAC and I was in the third one. I don't know who was in the first two, but they were rejected.

When I told General Seaman I'd decided to accept the assignment, he told me I'd made a wise decision. He said he didn't really want me to go, but if I turned that assignment down it would have been like him rejecting an appointment as Chief of Staff of the Army. He also told me that out in Hawaii I'd be working for one of the best commanders in the Army, Gen. Ralph Haines.

So in December 1968 we left Fort Meade, drove across the country, stopping in Illinois and Kansas for a few days to see our families, and then on to the West Coast. Mary stayed behind at Fort Meade and kept her job at the NCO club. She got herself a little apartment, and the Marine sergeant major who was in charge of security over at the National Security Agency promised to look after her for us. She joined us in Hawaii about six or seven months later.

≡ 9 ≡

A SERGEANT IS A SERGEANT

Once our orders for transfer to Hawaii were confirmed, I got a communiqué from Frank Wickham, U.S. Army Pacific sergeant major, telling me that within about ten days of my arrival—two weeks maximum—I'd be going on a trip with CINCUSARPAC (Commander-in-Chief USARPAC) into the western Pacific, so I'd need a passport. He also informed me I'd need a set of dress whites.

I went down to a uniform outfit on Glebe Road in Arlington, Virginia, and ordered my whites, then dropped by the Pentagon, which is just a couple of miles down Columbia Pike from there, to apply for my official passport.

The woman at the passport office asked me where I was going. I told her Hawaii, and she informed me I didn't need a passport to go there. I explained that I would be doing some foreign travel immediately upon arrival in Hawaii and that's why I needed the passport. She insisted I didn't need one. I asked to speak to her supervisor, who told me the same thing.

I went through four supervisors before I got to the chief. I explained to each one of them along the way why my new job required a passport and each time got the same answer. When I told the chief of the branch my problem, he said, "Fine. No problem," and took me out to the woman who'd first told me I couldn't get a passport. She processed my application. I got the passport about two weeks after that.

One thing I'd learned by this time in the Army was that a lot of people in the chain can say yes, but very few can say no, and this whole exercise just reaffirmed that principle. I think citizens everywhere, and especially soldiers, should remember that entrenched bureaucracy, whatever the level, *can* be overcome.

Then, just as we were getting everything ready to depart for

Hawaii, the flu bug struck. I had just gotten over a bout the month before, and now Hazel took deathly ill, so sick she could hardly hold her head up. We'd been moved into guest quarters at Fort Meade while we vacated our assigned quarters, and I had the duty of getting the old set ready for inspection.

Clearing family quarters on an Army post is a lot of hard work. No decent person wants to leave his dirt behind for the next person anyway, but the regulations require a thorough cleaning, and your work is inspected by the post housing officer.

About the second night I was working on this project, about seven-thirty or eight o'clock—it was already dark by then in December—I heard somebody holler, "Is there anybody in the house?" It was John Doherty, my adjutant general sergeant major. John had with him two buckets, some rags, some cleanser, and other stuff, and he asked, "Where do I start?" So John and I did all the walls, and I guess we must have worked until well after midnight that night. That was a four-bedroom, two-story house, and the two of us scrubbed it thoroughly in about six hours and it was ready to pass quarters inspection in the morning. But with Hazel in charge the place never got very dirty in the first place.

That was when I discovered that the best product for cleaning walls, woodwork, floors, and bathrooms is dishwasher compound mixed in a mild solution. You have to be careful how you handle it, because it's caustic, but you don't have to rinse it off and it cleans beautifully in a one-step operation. Wear rubber gloves.

They had a going-away ceremony at First Army Headquarters during which General Seaman awarded me my third Army Commendation Medal. I got a good send-off, honor guard included. I was replaced by Jim Rogers, another infantryman and Vietnam veteran.

We took Kat with us, and before we left I went down to the vet to get her a tranquilizer. We loaded the car—Mary accompanied us back to Illinois to visit her grandparents—and Kat got her hind legs up on some gear piled in the backseat, and one front leg on the driver's window ledge and the other on my left shoulder, and for the first forty miles down the road she was right in my ear, going "rowrrrr" about every five minutes. About fifty miles into the trip she decided it was time to go to sleep, so down on the floor she went, and she slept the rest of the way to Illinois. So much for tranquilizers for cats—it takes a while for 'em to work.

We visited with kin in Illinois and Kansas and then drove across the western part of the country. Going through Utah there was nothing but flat ground and an occasional pile of sugar beets mile after mile. We had a Buick Skylark by now, with air conditioning, a windshield washer, power-assisted brakes, power steering—that was such a good car we've still got it right out in the garage. In those days the speed limit was seventy miles an hour. I was just gradually easing my foot down on the gas pedal, going faster and faster, and I turned to Hazel and asked, "How fast do you think we're going? Don't look at the speedometer."

She guessed sixty-five. Then she looked over and saw we were doing 105. "You slow this thing down!" she cried, and I did. I should never have let it get up there in the first place, but I was just trying to see what it'd do.

We turned our car in at Oakland Army Terminal and were met by the USARPAC liaison officer. We flew out the next day on United to Hawaii.

We landed at Honolulu International, and as the plane was taxiing up to the gate, the stewardess came back and requested that we remain in our seats until all the other passengers had gotten off. She told us that was the request of Sergeant Major Wickham. When we got to the gate, which opened out onto the tarmac instead of into the terminal, we were met by photographers and given leis. This was Frank's way of providing us with a private welcome ceremony.

Frank took us to the VIP lounge in the terminal, where we were greeted by CINCUSARPAC himself, Gen. Ralph Haines, and his wife, Sally. That was a first for me, and we really got a stunning reception. That was the kind of officer he was, a tremendous individual, a great humanitarian. I guess I've been lucky over the years to get great commanders with whom I've had wonderful rapport. We were to remain in Hawaii three and a half years.

We spent the next two weeks, up to the middle of January 1969, getting settled in. We moved into a three-bedroom, two-story apartment with one and a half baths in a building with four units at Fort Shafter, about a fifteen-minute walk from USARPAC Headquarters. The building was on a hillside. Out back was a little tree that shed purple blossoms all year round, and the lawn was always covered with them. We also had gardenia bushes right outside the living-room windows, and their fragrance wafted through those quarters all the time. We stayed in those quarters about eighteen months.

Fort Shafter is up on the Likelike—that's pronounced "leaky-leaky"—Highway, which runs north from Honolulu to Kaneohe. Camp H. M. Smith, where the Commander-in-Chief Pacific, Adm.

John McCain at that time, has his headquarters, is just a little farther northwest.

USARPAC Headquarters was located in Building 100 at Fort Shafter on Palm Circle, a beautiful two-and-a-half-acre parade field that was absolutely breathtaking, with stately royal palms growing on its fringes. Shafter is right in the Honolulu suburbs in the foothills of the Koolau Range. The Koolaus are a volcanic mountain range underneath which are massive caves from which Honolulu gets its water supply. The water from those caves is so pure that the city doesn't have to chlorinate it. From Fort Shafter you can see the ocean and downtown Honolulu.

Shafter is a small post, perhaps only 350–400 acres. What got me at first, coming from the Midwest, where it gets awfully cold in the wintertime, is that here the water lines run on the top of the ground, because it never freezes. There were officer and enlisted clubs at Fort Shafter and a post exchange, but no commissary. For grocery shopping we had to go up to Schofield Barracks. The post is just down the hill from Tripler Army Medical Center, so it doesn't need a large medical facility.

USARPAC was the Army element of the U.S. Pacific Command. Admiral McCain, CINCPAC, exercised overall tactical command of our armed forces in the Pacific area. U.S. Army Pacific was an intermediate headquarters between the Department of the Army and our forces in the field, but its role was one of logistical support, not command and control. At that time the Army had troops in Vietnam, Korea, Japan, Okinawa, and Taiwan. USARPAC also operated all the rest and recuperation centers.

By the time I was to depart on the two-week trip to the western Pacific, we still hadn't received our household goods. Hazel had a car but no household furnishings. Well, I went on the trip. We went to Vietnam, Korea, and Okinawa, and the day after we got back our household goods came, so I was there to give Hazel a hand moving them in.

While they were unloading our stuff, an inspector came up from the transportation office. When I saw them unloading our things I told him I thought they were not supposed to repack any of the things they'd packed at Fort Meade—they were supposed to be shipped directly to Honolulu. I could tell they'd been repacked because they were in different containers from the ones I remembered they'd been put into at Fort Meade. In those days, shipping weight allowances were reduced because some household furnishings, such as refrigerators, dressers, and so on, were already available at your new station. That saved the government money. But they had repacked our goods, and I noticed a big hole in one of the shipping containers. I pointed that out to the inspector, and he got his camera. When they peeled the side off that box, there was our TV standing on end, and the neck of the picture tube was right where that hole in the shipping case was.

We took the set inside the apartment and plugged it in, and when we turned it on—nothing. They'd crushed the tube and ruined a twenty-three-inch Zenith I'd bought on sale—seems we bought everything on sale—in Columbus, Georgia. We got it fixed at government expense, and it lasted until we moved to the Soldiers' Home in 1979.

So we started to settle in at Fort Shafter. We got reacquainted with the Potrafkas, Donald and his wife, Vi, whom we had met at Fort Benning. Don was the G-1 sergeant major at USARPAC and by date of rank was the senior sergeant major in the headquarters. They introduced us to others—Bill Long, the IG sergeant major, and his wife, Virginia, and Sgt. Maj. Bill Yarborough, our sponsor, and the rest of the staff's sergeants major.

In those days the Army worked on Saturday mornings. On my first Saturday morning I was introduced to Lt. Col. Richard "Bucky" Harris, an engineer by branch and General Haines's executive officer. He was a very stern individual, and the advice I'd received about him from Frank Wickham was that he was a hard man to get along with because you never knew where he was coming from.

My first meeting with Colonel Harris was a good one. I told him that the general and I had talked on our trip and it appeared to me that he wanted me to operate the same way I'd been doing all along—be his eyes and ears, do the things he didn't have the time to do, look into the things he needed to know about, particularly in enlisted matters, unless he told me otherwise. "There isn't any question about your relationship with the boss," Colonel Harris said, "and I'm here to tell you now, unless he tells you differently, that you've got an open door going by me. If you've got something to discuss with the boss, that's up to you."

"I will never go through that door," I told him, "with something you need to know about or with something that's going to come back out here to you, without you knowing before I give it to the Old Man. We've got to work together. We're on the same team and we've got to keep the boss out of trouble, that's what we're here for." From that time I never had a problem with Colonel Harris and he didn't have any with me.

I think it was a matter of personality between him and Frank. I suspect Frank came on a bit strong with Colonel Harris. Colonel Harris himself was a strong personality, as was Frank.

Colonel Harris informed me at that first meeting that I had been in the third packet of nominees for the USARPAC sergeant major's job originally. Sgt. Maj. Joe Veneble, who had been General Haines's sergeant major at III Corps, at Fort Hood, Texas, before he went to Vietnam, had been selected for the job. He had been scheduled to go to USARPAC in November or October. He was the 1st Infantry Division sergeant major at the time. In September he and Maj. Gen. Keith Ware, along with other key staff, were killed when their helicopter was shot down in Vietnam. Colonel Harris told me that the first two packets that came to him were "unbelievable"—there wasn't anybody in either group General Haines would consider for the job. "I'll tell you one thing right now, Sergeant Major, you've got to prove that you're bad. Your record is awful good, and the Old Man is really looking forward to your being his sergeant major."

General Haines had already said that he wanted me to operate for him as I had for General Seaman. I told him that it appeared to me that there were a lot of things that I could do for him and the command on my own, and I wanted to discuss them at our Saturday-morning get-togethers, when I could bring to his attention things that had happened during the week he might need to know about—but as "finished products." I thought it was important that things that needed doing got done at my level—that he should not have to take a hand in them. "The things you don't hear about are more indicative of whether I'm doing my job than the things you do hear about," I said.

He agreed to that.

We had quarters problems at Fort Shafter, just as we did at First Army. There were places to put our noncommissioned officers but no rhyme or reason to the assignment procedure. We had a big meeting on the subject one Saturday morning, and a lieutenant colonel action officer in the G-1 said he didn't understand why I was "pushing" for quarters for senior noncommissioned officers because "*I* don't even have quarters." I told him I wasn't worried about *his* quarters, I was worried about senior NCOs' quarters. "That brigadier general down the hallway, the G-1, is your route to quarters, and he is also mine, but I am not competing for your quarters. That's not the issue. The issue is whether or not we're dividing them up right among the senior sergeants."

"Well, what about the staff sergeants?" the colonel asked.

"They want quarters too," I responded. "The staff sergeant understands what I am saying and is waiting until he becomes a master sergeant so that he can get moved into a set of those senior NCO quarters. The staff sergeant is not the problem, *you* are the problem, and you've got to get off of this business."

"Well," he said, "I may be the problem, but you can go up to the commissary at Schofield Barracks and they've got a sign there in the parking lot, for 'Any Colonel' and one for 'Any Sergeant Major,' but there's no sign for 'Any Lieutenant Colonel.'"

"The problem there is, sir," I responded, "you've got to get promoted."

That meeting ended right there. I can't remember that officer's name anymore, but that's the way I operate. I tend to forget those lieutenant colonels who only have a mission for themselves and don't care about anybody else. There aren't many like that, but he was one. But the deputy G-1 adjourned the meeting because he didn't want it to deteriorate any further or me to get into trouble.

This became a subject with General Haines, and we got it settled.

As an afterword to this tale, there were at Fort Shafter two sets of officers' quarters built during the 1940s. They were detached houses located near the post headquarters. General Haines asked me to take a look at those located at 313 Montgomery Avenue. "Just tell me if they'd be adequate quarters for you and Hazel," he said. Out behind the house was a big earpod tree—I don't know what its scientific name is; it's a great, large tree. The house had been everything, nurses' quarters, a dispensary, and so on. It was a wooden frame structure with three bedrooms and one bath. Also in the back was a big fenced-in patio with bushes all around.

There was a lieutenant colonel assigned to the G-1 living in those quarters at the time. General Haines said he wanted to designate those quarters as mine when the colonel and his family vacated them. While we were talking about that, I suggested he also designate the house next door, at 311 Montgomery Avenue, for the post sergeant major. The post headquarters was only about a hundred yards down the road from that house—it was in his bailiwick.

"I never thought about that, but that's a good idea," he said. As a result, Sgt. Maj. Leonard Deavers, the post sergeant major, got his quarters a little ahead of us, because its occupants moved sooner than the colonel at No. 313.

Well, the time came for that colonel to leave and the house was still occupied. At another of our Saturday-morning meetings, the general said, "Bucky, what happened to 313 Montgomery Avenue?"

"Well, I don't know, sir," Colonel Harris answered, and he said he'd check. Come to find out, the G-1 had extended that lieutenant colonel for six months and hadn't informed General Haines. From then on there were no more extensions approved without General Haines knowing about them. But that got fixed, and Hazel and I moved into those quarters.

That's where we were when we celebrated our twenty-fifth wedding anniversary. Our younger daughter, Mary, who joined us in Hawaii just before the occasion, planned it all by herself. She'd written to her sister, and Steve, Kathy, and the kids flew out for it. She got the preparations almost finished when she ran out of money, so she came to me and said, "Dad, I've got to tell you that I'm planning a twenty-fifth anniversary party for you and Mom, but I need money to finish it off." She'd arranged with Bob Troutman, the club manager, to cater the thing, and she'd put out a guest list inviting General Haines and all the people we went to church with. I made up the shortfall for her, of course.

The upshot of the question about senior noncommissioned officers' quarters was that the Navy was eventually committed to build a lot of new ones at Fort Shafter. We also got a new NCO club, and it's still there, up on the hill, a beautiful round concrete building with windows all the way around, looking down on Honolulu. Up behind there are the new NCO quarters, with a house on the very peak of the ridge designated for the USARPAC sergeant major. I never got into those quarters, but we had them for my replacement. I got to pick the spot where they were built.

That's an example of the things we accomplished at Fort Shafter not for Bill Bainbridge, but for all NCOs.

One day General Davidson, the deputy CINC, was conducting a staff meeting. Maj. Gen. Con Milburn, the USARPAC surgeon, was sitting in, and when it came his turn to speak, he announced that Brig. Gen. Hal C. Jennings—who thought I was one of his NCOs when he was hospital commander back at Fort Benning—was to be promoted to three stars and become the Surgeon General of the Army, skipping the second star entirely. General Davidson said, "That must make all of those two-star medical officers in the Army feel pretty rotten today, huh, Con?"

General Milburn said, "What about me, sir? I'm a two-star medical officer and I'm getting passed over!"

Jennings had been U.S. Army, Vietnam (USARV) surgeon and he went from there to be Surgeon General of the Army. He was the handpicked replacement for Lt. Gen. Leonard Heaton.

General Milburn went on to inform us that General Heaton had visited Tripler Army Hospital the week before "to keep his hand in." Now, General Heaton was getting pretty old about this time, and "to keep his hand in" he'd done an appendectomy. General Milburn told us, "He did very well, too—his hands were pretty steady."

General Davidson said, "What about the patient, Con? Were *his* nerves steady?"

"Well, sir, he was under anesthesia."

General Davidson was a great guy and he had a good sense of humor.

Over the next three and a half years I made sixteen trips to the western Pacific. All of them got into Vietnam, but I also got to go to a lot of other places. Mrs. Haines normally accompanied us on these trips. We flew in the last C-118 ever built, tail number 33305, and it had a VIP package put into it—quarters for the CINC in the tail section, bunks for the crew and passengers, an office space for the secretary/steno who accompanied us.

My first trip to Vietnam in this job was in January 1969. General Haines, Colonel Harris, and I flew into the Philippines, where we left the rest of the party and caught a T-39 jet to Vietnam. We attended the Saturday-morning intelligence briefing at the Military Assistance Command, Vietnam (MACV) Headquarters in Saigon. Later we went out to USARV and had another briefing, and later that day we started to get our itinerary sorted out. I went everywhere with General Haines, but as soon as we got to our destination, a fire support base or whatever, I split: I went one way, he went another, just as when I was with General Seaman at IIFFV.

For instance, we went into Da Nang and half a dozen noncommissioned officers I'd known elsewhere were there to meet me, and it was like that all throughout this trip. When we got on the plane fifteen days later to leave Vietnam, General Haines called me back and invited me to have dinner with him that night, and then he told me, "I want to tell you, if I had any concern about you having the right rapport out here in the western Pacific and in the Vietnam combat units, that's all been dispelled during this trip. Everybody out there knows you, knows where you are coming from, understands you. They like you, and they know what kind of a soldier you are. I'm just as pleased as punch that you're my sergeant major."

"With your permission, sir," I said, "I don't need any more briefings on these trips. What I need to do is lash up with the USARV sergeant major when we get in-country and you go your way. What you're looking for is not what I'm after, but what I am looking for you need to know, and you don't have time to get at it."

He agreed. From then on I only traveled to places with the CINC. I talked to the troops and he got the briefings. When we got into a firebase, for example, it seemed every command wanted to brief General Haines. I'd get with the first sergeant or the sergeant major and go down to where the troops were actually operating, whether at USARV Headquarters, division units, firebases or wherever—the 25th Division, the 1st Division, the 1st Cav Division, the 101st Airborne Division, engineer units, aviation units, artillery units—we had lots of units in there at that time.

We also visited small advisory detachments throughout the country. I wanted to know how well they were being supported. Of course, much of their support came from the Vietnamese, but I wanted to know if they were getting their mail, their cigarettes, their PX supplies. It was important, I thought, that besides visiting the big troop units we also get to what I call the "two-four-sixes," the detachments of only two people here or four there or six over that way. Most visiting VIPs never bothered with them. Those are the men who get forgotten, and I wanted to let them know they were still part of the Army. And I think those visits boosted their morale.

We visited Special Forces camps too, those out with the Montagnards.* While those Special Forces soldiers have great training and are oriented toward living primitively, it's pretty nice when they can get their mail on time, get a beer now and then. Those things are important to them too.

At one point I was due to visit USARV Headquarters, my old outfit. Ray Martin, the USARV sergeant major, told me later that he was a little bit upset with me because I hadn't arrived when I was supposed to. On that occasion I was out visiting some unit in the field and I showed up at the headquarters at about seven-thirty

---

*This is the French name for the aboriginal mountain tribes of Vietnam. These people were of Malayo-Polynesian heritage, distinct from the lowland Vietnamese, who generally looked down on them.

or eight in the evening, late for the little dinner the NCOs were going to host for me. Ray said he thought I'd just passed them by, and when I did arrive I had mud on my boots and was wet to my rear end, but in great spirits, and he was wondering what in the hell was the matter with me. He said I looked as if I ought to be miserable but I wasn't. He asked me where I'd been.

"Ray," I answered, "I've been out visiting your soldiers. I apologize for not getting here on time, but it was just a little bit more important for me to stay out where I was at Bear Cat." Ray told me afterward that he knew damn well I was the right guy in the right position because I knew something about soldiers and believed protocol could go hang if there was a soldier I could take care of.

That was nothing I had planned. I just felt good out talking to the troops where they were, because that's where you can find out what their problems are. You can't find out in a briefing room in Saigon what the guy in a platoon out at Bien Hoa or Bear Cat or Xuan Loc is doing, and that's what I figured we were over there for.

It wasn't that people weren't doing their jobs when it came to supporting our soldiers, but sometimes they just couldn't see the forest for the trees. Troops would complain to me freely about things that weren't going right, and I accepted those complaints because I could get something done about them. I could take it all the way one-on-one to the USARPAC commander, and that got lots of people's attention. And I did that when necessary.

From the very first time I ever worked for a general officer, I never went around the staff unless I was forced to, and not too many times did that happen. Most of the time, things can be resolved by the staff, and that's how I did it all the way up to the Sergeant Major of the Army's Office, because the staff guy or gal is the person who's going to have to work on the problem. If you give it to the staff as a problem, it gets to the chief or the general as a *solution*; if you give it to the commander as a problem, it becomes a hot potato to the staff and they wind up jumping through their rears trying to get something done because the commander has said *do* it. Things work so much better the other way—and not only do you get along better with those folks, but they respect you and they support you. And if they do that, the trooper is also getting supported.

This trip took place in 1969, and we'd had major ground forces in Vietnam since early 1965. This trip I sensed a difference in the attitude of the soldiers I talked to. When we went there in 1965, we went as full units, knowing everybody's capabilities at each level, what each man could do and what his shortcomings were and how we could work around them. But in 1969, with the one-year rotation policy well established, the forces in Vietnam had by then turned over completely four times. Sure, we had a lot of people back for more than one tour, but now, instead of having units filled with soldiers who knew each other, they were being filled with people from all over the world.

The caliber of the noncommissioned officers was different too. By then we were beginning to see some of the graduates of the NCOC coming to Vietnam. By 1969 the program was into all the combat arms, not just the infantry. Those NCOs were trained to do a specific job, and I think they were trained to do it very well. They didn't have experience in dealing with everyday garrison problems. Yes, there were garrison situations in Vietnam—base camps, division headquarters, and so forth. You had platoons from the 173rd Airborne Brigade involved in the pacification program, sitting in little hamlets in the countryside, trying to Americanize the Vietnamese, and soldiers aren't trained to do that. The 173rd was trained to jump into a combat zone and fight.

So we had a lot of troops with time on their hands, and we had problems with drugs and fraggings.* It wasn't that we didn't have good soldiers, but the experienced noncommissioned leaders, the men with ten or twelve years of service, had been killed off or promoted out of the ranks. So we had platoon sergeants who just didn't have the experience to run their platoons the way the old-timers did. From what I saw, the biggest problems were not in the combat units but in the base camps and in the big cities. The man out in the field didn't have the chance to get into trouble. Out there he was too busy protecting himself and his buddies and try-ing to get his mission accomplished, and he wasn't about to be caught smoking pot. But when a man had a chance to go into downtown Saigon every night and visit the bars and the brothels, he was primed for trouble.

We were getting enough strong leaders to carry us through that period, and I think we made it in a lot better shape than we've given ourselves credit for. I've heard from Korean War veterans that they went to Korea because even then it was easy to get drugs over there, and some men went to Vietnam for the same

---

*The attempted assassination or wounding of officers and noncommissioned of-ficers by disgruntled enlisted men. The term comes from "fragmentation gre-nade," but applies to the act without regard to the weapon used.

reason. We even had entrepreneurs. We had a former corporal who gave heroin-laced marijuana cigarettes to troops until he got them hooked and from then on sold them the cigarettes. He was killing his buddies as surely as the Vietcong. So we had an insidious group of people working on the inside of the Army, and it's hard to ferret those guys out.

Vietnam wasn't the only place we looked at while I was USARPAC sergeant major.

General Haines gave me the mission of checking out all the R&R centers in the western Pacific area. I visited every one of them. I'd been to Hong Kong when I was in Vietnam, and that place worked beautifully. I went to Kuala Lumpur, Sydney, Singapore, the Philippines—all the places where we had R&R centers. I even got to New Zealand. Although we didn't have an R&R program there, some of our guys got to New Zealand anyway.

I found that the R&R centers were run very, very well. Soldiers were able to relax, go to dances, or get a girl for a week. That may seem immoral, shocking, but we're talking for the most part about a lot of young, unmarried soldiers who'd never before been away from Indiana, Illinois, Wisconsin, wherever, and here they are in a faraway place with a bunch of people trying to kill them with anything at hand, from punji stakes to our own five-hundred-pound bombs rigged as booby traps. They let their hair down on R&R, and you really can't blame them.

I just take my hat off to all those folks who set up and ran the R&R centers, from the top of the Army right on down. That R&R program was one of the real success stories of the Vietnam War. When our troops are in combat, they deserve any relaxation we can give them. That's money well spent.

About halfway through my tour General Haines was called back to command CONARC (Continental Army Command), and General William Rosson, a four-star general, a brilliant officer, one of the youngest lieutenant colonels in the Army during World War II, a bachelor, and a tremendous friend of the soldier, became my boss.

Since General Rosson wasn't married, his deputy's wife, Mrs. Yarborough, became the "first lady" of USARPAC. Gen. William Yarborough was the father of the Special Forces—he organized them when he was a colonel.

My method of operating did not change one iota under General Rosson. I had a little session with him to find out what his guidelines were, and they were no different from General Haines's. I did find out that when you really wanted to put a glow on General Rosson, you scheduled a trip to visit the troops. He was not much of a headquarters type.

General Haines had a very good staff. I've mentioned Lt. Col. Bucky Harris. He turned out to be one of my best friends at USARPAC. He went on to become a two-star general. Another was Thelma Baker, who'd come from Japan several years before, where she'd been a secretary to Gen. I. D. White of IX Corps. When he came back to Hawaii he brought Thelma with him, and she stayed on when General White left. She was a tremendous individual. Her husband, Bill, was the education director for all of USARPAC.

So General Haines went back to CONARC and Gen. Bill Rosson came in to be CINCUSARPAC. In the meantime, Gen. Mike Davidson, who was the deputy CINC and chief of staff under General Haines, went to Europe, where he became a four-star general himself and U.S. Army Europe commander.

One day back in 1970, General Yarborough was talking about pin-on insignia of rank. We'd had them on the field uniform for some time, and I was saying that we ought to have them for other uniforms as well. "Sergeant Major," he said, "I'd like to see you wear the old chevrons of the days of the horse cavalry, so I could see you as my sergeant major all the way across the parade field."

I said, "General Yarborough, if you need to see a set of chevrons on an arm to know that I'm your sergeant major, you don't need me as your sergeant major. You ought to be able to tell me by this old mug of mine, and you also ought to be able to recognize me when I'm walking away, by the back of my head."

He looked at me for a moment and he said, "You know, you're exactly right. That's the squad leader in you talking, isn't it?"

"That's right, sir. You don't have to wear a name tag in my squad, because I can tell you wherever you're at."

"That's a good point, Sergeant Major."

"And you never wore any chevrons. I've worn them most of my Army career, and none of them have been worth a damn. You give me a cotton shirt and a wool chevron and the chevron shrinks faster than the shirt, so I've got a puckered sleeve and you're on my rear end because my uniform looks like hell, but yet you won't issue me a good set of chevrons. Then you change the system and you put little chevrons on my arm so you can't tell who I am unless you come up and shake my hand. Then you turn things around and you put blue chevrons on gold for support personnel and gold on blue for combat troops. What kind of deal is that? A sergeant is a sergeant! We've got to put a little common sense into this system."

General Yarborough admitted that I had made some valid points. He was the kind of guy who would listen to you. Today we use pin-on insignia on most of our everyday uniforms.

General Rosson and I were getting ready to make a trip throughout USARPAC. He told his staff that he wanted a page on every place we were going, a heads-up on the matters they wanted him to discuss with the commanders included on his itinerary. That was my first trip with him, and I could see the change come over him as he began to *glow* the farther he got from his headquarters.

We got airborne in the CINC's C-118, and the door to the CINC's quarters opened and he motioned for me to come back there. "Sergeant Major," he said, "look at this blankety-blank book!" He had two three-inch loose-leaf folders, and they were full of papers for him to read so he'd know what the staff wanted him to discuss when he got on the ground. "Here I am, all thrilled about going out to see soldiers, and it's going to take me all night to read this blankety-blank stuff and my eyes will be red and they'll think I've been drunk all night. This is terrible! It isn't going to happen again!"

When we got back to Hawaii, at the next staff meeting he told his staff, "I've been in the Army all week. I know a little bit about what's going on out there. You just give me a couple or three paragraphs from now on and I can handle it from there." The next time we went he had a one-inch folder about half full.

We were now into 1971, and the pullout from Vietnam was well underway. As the year began, we were down to only 280,000 troops in Vietnam. The 101st Airborne Division was at Phu Bai, in the I Corps area, the 173rd Airborne was in the II Corps area, and the 1st Cav and a brigade of the 25th Infantry Division was in the III Corps area. Now, instead of visiting division-size units (sixteen thousand men), we were visiting mostly brigade-size organizations (four thousand men), but the soldier problems were about the same.

This was my first experience in witnessing an army disband. We were trying to keep the men's spirits up, but it was not easy. My last trip to Vietnam was a memorable one. That was Christmas of 1971. We were over there in Christmas of 1970 too. General Rosson always wanted to be with the troops at a time when most folks wanted to be home, but he always made sure we had our Christmas when we got back to Hawaii. He'd take us down to Fort De Russy, where he had a set of quarters—this was before they converted the place to the Hale Koa Armed Forces Recreation Center. He invited his staff members and his aircrew and their families as well.

General Rosson knew he had to do two things. First, he had to get out among his soldiers and show them we were interested in them and didn't mind spending our Christmas with them. And he had to show his own staff the same spirit.

I can recall several dinners at General Rosson's quarters in those days. After the dinner he'd address the ladies and tell them they could go on up to the drawing room on the second floor for tea and coffee while we men remained downstairs for a cigar and "man talk." Then he'd say, "Word of warning. Don't come stumbling back down here until we call, because we might be talking about you." That wouldn't go over too well in today's Army, but all those ladies just loved that guy, and they all laughed and went on upstairs. Had I ever said anything like that even then, they'd have thrown rocks at me—but he could do it because those women knew he wasn't being disrespectful to them.

General Rosson had a bad back. One time he was in the hospital up at Tripler, and because one of his legs was just a little bit shorter than the other, they had him up in traction. He was lying in bed one day, reading an official paper, and when the nurse came in she saw this thermometer sticking out of his navel. She said, "Who put that in *there?*"

He said, "I don't know. I was reading and somebody came in here, stuck it in there, and left."

"Well, that's not where to put it."

"I didn't think so either," he said. Her supervisor came in, took one look, turned around, and got the chief nurse. "General Rosson," she said, "I need to know who put that in there, because that's just *ludicrous!* Why would anybody . . . ?"

"I don't know who put it in there. As I told the first nurse, somebody just stuck it in and left before I even knew what happened."

Well, he had the nurses on that ward just climbing the walls, trying to figure out who'd put that thermometer in his belly button.

But as I said, that last trip to Vietnam was a memorable one. Before we went I'd already gotten my tour in Hawaii extended six months, to give me four years there. Then I got a telephone call from Col. Karl Morton, General Haines's executive officer at

CONARC. He told me General Haines wanted, as the capstone of the Noncommissioned Officer Education System, a Sergeants Major Academy. General Westmoreland had given him the authority to do that but stipulated he'd have to take it out of his own resources. So General Haines picked Colonel Morton to be the commandant and recommended me to be Colonel Morton's sergeant major. Now when we went into Vietnam in 1965, the unit we relieved was the 2nd Battalion of the 18th Infantry, commanded by Lt. Col. Karl Morton. His sergeant major was Jim Knox, who'd been one of my company first sergeants. That's all Colonel Morton knew about me, but General Haines knew a lot more.

Colonel Morton told me that he knew I was on an extension of my tour in Hawaii but he wanted me to consider being his sergeant major nevertheless. I promised to think it over and get back to him. I talked to General Rosson. I told him I'd been out there since 1969, seen Vietnam build up to half a million troops, then dwindle down to a pretty small contingent, which was getting smaller, and now I had a new opportunity with this offer to be the sergeant major of the new Sergeants Major Academy. I said I'd been educating noncommissioned officers ever since I'd been in the Army and here we were getting this system set up, and I'd sure like a crack at being the first sergeant major back there. "I think I can have a lot of influence on not only what kind of system we build, but also on a lot of the noncommissioned officers coming through it. I'd like to get relieved from that extension you approved, because I think at this point I can do more good for the Army there than here. I feel that my mission out here is completed."

General Rosson replied, "I agree with you. There isn't any question that's where you belong."

So we made this last trip to Vietnam at Christmas 1971. Meanwhile, I was talking about the new academy, talking about what it would be. At the same time I was looking for people that I knew we'd need there.

In Vietnam that last trip, we visited a brigade of the 101st, a brigade of the 1st Cav, an aviation group down in the Mekong Delta, and a corps headquarters. On Christmas Eve we were at Fire Support Base Arsenal, right on the DMZ. It was the 101st's forward fire support base. We got in to the division base camp in the midafternoon and learned that they had a dinner planned for us at the headquarters that night. General Rosson said, "No, the dinner is for the rest of you, because the sergeant major and I are going up to the FSB tonight." General Rosson's executive officer said he'd get a chopper for us and the three of us would go on up there then. General Rosson said, "No, the sergeant major and I will go up to the fire support base and the rest of you will stay here, and we'll see you in the morning."

We spent Christmas Eve on Fire Support Base Arsenal, within eyesight of the DMZ. The Vietnamese fired every one of their red and green flares for Christmas Eve celebration. General Rosson and I were quartered in dug-in CONEX* containers. We had cots and sleeping bags. We walked the line after dinner—hot dogs—and didn't get to bed until after midnight. We spent the entire evening talking with the troops, asking them about their duty and where they wanted to go when they got home, the things soldiers talk about.

On December 25, just at daybreak, a chopper came in and we started our trip south, toward the Delta. The trip ended that evening, three Christmas dinners later. We visited every American soldier in every hospital in Vietnam. There weren't many of them left, maybe 150 or so, but we hit every hospital, and we used every kind of transportation that day, from elephants to T-39s, to get there. It was really a poignant trip. I knew it was my last. But we did what we'd been doing all along, taking care of soldiers and finding out what their wants and needs were.

An aviation company commander and I were talking about the Sergeants Major Academy at dinner that night. I was telling him that one of the nice things about the concept was that for the first time commanders in the field would not be able to keep their first sergeants and master sergeants from going to the course. When orders came down, they would go to the school, because it was to be a permanent change of station assignment, just like the War College or the Command and General Staff College for officers. I thought that was a real step forward, because the selection process would pick the best to go and then they would go because their field commanders couldn't stop them from going.

The major said that didn't seem fair. The conversation went something like this: "You mean to tell me that if First Sergeant Johnson here, my first sergeant, is selected I wouldn't be able to keep him?"

"That's right. You'd *have* to let him go. But the orders would

---

*CONEX comes from "continental exchange." CONEXes were large corrugated metal shipping containers used for storage and transport of equipment. They were eight by eight by eight feet.

be cut at the end of his tour and you'd lose him when you'd normally lose him anyway."

"Well, what if I wanted to extend him?"

"You wouldn't be able to do that. He's going to go to that
course."

"That isn't fair!"

" 'Course it's fair. That man needs to go to that course—he's
been selected as one of the top people in his field."

"Well, it isn't fair because I depend on my first sergeant."

"Let me put it this way, Major. I'm going to have dinner with
the brigade commander tonight and I'm going to recommend to
him that if you come out on the Command and General Staff College selection list, he should just keep you here because it's important for him to have you here."

"Oh, that wouldn't be fair!"

"But you just told me it was all right if your first sergeant
didn't get to go to the Sergeants Major Academy. What's fair for
the goose is fair for the gander."

That company commander probably never saw the light, but
thank goodness most of the officers in the Army have.

This trip also took us to Japan and Korea, and I was to pick up
two key people for the academy. One was S/Sgt. Don Kelley, later
to be a command sergeant major, and at the time I tapped him he
was the protocol NCO at U.S. Army Japan. Don had his family
with him and was also on an extension. I picked him because I
knew that he was discreet. He was also a forward-thinking young
staff sergeant and knew his business, and I needed a protocol man.
Don talked to his wife, Betty, and they decided to come to the
academy.

In Korea I picked up Sgt. Maj. William Sweeney, the G-3
operations sergeant for the Eighth Army.

Korea was always a place that concerned General Haines and
General Rosson. We still have people in quarters over there that
do not have bathrooms. We've been there since 1950, and we still
have people going outside to hit the john in the middle of the
night. We also wanted to get more family members over there.
The family separations caused when men went to Korea generated
a lot of problems. It seems that there were a lot of married men
picking up girlfriends over there during their one-year separa-
tion—"yobos," they called them. Some of the guys would get to
Korea and they couldn't stand prosperity.

My comment on this during one of General Haines's Saturday-morning conferences was that a lot of our people "had wives who were married but they weren't." And it wasn't just the enlisted men, it was across the board. Of course, you can't blame the single guy who wanted to shack up. Many of those Korean women were second-class citizens in their own country, but if they could manage to get an American boyfriend, they became first-class citizens. You can't blame a Korean gal for wanting to live like a human being for a year.

We were able to address some of that. The VD rate went down during that time, and the alcohol abuse problem diminished, because we were bringing in more families for two- and three-year tours. The KMAG* people had their families with them all along, but we got some families into the Seoul area for the men in the troop units.

Korea was a great training ground, because the commanders had their soldiers 100 percent of the time. We had the same situation in Desert Shield/Desert Storm, because there were absolutely *no* off-duty distractions for the troops while they were in Saudi Arabia and in the Persian Gulf.

During this time we were getting ready to pull our chemical munitions out of storage on Okinawa. Part of the arrangement made for handing the island back to the Japanese was that we had to move those munitions. That generated Operation Red Hat. The 515th Ordnance Company was handling those munitions out there. All of it was to be loaded up on ships, along with the company, and moved to Johnston Island, six hundred miles southwest of Honolulu, in the middle of the Pacific Ocean. General Rosson and I were on Okinawa, and we watched the unit load up everything, including its mascot, an old dog.

The Johnston Island base had been set up by the Atomic Energy Commission way back in the 1950s. They had some Air Force people there and a few quarters and other facilities, but it was an isolated tour. Johnston Island covers 650 acres. It was only a 65-acre atoll to start, but the Army engineers dredged up all the coral and built the island up to about four feet above sea level. The atoll itself gives the island some protection against the sea, but on occasion they've had to evacuate the place because of violent storms. There's an airstrip there that'll take about anything.

*Korean Military Assistance Group, the U.S. military command in the Republic of Korea that provided military advice and logistical assistance to the Republic of Korea armed forces.

But for the most part it's in an area where storms are not a problem.

Well, we watched them load up, and later on we were on Johnston Island when they came in to unload. They were really pleased to see us there. Off came the company from its planes and off came the old dog.

From that time forward, I had a big soft spot in my heart for Johnston Island. As Sergeant Major of the Army, I visited Johnston Island every year I was in office. That's one of those "two-four-six" places. It's not the best place in the world to do your service, but a lot of the men stationed out there extend their tours. You can complete a high school or college education in a year out there. There were good recreational facilities, but it was pretty isolated and an all-male environment.

Witnessing that outfit move from Okinawa to Johnston Island and do it in such a professional manner was one of the highlights of my tour at USARPAC.

Before this tour I had never been to Australia or New Zealand. The first time we went to Australia we visited Duntroon Military College, just outside Canberra. When we flew in afterward we always landed at Darwin, to refuel, and then we'd fly across the country to Canberra. That's a long flight. Australia covers more than 2.9 million square miles; the United States is only 3.6 million. It usually took us a whole day to make the flight in that C-118.

Duntroon is the West Point of the Australian Army. We stayed in downtown Canberra in a hotel, but I was invited out to the sergeants' mess at Duntroon. My host was Sgt. Maj.* Norman R. Goldspink, a fellow about six feet nineteen, rawboned, a party lover and a great guy. He sponsored me at the mess. I went out the first night and knew right off what was going to happen—they were planning on putting me under the table. Australian beer is potent, but they did not succeed, although I could not buy a drink the whole night. The young sergeant who was running the bar kept telling me, "Sarn Mayjer, I kin give you a beer but I cain't take yer money."

I walked out of that club at the end of the night, because I never sat down the whole evening. I stayed up with them all night, because I knew that with what I had drunk, if I did sit

*Sergeants major in the Australian Army are warrant officers designated WOI and WOII, regimental and company sergeant major, respectively.

down I'd be in trouble. What they didn't realize is that I wasn't drinking one-for-one, but hedging the drinks.

The next day I got a telephone call inviting me back for dinner that night. They confirmed the plot of the evening before, and the word was out that they couldn't "unbend" that guy Bainbridge, because he could hold his own—"But we suspect he wasn't drinking as hard as we were!"

That started friendships that have lasted through the years. The next time I went out I was invited to stay in the mess.

The sergeant major in the British Commonwealth armies occupies a very special status. For instance, the close-order drill given to the cadets at Duntroon is the realm of the sergeant major. One day, unbeknownst to Norm, his brigadier had given permission to a group of frosh from a girls' college to serve tea to the cadets on the parade field, as part of their freshman initiation. Norm told me, "I was aghast! I was prepared to drill the cadets and here were all these young ladies, getting ready to serve tea and cookies! I accosted them and asked what they were doing there on my parade." They informed him they had permission from the brigadier to be there. Norm said, "I am sorry, ladies, you may have the brigadier's permission, but by God, you don't have mine," and he dismissed the corps.

Norm proceeded to his office and penned a note to the brigadier and had his runner take it over to him. He knew he was finished as the sergeant major at Duntroon, but he wasn't about to go out without a fight. An hour later the brigadier sent a note back, apologizing for getting into his business. "And Sergeant Major," he wrote, "it won't happen again." "And by God," Norm told me, "it hasn't."

It seems every town in Australia has a Victoria Barracks. We went to Victoria Barracks in Brisbane, and I toured the training site there. They had a little reception and dinner at the mess, and when I entered the place I was given a little slip of paper with a number on it, for the door-prize drawing. I stuck it in my pocket and forgot about it until the drawing. When they called out the winning number, their Sergeant Major McLaughlin asked me what mine was, and I gave him the paper.

"Here's the winner!" he shouted out, holding up my slip of paper. The prize was a quart of Johnnie Walker Red scotch. In those days I was a scotch drinker, and the Australians knew it.

"Wait a minute," I said. "I come over here on a visit, you wine me and dine me, and then you rig it so I win the door prize."

"Let me tell you something, Bill," McLaughlin said. "We appreciate your trip down here and we wine you and dine you because we like you, *but,* when it comes to Johnnie Walker Red, we like it too, and mate—you won that one fair and square!"

That same night they decided to invite General Haines and his party down for a drink at the sergeants' mess, so they closed the bar, thinking to open it with a flourish when he arrived. We waited and we waited and we waited, it seemed like an hour or an hour and a half. The party finally arrived and the bar was opened.

In the party was a Colonel Underwood, the USARPAC public affairs officer. Colonel Underwood struck up a conversation at the bar with an Australian female sergeant major. He said, "I really appreciate that you invited us in for a drink and closed your bar for a few minutes, so you could open it when we came in."

She said, "A few minutes me arse, Colonel—we waited well over an hour for you to appear."

I also got a chance to visit the Canungra training area, where the Australians trained troops who were going to Vietnam. Their men couldn't go to Vietnam without one full year of training. They couldn't understand why we sent our people over there with such little training, and I explained that we couldn't afford otherwise because of the size of our force in Vietnam.

I also visited Australia and New Zealand one year during ANZAC Week, in honor of the Australian and New Zealand Army Corps first formed during World War I. In New Zealand I always got into the controversy over whose beer was better, theirs or Australia's. The sergeants' messes in those countries have old traditions—special silver used only on ceremonial occasions, formal rituals employed, and so on—imported from Great Britain.

My host in New Zealand was Jack Flowerday, a regimental sergeant major in the New Zealand Army. At that time New Zealand had an army of about five thousand men (Australia had nearly fifty thousand).

I went to the club with Jack one evening and they got me into a dart game. I'd never played before in my life. They had what they called "livers-in" and "livers-out" in the messes. The "livers-in" are the sergeants who have their rooms at the mess, and the "livers-out" are married or live off post. I played with the livers-out that night. I scored the highest three-dart total anybody had ever scored in that club—by accident. There's this little tiny ring in the middle of the board, and I got one dart in there, and there's another around that, just about big enough for the dart to get in between the wires, and I got two in there.

The livers-out won, based on my sterling performance. They always afterward accused me of being a darts shark. The next time we went back, Mary Robinson, a regimental sergeant major, presented me with my own set of darts. She said anybody who could throw like me should have his own set. I still have it, brass darts with stainless-steel points.

Those are some really hospitable people down there. On my second visit I was offered three different caravans—trailers—if I'd bring Hazel down and go on a tour of the country. I declined, of course, pointing out how impractical it'd be—I'd have to drive all the way back down to turn the caravan back in to its owner. "No, no," this one fellow said, "you take my caravan, do your traveling, and then call me when you're finished and tell me where you left it and I'll just pick it up myself."

I put those New Zealand and Australian folks, so far as their outlook on life goes—and that was nearly twenty years ago—in the same category as our Old West. They still have that pioneer spirit of playing hard and working hard. And once you get them on your side, they're on your side forever.

New Zealand consists of two islands, the North and the South Island. Auckland and Wellington, the capital of the country, are on the North Island, and Christchurch is on the South Island. When I visited Waiouru, the main training center in the middle of the North Island, I failed to do my homework—I presented my hosts with a Hawaiian tiki, a small sculptured figure or amulet representing a Polynesian god, not realizing that the native Maori people of New Zealand, who are also Polynesians, have them too.

Taiwan was also a place I liked to visit, because we had some isolated signal units stationed there on mountaintops. It took a whole day to reach some of those sites. Again, two-four-sixes in places where normally nobody ever came up to visit. Frankly, I found the morale in those places better than down in the lowlands, where the troops could mix with the civilians.

I came within an inch of getting a hole-in-one on a golf course in Taiwan.

The Taiwanese are great people too. I got to visit Quemoy and Matsu islands, where in those days the loudspeakers were still going, blasting propaganda to the Chinese mainland.

One of the most satisfying events of my three years in Hawaii involved the special education program at Fort Shafter. The wife of the sergeant major at Tripler Army Hospital taught these children,

and she couldn't get all the supplies she needed for her classes, so
in conjunction with the NCO club manager, Hazel organized a
Monte Carlo Night to provide funds.

We bought play money and overprinted it so nobody had to use
cash in the games. Everybody pitched in. We had faro dealers,
craps, poker, every kind of gambling game. We made something
like $4,800 for the kids. We did that two years in a row and pro-
vided more money for that program than the state of Hawaii
provided in its budget.

That's the sort of thing Hazel did while we were in Hawaii.
Over the years she's devoted many thousands of hours to Army
community service work. It wasn't all Bill Bainbridge's effort that
made mine a successful career—a lot of it was Hazel Bainbridge's. As General Haines wrote in the official history of the
Sergeants Major Academy, there was no doubt in his mind that
the reason I became Sergeant Major of the Army was Hazel Bainbridge.

≡ 10 ≡

ONE FIRST SERGEANT, MANY SERGEANTS MAJOR

On October 8, 1972, Hazel and I sailed for the States on the SS *Mariposa*, a cruise ship owned by Far East Lines. This was while surface transportation was still authorized for military personnel returning from duty in Hawaii. Right afterward the government discontinued the practice because it was expensive.

Sgt. Maj. Howard Shaw, the U.S. Army Hawaii sergeant major, and his wife, Mary Ellen, accompanied us. The voyage to San Francisco took five days and four nights. The *Mariposa* was returning from a six-week cruise to the Far East, and we boarded when she docked at Hawaii. The other passengers were people who had a lot of money.

We went to dockside the day before the ship sailed and they drove our car right onto the ship. We had a first-class cabin above the waterline with a porthole to the outside world. It was the typical ocean cruise—they started feeding you at six o'clock in the morning and kept it up until five-thirty the next morning. You could have a "prebreakfast" and then breakfast; there were three sittings in the dining room for each meal. We were all assigned a table so we knew who our messmates would be. The evening meal was a formal affair that required a coat and tie. The Shaws sat with us and we really had a good time.

There was plenty of entertainment, and for an old infantryman like me, it was really something. The *Mariposa* operated a little bit differently from a troopship—nobody came around and pounded on your door to remind you of your troop details. In fact, we had somebody to make our beds and somebody else to ring a bell when it was time to eat, as if I could ever forget my mealtimes.

We sailed in under the Golden Gate early one morning. What

a sight! We docked about nine-thirty and within ninety minutes our car appeared, we loaded our cabin baggage, and we were off for El Paso, Texas. We didn't bother to go back to Illinois at that time because we'd been home on leave while we were in Hawaii, our older daughter had visited us twice, and my mother-in-law had visited twice.

We drove east to near Stockton, where we picked up I-5 and took it south to Interstate 10, which goes all the way east to El Paso. We drove all that day and stopped for the night in Arizona. The next day we drove on and stopped for fuel at what has become one of my favorite places, Las Cruces, New Mexico, about forty miles north of El Paso. It was around three o'clock in the afternoon, and it was *hot*, so we decided to stay the night, since if we went onward we'd just arrive at Fort Bliss at quitting time. Instead we could get a good night's rest and report in the next morning.

We stayed at a nice place called the Blue Bird Motel. They gave us a chit for a drink with our dinner and another for a continental breakfast the next morning. I think it was the hospitality of the people at the Blue Bird that endeared that town to us, and we went back to the place every chance we could.

I have a little story about the people at the Blue Bird that illustrates how honest and conscientious their employees were. One time Hazel and I were taking a short vacation at the Kilauea Military Camp on the big island—a recreation center that offered cabins and other accommodations, tours, all kinds of recreational opportunities—and because it was chilly that day, Hazel bought me a nylon windbreaker to wear on the golf course.

After we got moved into our new quarters at Bliss, one day I was looking for that jacket and couldn't find it. I knew I'd had it with me when we'd left San Francisco. We looked all over the place. I finally concluded that I'd left it at the Blue Bird Motel. By that time it had been a good two months since our stay there, and I didn't think a call to the manager would do any good. But Hazel persuaded me to spend the forty cents on the call. The manager promised to look for the jacket. About five days later we received a registered package, and in that package was my jacket.

I still have that windbreaker hanging in the closet, and I wear it every once in a while.

Fort Bliss is on the outskirts of El Paso, a city of around 515,000 people just across the Rio Grande from Juárez in Old Mexico. The U.S. government first established a military post there in November 1848. Originally known only as the Post of El Paso, in March 1854 it was renamed Fort Bliss in honor of William Wallace Smith Bliss, a veteran of the Mexican War. The place is over 3,400 feet above sea level.

Fort Bliss is in the extreme southwestern part of Texas. I recall that when the Student, Staff, and Faculty Company first sergeant, Jesse E. Mills, who came out from Fort Dix, New Jersey, reported in he said, "Sergeant Major, I've been driving for three days in Texas and I still lack six miles of getting out!" He said he spent as much time driving across Texas as he spent driving from New Jersey to Texas.

The Spaniards named the place Pasa del Norte, or "Pass to the North," where the Rocky Mountains cross into the United States. Just to the west of Fort Bliss is Mount Franklin, which rises about 6,100 feet above sea level. We found El Paso very different from anything we'd known in Honolulu. The Koolaus behind Fort Shafter are plush, beautiful, forested mountains, but there isn't a single tree on Mount Franklin and damn little grass.

Fort Bliss is the home of the air defense school. The Germans have a large contingent there as well, with their own grade school staffed with their own teachers right on the post. The air defense school serves the forces of the entire free world, so we always used to have foreign students at Fort Bliss, many of whom we invited to our affairs.

The weather there is great. The El Paso paper always ran a little box on the front page that would tell you how many consecutive days of sunshine there had been. If the sun just peeked through for an instant, it counted. The climate there is sunny, hot, and dry. There's lots of water under the ground, because of the great aquifers, but it is desert country. You never have to worry about parking space out there—space is one thing they've got a lot of in that part of Texas.

Fort Bliss was also home to the 6th Armored Cavalry Regiment, which moved from Fort Meade while we were at Bliss. It also hosted basic and advanced individual training and various school courses for the different missile systems.

Bliss is a beautiful post that abuts right up against the city of El Paso. You just drive off the south end of Fort Bliss and you're in El Paso. For all the water in the Rio Grande, you can walk across it most of the time, because most of the water is behind Elephant Butte Dam north of Truth or Consequences, New Mexico. Access to Mexico is freely permitted, with just a cursory customs check as you cross the border. I'd estimate that El

Paso–Juárez is home to about one million people, most of them in Juárez.

There are a lot of retirees living in El Paso, drawn by the reasonable cost of living and the weather. For an out-of-the-way place, it's still probably one of the easiest places to get to; I think four major international airlines still serve El Paso.

In short, El Paso is an oasis in the desert, and the people who live there are great folks. I found the Mexicans to be a very agreeable group of people.

When we went there the Army was still leasing Biggs Field from the Air Force. It had been a SAC base at one time, and just before we took it over it had been home to the Defense Language Institute Southwest. The U.S. Army Sergeants Major Academy (USASMA) took over a lot of those old Air Force facilities. The former base exchange became our learning resources center, the briefing room became our auditorium, and some of their assembly areas were converted to classrooms.

We reported in about noon. Col. Karl Morton, the USASMA commandant, informed me that my quarters were not yet ready. I'd been under the impression that we could move in when we got there. Fort Bliss thought they were ready, but Karl Morton didn't think so. He was upset with the post because the engineers hadn't painted the place properly and had left some repairs undone. They were a nice set of quarters at 3044 Hero Avenue. What an address, and right on the third tee of the post golf course! All I had to do was hop over the fence. I'm not much of a golfer, but I was to play a lot at Fort Bliss.

I asked Colonel Morton what Hazel and I should do until the quarters were ready for occupancy. "You're gonna move in with my wife and me," he said. I declined the offer at first, but he insisted. He had a big place up on the Main Post, he said, more room than he and his wife needed actually. So Hazel and I moved in with the Mortons and their son, and we stayed with them about three weeks. They gave us a room with a bath, and we took our meals with them. He and I traveled back and forth to work together, and we developed one of the greatest commander–sergeant major relationships I've ever had. Colonel Morton is retired in Tucson, Arizona, and today I consider him one of my very best friends.

The quarters in our neighborhood had been started by a contractor who never finished them. Some had roofs and some didn't, for instance. They just sat there unfinished for a good while before the government could get another contractor to finish them off. They were nice homes in a nice area, just five minutes from the Main Post, ten or fifteen minutes from the USASMA. Ours was a one-story with three bedrooms, one and a half baths, and a carport. The heat was natural gas.

The typical cooling plant for homes in that part of the country is called a "swamp cooler." Refrigerated air conditioning is not needed in the southwest. Out there you need to put moisture *into* the air rather than take it out, as is the case in more humid climates. As I recall, the humidity in that part of Texas is between 7 and 12 percent. A swamp cooler is mounted on the roof. It contains excelsior pads soaked in water, and the air is drawn through those pads and moisturized. Ours did a fine job of cooling our house.

The U.S. Army Sergeants Major Academy (USASMA, or "Yousassma," as it's called) was authorized by Department of the Army General Order 98 of July 15, 1972. The academy's mission is to prepare selected senior noncommissioned officers to assist future commanders at the division level and higher.

At that time a committee was convened at Fort Bliss to develop a plan of instruction. The committee consisted of ten command sergeants major from major Army commands and thirteen educational personnel, military and civilian, from places like the War College (Carlisle Barracks, Pennsylvania); the Command and General Staff College (Fort Leavenworth, Kansas), the Army signal school, the chemical school, and so on. The group was a cross section of senior educational experts and senior noncommissioned officers.

I was in the group, although at that time nobody knew I'd already been tapped to be the first sergeant major of the academy. We had about a two-week session figuring out what the curriculum should be. Col. Dandridge Malone, a War College instructor for years and a noted authority on military training and education, was also included. Col. Karl Morton, the commandant designate, was also there.

Out of that group there was only one man who at that time had been officially assigned duty at the academy, M/Sgt. Benny Harris, and he was there as a kind of coordinator.

The curriculum we developed included courses on leadership, world affairs, human relations, military management, military organization and operations, and various electives. The only problem we had was getting world affairs accepted. For some reason, a good number of people throughout the Army hierarchy were dead set against noncommissioned officers studying world affairs.

I am not really sure why this was. Perhaps some officers thought that noncommissioned officers should be educated along strictly practical military lines—tactics, operations, logistics—and shouldn't spend any time on current events. I think also there might have been a degree of jealousy involved, a feeling that if NCOs studied the world political situation, they would be usurping the prerogatives of the commissioned ranks. Colonel Morton and the rest of us thought that this subject belonged in the curriculum because, as General Haines had said years before, noncommissioned officer education was a good thing—he knew his NCOs read the sports pages and the comics, but a good education might get them to read the editorial pages as well. As I've said many times throughout my own career, there's nothing wrong with smart sergeants. But I don't think every officer in the Army at that time believed it. Take that aviation major in Vietnam on my last trip there as USARPAC sergeant major, the one who thought his first sergeant shouldn't go to the academy because he needed him in his little company.

Eventually this controversy went all the way to Gen. Creighton W. Abrams, Chief of Staff of the Army, before it was resolved. It came up during a meeting at the Pentagon in the late fall of 1972—the first class was scheduled to begin in January of 1973. General Abrams had been following the development of the academy ever since General Westmoreland had given General Haines the go-ahead to establish it. Col. Victor Hugo (a direct descendant of the famous French writer), who was later to become a general officer, was present at the meeting. He said the pros and cons—mostly cons—of the proposed course of instruction were discussed.

Finally, General Abrams said, "Let me tell you something. When I was COMUSMACV,* every Saturday or Sunday afternoon I had some of my senior NCOs into my quarters for lunch and we'd sit around and talk about things, thoughts that were on their minds and just soldiering in general. Gentlemen, I learned many things from those sessions, and I think you would be surprised if you sat down and started talking to a similar group of senior NCOs. Let the commandant at the academy do his thing."

World affairs stayed in the curriculum, although critics continued to pick on it all the time I was there.

I think General Abrams realized there's nothing wrong with

---

*Commander, U.S. Military Assistance Command, Vietnam.

smart sergeants. Every bit of education you can give a soldier helps him do his job better, and that includes studying the things that will affect him. After all, the Army is a tool of the government, and if it sends soldiers overseas, as it did recently in the Persian Gulf, and they understand why they have to go, there's no question in my mind they're going to be better soldiers for it. It's just good common sense. We NCOs were not trying to infringe on anyone's prerogatives with this course. The good NCO only wants to support his commander, because if his commander goes down the drain, there goes the unit.

With that behind us for a while, we proceeded to recruit instructors and build files for the courses. Until full-time staff and faculty could be assigned, we borrowed people from all over the Army's educational system to write the lesson plans for the first class.

Continental Army Command (CONARC) had originally proposed that Maj. Gen. R. L. Shoemaker, commanding general of the Air Defense Center and Fort Bliss, be the commandant of the Sergeants Major Academy and that Colonel Morton be his deputy commandant. General Shoemaker pointed out that this proposal made no sense. His school taught air defense artillery, and the Sergeants Major Academy was like the War College. "Karl Morton," he said, "doesn't need me to be meddling in his business. He works for the CONARC commander, as I do, and he knows what he wants to do. All he needs from me is support."

This arrangement worked out beautifully. General Shoemaker gave us support above and beyond the call of duty. He saw to it that we got good service from his folks, the engineers, the housing people, the training aids office, and so on. I had a good working relationship with the post sergeant major—I didn't bother him and he didn't bother us, but he did support us, and we always included the post senior people in our social events.

We worked hard to get ready for that first class. At a meeting near Thanksgiving Day 1972, Colonel Morton told the entire staff that they *would* take Thanksgiving Day off. We had a lot of "geographical" bachelors—married men without their families—who couldn't go home for the holidays, so those of us who did have our families arranged to have these men over to share Thanksgiving dinner with us. Colonel Morton told everyone that he didn't want to see anybody back out at work after Thanksgiving dinner. He wanted them to take the whole day off. He warned them that he and I would check up on them. They didn't think he meant it, but he did. We found about seven people who had sneaked back to the academy area to work on lesson plans, and we ran them off.

A couple of weeks before I arrived there to assume duty as the sergeant major, General Haines had visited Fort Bliss and Colonel Morton had told him he was not going to be able to start the course on time. He explained that he just didn't have the people to do the job, and he, as the commandant, was not going to start the course unless he could do it right. General Haines asked Colonel Morton what he needed and promised to provide the people. As a result, that team was pulled together from all over the Continental Army Command to go to Fort Bliss and put the curriculum together. Those are the people we had to chase from work on Thanksgiving Day afternoon. They believed in the concept of the Sergeants Major Academy and gave their all to helping us get it started.

The approved staffing for the academy consisted of 120 personnel: forty-seven officers, one warrant officer, forty enlisted personnel, and thirty-two civilians.

Later we got some people who proved key assets in getting the course off the ground. One was Lt. Col. George R. Stotser, deputy commandant for education, who retired as a Lt. Gen. He was ROTC, University of Tennessee. He was told by his faculty adviser at the U.S. Army War College, at Carlisle Barracks, not to take the assignment, that it would be "the kiss of death" to his career. Colonel Stotser did not believe his adviser and took the job because he believed he could make a difference in what we were trying to do. Thank goodness for George Stotser. He did make a difference. He tailored the curriculum to make sure that the right material was presented and that the proper balance between classroom and study time was achieved. He got the division chiefs to cut their classroom schedules—a herculean task, because every instructor wants to *add* time to the schedule—to six hours a day. That's how we avoided classroom burnout.

Another was Lt. Col. Ronald R. Rasmussen, the deputy commandant, who also came to us from Carlisle Barracks.

With Karl Morton and those two guys we were able to put together one hell of a coalition of instructors. We got people from all over the Army to be interviewed as faculty group members—FGMs or "fuggums," as they were called, reflecting the soldier's penchant for making words out of abbreviations and not necessarily ones that can be used in mixed company. We were looking for good soldiers, senior soldiers, master sergeants (E-8), and sergeants major (E-9), who had some instructing experience in their backgrounds. We wanted them from all across the board—people from all sorts of Army jobs, not just combat arms. The Sergeants Major Academy was intended to be the capstone of the Army Noncommissioned Officer Education System, and its curriculum could not be oriented toward only one specialty.

The NCOES, as it was operated while I was on active duty, consisted of six courses of instruction covering each stage of a soldier's development as a noncommissioned officer, starting with basic combat and advanced individual training. Next was the primary leadership development course, or PLDC, which emphasized how to lead and train and the duties, responsibilities, and authority of noncommissioned officers. The PLDC prepared soldiers for leadership positions in the grade of sergeant (E-5).

Soldiers in the grade of staff sergeant (E-6), or those in line for promotion to staff sergeant, attended the basic NCO course, which taught them how to lead and train soldiers in combat. Soldiers in the grade of platoon sergeant or sergeant first class (E-7) attended the advanced NCO courses, which concentrated on technical and advanced leadership skills. To be selected for promotion to master sergeant (E-8), a soldier had to have completed this course.

And then there was the U.S. Army Sergeants Major Academy. Of course, the NCOES consisted of many other kinds of training, such as the first sergeant course for soldiers selected to fill that position at company level, and various functional or technical courses—operations and intelligence, basic and primary technical courses—designed to make soldiers more proficient in the technical aspects of their jobs. Then there were correspondence and extension courses, and, of course, the traditional NCO academies, which instilled self-confidence and a sense of responsibility.

Take all these aspects of the NCOES together and what the Army had developed was light-years beyond what passed as training in World War II.

I mentioned earlier my efforts to recruit men like Don Kelley out of Japan and Bill Sweeney out of Eighth Army. We also got men like Sgt. Maj. Virgil "Mac" McNeill, who was the sergeant major of my old outfit, 1st Battalion, 28th Infantry, out of Fort Riley, Kansas. He was a tremendous person. Mac had been all over the Army, he had ROTC, infantry, and instructor experience, and he was just one hell of a good soldier. He came down for an interview, and when he left, he was overwhelmed and wasn't sure he would be coming back. We all knew that he was. He told me later that he, like a lot of us, hadn't had the opportunity to attend schools like this, that he had only his Army experience to offer. But that was exactly what we were looking for. About six weeks afterward, Mac and his wife, Maxine, and their five boys reported for duty at the academy, and he became one of the first and best faculty group members we recruited.

Later, when I was Sergeant Major of the Army, Mac, after a tour of duty in Korea, returned to the academy and became its first enlisted company commander. A captain, Harry W. Durgin, had held that job when Mac and I were there the first time. Virgil retired from that assignment. Those were the kind of people we had.

We recruited Sgt. Maj. Bob Steyer, one of the few enlisted men with a master's degree in education, although he was a medic by MOS (military occupational specialty). Bob's gone now. While he was not a very gung-ho soldier, he had his head screwed on right.

We got another man out of Korea, Sgt. Maj. Bob Foreman, who proved to be one heck of a good instructor.

But back to the lesson plans. Here it was, December 1972, and the members of the first class were beginning to report in. The pilot class was to consist of one hundred students, although the plan called for regular classes of two hundred students after that first one. Well, it turned out to have 105 students. We wanted accommodations to be as good as possible, so we had arranged for family quarters for the married men and bachelor quarters for the singles or for those who elected not to bring their families.

We had a sponsor program,* but we had more people coming in for that first class than we had faculty to support, so each faculty member ended up with four or five students to sponsor. We had to pick them up at the airport and so on. We were hauling dogs and kids and suitcases, and baby-sitting. We'd made arrangements with the post billeting office to have the keys to the married quarters handed over to us, so when a new student came in, the

---

*Under this program every NCO and officer coming into a new unit is assigned someone of comparable grade to help with the myriad details of settling in. Ideally, contact between the incoming soldier and his or her sponsor begins by mail or telephone several weeks before moving. The sponsor's duties include arranging for temporary quarters, helping with the required in-processing activities, and even providing transportation and baby-sitting services. For the individual or family arriving at a strange post, the sponsor is an angel in uniform, and many sponsors, cringing in anticipation of their onerous tasks, have been pleasantly surprised to see this official duty bloom into lifelong friendships.

first sergeant gave him several sets of keys and told him to go and pick out the quarters he liked best.

These people got first-class treatment, and none of them had ever been treated like that before in the Army. We wanted them to have a good taste in their mouths when they got ready for the course. This sponsorship program was one way we did that.

Of course, not everybody chosen to attend the first course was terribly enthusiastic about it. One day I was informed that a selectee in Europe wanted to decline. The man was in a Signal Corps outfit. He'd called the academy and talked to one of my sergeants, and I told the sergeant to let me make my own call before he got back to the signalman. I telephoned Ted Spellacy, the sergeant major of the U.S. Army Strategic Communications Command at Fort Huachuca, Arizona.

"Ted," I began once I got him on the telephone, "I understand you support the academy and all we're trying to do down here, isn't that right?"

"Oh, you know I do, Bill!" he replied at once.

"Well, then how in the hell come there's this guy in Europe doesn't want to come to the academy?"

"Who's that?" I told him. "I'll call you back tomorrow!" he said, and the telephone went *click*.

Before Ted could call me back, this fellow in Europe called his sponsor to inform him he'd changed his mind "because I've just talked to the sergeant major of the STRATCOM. I've changed my mind—I'll be there." Ted had told this master sergeant there was no way he *was not* going to the academy, and he gave him an order to pack his bags and his family and head for Fort Bliss. He did show up, lock, stock, and family.

That is representative of the support we had throughout the Army.

So on January 15, 1973, the first class of 105 people was convened. The class president was Sgt. Maj. Harold L. Billips. He was a bachelor and the senior man in the class. I'd decided that the senior student (by grade and date of rank) in the class, regardless who he or she was, would be class president and that the position would be a duty assignment. It was a tough assignment, because the president had a lot of administrative details to attend to, such as coordinating the class ring procurement project, organizing dining-in and dining-out functions, and chairing the class yearbook committee.

Another rule we established was that each student would attend the opening ceremony, the formal dining-in and the dining-out, and the graduation ceremony. Unless a student was in a casket, there were no excuses. Those events were command performances.

The students themselves were totally responsible for organizing and conducting the dinings-in and -out. Those activities, by the way, had always been a tradition with the officer corps but not with the NCO corps. The ones we conducted at USASMA were the first of their kind, so far as I know.

The dining-in is a highly formal military social function that requires a high degree of discipline in carrying out its traditional protocols and enduring its lapses of sanity, depending on how well they're organized, of course. It is a stag affair, meaning only students, regardless of gender. Even though we had female soldiers—M/Sgt. Betty J. Benson* was a member of that first class—no family members or dates were included, only the students.

The dining-in serves several important purposes. It brings the soldiers of a unit together, strengthens their bonds as members of an elite corps, enhances their sense of military tradition, and teaches them it's okay to own and wear a set of dress blues.

We held our first dining-in on March 22, 1973.

The dining-out is different in the sense that wives and husbands and other civilians are included, but it is still a formal affair. A mess president still presides at the head table, and the vice president of the mess ("Mr. Vice") performs his protocols. Small fines are still imposed against persons who violate the rules of the mess, and it is surprising how during the course of an evening they can add up to a considerable donation to a local charity the next morning. Mr. Vice determines how much the fines are, and the president arbitrates.

While I was USASMA sergeant major we always invited the Sergeant Major of the Army to be our guest speaker at the dining-in. That worked very well, because he could transmit his message in very plain language. While I was SMA I went down there for every one.

We also invited Sgt. Maj. Allen Snedden of the Australian Army down from Washington, where he was attached to the Australian embassy. "I'll tell you, Bill," he said after attending our first dining-in, "I've been to lots of these, and this has been the

*Betty lived in the BEQ, and she had two little dogs, Tina and Tinker. One night somebody broke into her rooms and managed to steal her blind without waking up Betty or either of those dogs.

most professional one I've ever seen." I felt very good about that, because he came from a background where these functions are put on routinely. I believe the academy is primarily responsible for instilling in the Army's corps of senior noncommissioned officers an appreciation of our military traditions, and this is one of the most important things we've ever done.

My personal role at the academy, as the senior NCO on the staff, was to advise and assist the commandant, but I also had a lot of input to the curriculum and the selection of the faculty group members, all of whom I interviewed.

When interviewing we'd ask the prospective faculty members what they thought of the academy as an educational system, what they thought it would do for the Army, whether they supported it or not. A person could be a hell of a good soldier and have all the qualifications we were looking for, but if he didn't support what we were trying to do, he wasn't going to be on the faculty. We didn't find many like that, incidentally.

Through the interviews we got a good cross section of Army skills, men in every job the Army had. From Special Forces we got Sgt. Maj. Bill Craig and a sergeant major I will call Rodney Southpaw.

Rodney Southpaw was a case history of sorts. He was retired in Florida, last I heard of him. He had a lot of schooling in Special Forces and was keen on the academy as an instructor. While he had a good training background in Special Forces, he had never served in a regular unit. The normal tour for faculty at the academy was two years. Rodney came there as a master sergeant, and after he got promoted to sergeant major he got itchy feet and wanted to go back to Special Forces.

I advised him to spend his two years at the academy, then go to an infantry outfit, to a battalion assignment, and then after that go back to the Special Forces. That way, I thought, he would have a chance at appointment to command sergeant major. I told him that if he went directly back to Special Forces from the academy it might cost him the wreath of the CSM chevron, because in picking sergeants major for CSM the Army looks for broadly experienced men and women.

Rodney thought about my advice for about six weeks and decided he wanted to return to Special Forces. Rodney is an example of what not to do if you want to be a good senior noncommissioned officer, and he will crop up again in this story a bit later.

One of the graduation requirements was that each student submit a 2,500-word essay. Each had a faculty adviser who would help with the project. Writing a 2,500-word essay is not really that difficult—you could write one on an anthill if you really set your mind to it. But we had one student who came to me and confessed that he just couldn't get his paper together. He said he had a wastepaper basket full of false starts. He'd discussed his dilemma with his faculty adviser, who had told him to keep trying, but he hadn't at that time shown him anything he'd written. I told him to take his stuff to the adviser—maybe he could spot the glitches that were holding him back and help him get started. "Naw," he said, "this is too much for me. I'm gonna retire."

I told him he was making a big mistake. He had twenty-one years in the Army and two kids not yet out of school. "What are you going to do on the outside?" I asked him.

Well, he took leave, stayed in his quarters at the academy during that time, and went to work for Ma Bell and found out that digging ditches and setting telephone poles is hard work. About a week or ten days before his retirement orders were to take effect, he came to my office and said, "Sergeant Major, I've really got a problem. *Now* I understand what you were trying to tell me, and you're the only one who can help me now. I've changed my mind and I want to stay in the Army."

"Well, if I'm the only one who can help you," I said, "then you're in bad shape, because I am not going to help you."

"Why?" he asked.

"Because," I told him, "we tried to help you up front, and you didn't accept that. Now you've decided I gave you good advice, after you found out what it's like on the outside, and I'm not going to support you because the next time you run up against a wall you'll quit again. I don't need quitters in my Army. You just go on home." And he did—he retired.

If you can't take good advice, don't try to come back and get fixed up. Here this man had spent the Army's money to come down to the academy and he didn't want to see it through.

We even had some officers who thought they couldn't finish their assigned tasks. A lieutenant colonel and a major, some of our borrowed folks, were to put together a course on tactics. They came to Colonel Stotser after a while and confessed they just couldn't design the course to be taught by the small-group method.* Colonel Stotser said, "Well, if that's what you believe,

---

*A method in which the students learn through practical exercises instead of listening to an instructor explain the lesson from a podium.

obviously you've been given a task that you're not up to. We'll have to figure out another, less effective way to do it. You're telling me you're going to quit?"

Those two officers were furious with Colonel Stotser for that remark. They went back to the drawing board, and because he had challenged them, called them quitters, which they really weren't, they came up with a plan that would work, tossed it on his desk, and said, "Here's your goddamn challenge!"

That's just what Colonel Stotser wanted. He forced them to use their abilities for the academy.

Some things were slow getting started. Take the Resources Learning Center. When the first class began, the books we had on hand weren't even on shelves yet, so when a student asked for a reference, the librarian would direct him to Box 42 at the rear end of the building. We established our library as we went along, at first relying exclusively on donations. The chemical school, at Fort McClellan, Alabama, for instance, gave us its entire nontechnical collection, and the Special Services in Korea gave us two thousand volumes. Colonel Morton, the librarian (Miss Barbara Stevens), and I went to the War College for books. The War College let us go through its library, and if we found something we could use and the War College had a duplicate, we were permitted to take that volume with us.

We tried to get an Army flag for the academy. We went through channels and were informed that NCO academies weren't authorized copies of the Army flag. We told the people up the channels that the USASMA was not an "NCO academy"—we weren't teaching soldiers to shine shoes, polish brass, make beds tight. Enter, again, Victor Hugo, who was a friend of Karl Morton's. Colonel Morton called him and said, "Vic, what the hell's going on here? How come we can't get an Army flag?" Vic Hugo said he saw no reason why we should not have one and promised to work on the problem.

Two weeks after that conversation we got an Army flag, with streamers.* Eventually we got one from each service, because later on we had students from the other services.

We also got the crest and coat of arms for the academy approved. Colonel Morton and I made several trips to the Army In-

*This is no ordinary flag. With campaign streamers—one for every significant battle the Army has fought from the American Revolution to the present day—each copy is worth thousands of dollars.

stitute of Heraldry at Cameron Station, Alexandria, Virginia, to get it approved. We dealt with Neil Potter up there. One day I was talking to him, and I was wearing the CONARC crests, not being authorized any for the academy yet. They are an absolute apparition, big, ungainly things that try to symbolize everything CONARC is about. You list to one side as you put them on, until you get both up on your shoulders to balance yourself.

Mr. Potter himself is a little old guy who must weigh all of ninety-eight pounds soaking wet, a World War II Marine, and we always ribbed each other over which was the "better" color of green, Marine or Army. Mr. Potter got the challenge of designing the coat of arms for the Sergeants Major Academy, and I said, "Mr. Potter, just do me one favor. Will you look at these CONARC crests? When you get this coat of arms for the academy put together, will you have it designed by a jeweler instead of a blacksmith?"

Well, he really did an outstanding piece of work, and the design was in fact crafted by a jeweler. The crest consists of a dark blue flaming torch, to indicate zeal, superimposed on a crossed sword and quill over an open book. The book signifies knowledge and instruction, and the sword and quill represent the combat and administrative services from which the academy's students are drawn.

The shield consists of three green and yellow embossed chevrons on its lower half, the basic symbols of the noncommissioned corps. Over them is a star within a circle over a wreath; gold links are fastened left and right to the circle. The links refer to the role of the sergeant major as the link between the soldier and his commander. The star signifies command and the excellence required of those who attend the academy, while the laurel wreath signifies the high degree of meritorious performance that qualifies soldiers for selection as students.

The experts at the Institute of Heraldry made us a Grant of Arms with fleur-de-lis and ribbons drawn in color on a big piece of poster board about two and a half by three and a half feet. I was up at Cameron Station and took it back to Fort Bliss with me. I carried it with me onto the airplane at Washington National Airport, and the stewardess told me the Grant would have to travel in the baggage compartment.

"Are there seats in the baggage compartment?" I asked.

"Oh, no, of course not!" she answered.

"Then this is not going down there, because this goes where I go, and I got a ticket." She asked me then what was in the package, and I told her and added, "It's not getting out of my sight until I get to Fort Bliss."

"Sergeant Major," she said, "I'll put it in first class, but *you'll* have to fly coach." So it flew behind the last seat in the first-class section of that airplane, and today it's still hanging on the wall in the auditorium at the academy.

Criteria for selection of students for the first class, which was done at the Department of the Army, were that they had to be first or master sergeants with between fifteen and twenty-three years of service with a primary military occupational specialty test score of 100 or more, a general technical score of 100 or more,* and demonstrated professionalism and good character. Selectees on the promotion list for sergeant major were still eligible, as long as they hadn't been promoted by the time their class started. We had a lot of people promoted to E-9 while students, selected before coming to the academy. Generally, the criteria for academy selection were pretty much what it takes to get promoted from sergeant first class to master sergeant or from master to sergeant major.

The first academy course consisted of 632.5 hours of instruction, most of it in the classroom. We had some physical training, which included "drown-proofing" courses in the swimming pool. Colonel Morton had lost a soldier at one time because he couldn't swim, so one of his requirements for each student was that he get across the swimming pool with all his gear on. That caused a lot of consternation, but each student did it.

Classes began at eight in the morning. We had no mess facilities, so the students who were single or didn't have their families with them had to eat breakfast at the snack bar or the NCO club or wherever. Classes continued throughout the day until about three-thirty in the afternoon. As happens in all new courses, we experienced "curriculum creep," and by the end of the second class it developed into a real problem, because we had loaded too much on the students.

Two days a week we had elective courses, which were college courses taught by instructors from El Paso Community College, who came out to the academy to give them on government time.

---

*General technical, or GT, score is the Army's version of an IQ score. It is derived by averaging a soldier's scores on the Verbal English and Arithmetic Reasoning test segments of the Army General Classification Test. A GT of 100 is considered average.

Those college instructors were amazed because none of our people were reading newspapers during class, none had on Walkman devices, none were asleep, none failed to get their assignments in on time. As a matter of fact, some of the instructors told us, they had to study harder to get ready for those classes than for any they had to teach back on the campus, because our people had come to school to learn.

One day a week we had physical education.

We had testing, but not to flunk anybody, rather to bring people back up to speed. We were trying to get people through the course, not eliminate them.

In the first class there was a first sergeant from Fort Bragg, North Carolina, and about four or five weeks into the class the education people at Fort Bliss got hold of his records, and they noted that he had earned a high school GED when he was a staff sergeant. You had to have at least a GED to be accepted as a student for the course. The education people reviewed his GED scores and said they were too low for a high school to have awarded him a GED. However, through administrative error, he had been awarded a certificate. The education people said he would have to be dropped from the class.

I said, no way. The man thought he had a GED. Somebody had made an administrative error, and he wasn't going to be put out of the academy for that. I told them we would fix it up by having him retake the test.

Colonel Morton told them to administer the test, and if he didn't pass it, he wanted to know why—we would school him in those areas until he could pass it. That old first sergeant passed that test with flying colors. He got his GED, and when he left the academy he had a two-year associate degree on top of that, because he did extra work to get it.

The moral of this story is that when that first sergeant gets back to his unit and Staff Sergeant Bainbridge comes into his orderly room complaining that he doesn't want to go to take some course himself, he's going anyway, because the first sergeant will know the value of education to the man and to the Army and he won't accept any academic quitters.

Now, this man had been a first sergeant back at Fort Bragg, but while he was at the academy he did not enjoy that status, and he wore master sergeant's chevrons. Everybody who went there as an E-8 had to be a master sergeant. This was so because even though the first sergeant has his own distinctive chevrons, his is a rank, not a pay grade, and it is authorized only in units whose manning tables call for it. Besides, we already had our own first sergeant at the academy, Jesse Mills. Of course, some people wanted to test our system. Those people were referred to me at the time, but at our first assembly the question came up: I came here as a first sergeant—why can't I wear my first sergeant's stripes? The question was asked of the commandant. Colonel Morton deferred to me. I explained there was only one first sergeant to a unit and we already had one. "And if you were in his shoes, you wouldn't want it any other way."

We did allow the first sergeant students to keep their chevrons on their dress blues, so they could wear them on formal occasions, but in class everyone was either a master sergeant or a sergeant major. That way there was only one first sergeant, Mills. You can't have twenty-five first sergeants running around, because the term dictates there is only one first sergeant. You *can* have several sergeants major in a headquarters outfit if the tables of organization and equipment (TO&E) call for them, but you can have only one first sergeant.

That first class had its trials and tribulations, as does everything starting out for the first time. For instance, CONARC Headquarters wanted us to operate a command sergeants major refresher course. We didn't want it, because we didn't think we had the time for such a course of instruction. It was only going to be a two-week course, but we were too busy to do it properly. Our reasoning was that by the time the Army took a sergeant major out of his unit, got him processed in at Fort Bliss, and then got him processed out once the course was over, he'd have gotten only maybe six days of instruction out of the two weeks allowed for the course, and we thought it would be better to teach young dogs new tricks than old ones. Not that it might not have done some good, but we didn't think the effort was worth what it could cost everyone involved. But CONARC ordered us to do it anyway.

On February 22, 1973, Washington's Birthday, Gen. Creighton Abrams, Army Chief of Staff, visited the academy. I was conducting the briefing on what we were doing at the academy, and the CSM refresher course came up. "Wait a minute, Sergeant Major," General Abrams said. "What is that all about?" I told him what higher headquarters wanted us to do, and Colonel Morton chimed in that we had been ordered to implement the program. "Well, I don't think it's worthwhile," General Abrams said, "and I'll send a message to CONARC when I get back to the Pentagon." End of CSM refresher course.

General Abrams was a practical guy, and he saw at once that

we were not ready to conduct this course of instruction. We now
do have such a course, although it's a little different in concept
from the original. It came about because of that *Parameters* article
I mentioned in Chapter 8 by Brig. Gen. "Doc" Bahnsen, exco-
riating the CSM program. Neither General Bahnsen nor his coau-
thor had a clue as to what it was really all about, although General
Bahnsen gave some good lectures when he came to the academy.

We lost five people out of that first class. One because his photograph in his file revealed at least three decorations, one of them
the Purple Heart, that he was not authorized to wear. He had been
a master sergeant (E-8) on the promotion list to sergeant major
(E-9), but he left the academy as a sergeant first class (E-7). The
irony was that the photo wasn't even the official one but just
something he'd stuck into his record to impress people. Well, he
did manage to "impress" a lot of people.

I mentioned Bill Craig a bit earlier.* Bill had a Special Forces
background when he came to the academy as a faculty group
member, and he was a good one. He was a rather verbose individual who came up the hard way as a hard-fighting, hard-drinking,
kick-their-rear-end type of guy, but a bright one. I had a lot of dis-
cussions with Bill, but he was not successful in making the Sergeants Major Academy an adjunct to Special Forces training. I'm
not entirely sure Bill was 100 percent behind the system, but he
was never a problem, and he turned out to be one heck of a good
faculty group member.

I like Bill and he's a friend of mine. Rodney Southpaw's a
friend of mine too, although it might be a little hard for him to admit that.

Two key FGMs were Sgt. Maj. Joe Offutt and Sgt. Maj. Henry
Ferris, who after two years at the academy became command sergeants major and went on to other assignments. Joe had an armor
background and Henry was an infantryman.

And then there was Sam Walsh.

I first met Sam when he was a young SP5 at USARPAC (Fort
Shafter, in Hawaii), working for the secretary of the general staff
(SGS) there. Sam is a practical guy, and I remember him getting
so hacked off at the SGS, Colonel Blewett—what an appropriate
name!—that he'd come into my office just down the hall and say,
"That SOB is always blowing it!" I guess Sam became my

*Author of *Scare Time*, a Vietnam War novel (Ivy Books, 1990), and *Lifer*
(1994), a memoir of his and his father's more than fifty years of enlisted service.

protégé, although at the time neither of us realized it. We hit it off pretty well. I helped keep him going and maybe kept him out of trouble, too, because he always wanted to raise sand about things and I tried my best to cool him down. Over the years I've really come to love that guy. He's one hell of a soldier.

Sam went to Europe from Hawaii and after that tour went back to CINCPAC. One day I got a call from him. "Top," he said, "you've got to get me outta here!" He had a job in the J-4* (logistics) shop somewhere, a job where he was practically his own boss, but typical of Sam, he'd organized his work so well the challenges had all been overcome, and he'd gotten bored with the place. He said he wanted to come to Fort Bliss and work for me.

Well, we had an administrative slot at the academy, and I thought I could work him in, so after half a dozen calls back to the Pentagon, we finally got him orders and got him transferred to Fort Bliss. Sam went with me when I left there to become the Sergeant Major of the Army, and I'll have more to say about him later.

I also picked up SFC Herbert LeRoy Carman, an ex-infantryman turned personnel man. Sam and Herb worked together and commuted together, and with those two in cahoots, I really had a problem. They worked in the admin shop, where there were always a million and one things that needed doing, and they were absolutely top-notch noncommissioned officers.

I'd always get to work before those guys, and as soon as I got in I'd open all the doors and windows in their office so it'd be colder than hell in there when they arrived. It helped get their circulation going first thing in the morning so they'd be productive the rest of the day. And when Sam found out Carman liked to be called Lee instead of Herb, he called him " 'Erb" every chance he got. The last I knew of Herb, he was a CSM in a unit in Germany. Wherever he is now, I wish him and his family well. He was a fine soldier.

We had a tremendous family program at the academy. General Haines wanted the families involved, and Hazel, with plenty of help from Jean Morton, the post commander's wife, and the other FGMs' wives, set up what I consider one of the most unusual programs ever in the Army consisting of "classes" for the wives in everything from basket-weaving to painting. They held teas and

---

*On a joint staff—two or more military services—the staff designations take the letter "J." The U.S. Navy is executive agent for CINCPAC.

coffees and class presentations and raised money for class activities and put out cookbooks. It seems every class put out a cookbook. When we had our dinings-out, the wives got themselves new dresses and came with their husbands, and they became part of academy life.

One of the student wives, Rose Notter, had never touched a paintbrush to a canvas before she came to Fort Bliss. By the time she left she'd become a pretty darned good artist. Later they went to Fort Riley, where Rose had her own show. We have hanging in our bedroom right now a painting Rose gave to Hazel, and she gave it to her because Hazel got her started in the class.

Hazel held classes in Army protocol, and in how to serve tea—she wanted all the wives to understand that being asked to pour is an honor, not a detail. One of the reasons General Haines wanted this course to be a permanent change of station was to get the families down to Fort Bliss and make them part of the community.

The program also included tours and shopping trips to places like the Carlsbad Caverns, White Sands Missile Range, and Juárez, Mexico, as well as softball, bowling, and golf.

In volume one of the official history of the academy, covering the period July 1972 to December 1974, Hazel is described as "the prime helmsman of this program, and the success of it is entirely attributable to the tremendous load she assumed, carried, and adroitly discharged." General Haines went so far as to note in the history that one reason he concurred with Colonel Morton's decision to pick me as his sergeant major was "the organizational ability and professional drive of Mrs. Bainbridge."

When Sgt. Maj. Henry Ferris and his wife, Yoko, got their orders to leave the academy, Yoko told Hazel, "When I came here I knew nothing about what a sergeant major's wife should or could do. Now I can be a sergeant major's wife in any unit in the Army." She said she really appreciated what she'd learned at the academy. If the wives' program didn't do anything else, Yoko Ferris knew she could handle her side of the team wherever she and her husband went.

When we came to live at the Soldiers' and Airmen's Home, the Ferrises visited us several times, because Yoko developed cancer, which required hospitalization and treatments at nearby Walter Reed. Henry would come with her, and we'd get together and go out to dinner. Yoko passed away in 1985. In 1986, Henry's daughter, Frances, who's an engineer with NASA, came to town for a conference, and he joined her but stayed with us. He wrote a letter beforehand, asking if he could come out to see us while he was in town, and I replied, "Henry, you come and stay with us," and he told me he was hoping I'd say that.

We were all sitting on the porch one evening, talking about Yoko, and he told us, "Bill, I really miss that lady." That was in June. In August, Henry died. If anybody ever died of a broken heart, it was Henry Ferris. When Yoko's and Henry's ashes were interred at Arlington National Cemetery, Hazel and I stood in for Frances and her sister, Mary, who couldn't make it from California. Yoko's ashes were brought up from Fort Benning so they could be buried together. Henry was buried with full honors by the 3rd Infantry, "The Old Guard." The ceremony included a caisson, riders, and an honor guard. Henry's ashes were on the caisson, and behind it were two escorts and an urn bearer with Yoko's ashes.

Jean Morton, by the way, was Colonel Morton's second wife, and she knew absolutely nothing about the military and didn't care to learn anything, particularly when it came to protocol—she considered everybody equal. Jean never had any problem helping sergeants and their wives getting things done.

In my view, Karl Morton forgot more about Army noncommissioned officers and what they are than most officers will ever know. We both thought the same way, we both wanted to take care of our soldiers, and there was never any doubt who was in charge of the enlisted activities at the academy. I was. But he was the heart and soul of the academy, and he was the one who made it work.

I believe that had it not been for an incident that occurred in Vietnam, Karl Morton would surely have been a general officer. He was a brigade commander in Vietnam, and one of his subordinate units fired some mortar rounds into a village. Earlier I noted that during my time in Vietnam the Vietcong would shoot at us from the villages but we were not supposed to shoot back, and whenever we did it always seemed we killed "friendly" people.

Colonel Morton was told to relieve the battalion commander whose unit had fired those rounds. He refused to do it and told his division commander that if superiors fired the officer they'd have to fire him also, because he considered the officer's actions appropriate and supported him. As it turned out, neither was relieved, but because Colonel Morton refused to sacrifice his subordinate, he was never promoted again.

He had a great feel for soldiers and knew the Army backward and forward. He was the ideal man to be the commandant at the USASMA, and General Haines knew it, having had him as his executive officer. Colonel Morton was not only a hell of an officer, he was a hell of a man.

Without a doubt, the student with his family was 100 percent better off than the student who left his family elsewhere and came down as a geographical bachelor. If your family's at Leavenworth, for instance, and you're at Fort Bliss and your daughter breaks her arm, your wife might tell you she's doing fine, don't worry, but who wouldn't worry? And a worried student is a poor student.

The hardest thing for the students was to budget their time. As a first sergeant or a staff NCO, if you can't get something done by quitting time, you work overtime, until it's done. But for many of the students, the academy was their first experience of an environment where they *had* to get things done within a certain time. One student told me that he couldn't even go to the movies with his family because he had to study so hard. "Why not get up at four o'clock in the morning and study two hours before breakfast?" I suggested. "Then you can go to the movies at night." He'd never thought of doing that.

During my time at the academy we increased the classes from one hundred to two hundred students and graduated two classes per year. At the end of the second class, we decided we were giving the students too much work. When you get beyond six hours of class work in one day, you've lost it—you've just got to get out of the classroom. The classroom was only part of the day—there were at least two hours on either end of preparing and studying. When we added everything up the students were putting in twelve-to-fourteen-hour days.

Lt. Col. George Stotser called a meeting of the department heads and asked each to shave five hours off the curriculum. Each one said it was impossible, but the colonel insisted. So they went to work and cut out five hours of "fat," and claimed they'd really pared those courses down. Colonel Stotser was so impressed he told them to cut five more hours. And they did it—they streamlined their courses and eliminated a lot of repetitive and unnecessary work.

As the credibility of the academy grew, we got more and more into the things that affected the Noncommissioned Officer Education System and how it was conducted. We developed the qualification test for command sergeant major. We brought together a group of command sergeants major to develop the best test. Had it not been for men like Sgt. Maj. Johnny Jones, for instance, we would never have caught certain details. Take frostbite. In most cases, frostbite turns a man's feet ashen white, and that's one way to recognize when a soldier has it. But Johnny Jones pointed out that his feet wouldn't turn "ashen white" but *gray*, because his skin was black. Because we had regular people, not psychiatrists and psychologists, putting the test together, we got to the practical side of soldiering instead of the theoretical.

Initially we were required to submit 250 sample questions to the test center at Fort Benjamin Harrison, Indiana, and their psychologists, their "experts," got together and picked the 125 that would be on the test. The second year, based on the results of the first year's work, we were told to submit only 125 questions and they were accepted without question.

Today nothing happens in the Noncommissioned Officer Education System until it's checked by the academy. That makes sense. But had the academy's credibility not been as well established as it was under the leadership of Karl Morton, George Stotser, and Ron Rasmussen, who is now deceased, it might never have achieved more than the status of another NCO academy.

While I was sergeant major of the academy I was invited to the sergeant major conferences hosted by the Sergeant Major of the Army. Although the SMA's conferences were for the major Army command sergeants major, and we were subordinate to the Training and Doctrine Command (TRADOC, formerly CONARC), the institution was so new that I went up to brief them on what was going on down at the academy and let them know what they could do to help us.

Sgt. Maj. Farrel Graham, who had been the Eighth Army sergeant major and who had replaced me at USARPAC, came to Washington with me for a conference in 1974, when Sgt. Maj. Leon Van Autreve was SMA. We stayed in the Arva Motel, across U.S. 50 from Fort Myer. A group of us were sitting around one night, talking and having a few drinks, and when everybody left there were cigarette butts in the glasses, and I emptied them out in the toilet and flushed it. Farrel went into the bathroom and was talking to me over his shoulder while relieving himself, and suddenly he hollered, "You SOB! Look what you did!"

"What'd I do?" I asked.

"You threw my bridgework into the john!"

"I didn't do that," I protested.

"Come look!" Farrel shouted, and sure enough, there it was. It must have been in one of the glasses I emptied.

I suspect that to this day he believes I did it on purpose. I told him at the time, "You are lucky your mouth is so damn big—otherwise you'd have lost it."

At the end of the conference we were invited to SMA Van Autreve's quarters for lunch. I'd told everybody the story by then. As we came in the door we each gave Rita, Van's wife, a small peck on the cheek, and I told her that when Farrel came in and started to peck her, she should turn her head away from him. Sure enough, when he went to kiss her on the cheek, Rita drew away from him, and he shouted at me, "You told! You told that story, you SOB!" That story circulated around the Army for several years afterward.

Farrel retired in Hawaii and became the postal inspector for the Pacific basin. Two or three years ago when I was out there I called Farrel about nine-thirty or ten in the morning, just to say hello, and I got him out of bed. Naturally I said, "Gee whiz, Farrel, I'd sure like to have your job."

In early 1975 I was nominated to be Sergeant Major of the Army. That was the second time for me. The first time was in 1973, and I made the final five on that occasion. I went up to Washington for the interview, as did Sgt. Maj. Johnny Jones, the Fort Bliss sergeant major; Sgt. Maj. John Spooler, who was the Engineer Center sergeant major at Fort Belvoir, Virginia, and who replaced me as sergeant major of the academy; CSM John LaVoie, of TRADOC; and CSM Mel Holifield, from Fort Sill, OK, and one other. We were interviewed in May, and the Chief of Staff, Gen. Fred Weyand, picked me to be his SMA.

The interview board has certain guidelines to follow in making nominations from those interviewed. When I was selected, one of the criteria was that the candidate have passed his MOS test—we still had one then for command sergeants major. Others were that one have so many years of service and be serving as CSM. Each man's records were then screened administratively, which reduced the running to twenty or twenty-five people. They checked each person's family history and background.

Hazel played a big part in the process, because the way she interacted in the community had a big influence on how people viewed my role as a senior noncommissioned officer everywhere we went. It's important, and every board knows it, that you have that kind of husband-wife team at the highest levels. When the SMA travels, his wife often goes along, and she learns things on those travels, talking to the wives and families of enlisted people, that the SMA might not pick up—same as I did for my bosses on the military side. If it were left up to me, nobody could be Sergeant Major of the Army who wasn't married.

The interview panel consisted of a lieutenant general as president, three major generals, and the incumbent Sergeant Major of the Army. After looking over the data, they narrowed the field to ten or twelve people, and those were the men who actually appeared before them. In my case the interviews reduced the nominees to five men, and from them the Chief of Staff selected his SMA.

I can recall two questions that the board asked me. Maj. Gen. John W. McEnery, commanding general of Fort Knox, a big, tall guy, said, "You're not a very big man, Sergeant Major. If you are selected to be SMA, do you think your physical size will cause any problem?"

"No, sir," I responded. "I may not be big physically, but I've got as big a heart as there is in any soldier in this Army."

"No further questions," he said.

Another question had to do with my education, which went only as far as one year of college. I was asked why I hadn't attempted to get more college. I answered that I'd had some pretty tough assignments with a lot of time in the field and traveling, and that hadn't left me much time for school at night. "But I can tell you one thing," I said, "I've got a 'doctorate' in *soldiering*, and I think that's important."

When I left town I didn't know I'd been selected for the job, but I felt comfortable with my appearance before the board. General Weyand and I really didn't know each other that well. He was one of General Seaman's favorites, and when I worked for General Seaman as the IIFFV sergeant major we used to visit Weyand at 25th Division Headquarters. That was really all the contact I'd had with him.

Privately, I thought I had a good chance for the assignment, because I'd been nominated before, and certainly I had a varied background, perhaps the most varied up to that time of any of the nominees. I'd been in all kinds of units at all levels in the Army, I'd worked from the lieutenant colonel level right up to the four-star level, and I think it was evident I'd done a decent job in all those assignments. During all those jobs I'd been the senior NCO in every unit to which I'd been assigned.

About three weeks after I'd gotten back to Fort Bliss, Maj. Gen. C. J. LeVan, the post commander, called me to his office. My boss at that time was Col. Eldon "Tiger" Hunnicutt. Colonel Morton had retired in 1974 and was then living in Tucson. Colonel Hunnicutt had come to us from Fort Campbell, Kentucky, where he'd commanded a brigade in the 101st Airborne Division.

When I stopped by Colonel Hunnicutt's office to tell him I'd been called up to see General LeVan, he informed me he'd also been called up there. We waited maybe fifteen or twenty minutes outside the general's office, and when we finally reported to him he sat us down and informed us that the commanding general of TRADOC was coming in and there was trash all over our area and he wanted it cleaned up before the CG arrived.

Then he grinned and said, "I don't know why I'm trying to pull this old crap here. I guess it's just a tradition," and he handed me a back-channel* message and told me to read it.

It was from General Weyand and announced that he'd selected me to be his Sergeant Major of the Army. General LeVan was authorized to let my commander and me know, but the official announcement would be made by Department of the Army headquarters.

Well, for the next four or five hours I didn't leave any footprints wherever I went—I was walking about eight inches above the ground. We went back out to the academy, but nobody was fooled—they knew when we were called up to post headquarters what the news would be. The official announcement was made the next day. About a quarter past five the next morning, Virgil McNeill knocked on my door to congratulate me. "I knew damn well you were going to make it," he said.

I was asked later what I planned to do when I became the SMA, and I answered that I'd do the same thing I've always done, except that now I'd be doing it for the whole damn Army, not just one unit.

---

*Back channels are private and personal messages that are sent between general officers and are given extremely discreet handling.

≡ 11 ≡

SERGEANT MAJOR OF THE ARMY, 1975–1977

The first Sergeant Major of the Army was William O. Wooldridge, who was sworn in on July 11, 1966, by Chief of Staff Gen. Harold K. Johnson. The Marines had had a "Sergeant Major of the Corps" since May 23, 1957. The Navy appointed its first Master Chief Petty Officer of the Navy on January 13, 1967, and the Air Force followed with its Chief Master Sergeant of the Air Force in April 1967.

General Johnson was responsible for creating the office of the SMA. He said that if the Army was going to talk about noncommissioned officers being the "backbone of the Army," then "there ought to be established a position that recognizes that this was in fact the case." General Johnson demanded that the SMA be his adviser, not an "operator," and he thought of the SMA as an "ombudsman," or a spokesman at the highest levels of the Army, to provide the Chief of Staff with an enlisted voice on all matters pertaining to enlisted soldiers.*

I was preceded in office by SMA Bill Wooldridge, SMA George W. Dunaway, SMA Silas L. Copeland, and SMA Leon L. Van Autreve. I've been followed by SMA William A. Connelly, SMA Glen Morrell, SMA Julius W. "Bill" Gates (who when he retired took my old job at the Soldiers' Home), and the incumbent SMA Richard A. Kidd.

Before I left Fort Bliss to go to Washington, Gen. C. J. LeVan gave me, framed, the original back-channel message from the Chief of Staff announcing my selection as the fifth Sergeant Ma-

*The historical information in this section is from Dr. Ernest F. Fisher's *Guardians of the Republic* (Ballantine Books, 1994).

jor of the Army. I kept it on the wall behind my desk at the Soldiers' and Airmen's Home until I had to take it down when the building caught fire. It's one of my favorite mementos. Back-channel messages don't often get framed, but this one's *mine*.

The academy gave me a grand send-off by having a little roast for us. I'd always been adamant that nobody was to receive a diploma from the Sergeants Major Academy unless he went through the course; we weren't in the business of handing out "honorary" certificates. To me, that would have taken away something from the effort of those who'd gone through the course. But Colonel Hunnicutt, the commandant, said that while he understood fully how I felt, whether I liked it or not, I was going to be the first honorary graduate of the USASMA.

Before I went up to the Pentagon to appear before the SMA selection board, I'd confided to Sergeant First Class Sam Walsh that if I was chosen for the job, I wanted him to come with me and be my administrative assistant.

I also inherited in that office, from SMA Leon Van Autreve, Raylene Scott. I believe Raylene became the secretary for SMA Silas Copeland, and Van kept her in that job when he became SMA. He thought very highly of her, and I'd attended several conferences when she'd been taking care of the agendas, so it was obvious she would remain in that job. She proved a real mainstay.

We hosted those conferences each year. They started way back with the first SMA, and the process got more refined each year. The "major commands" were Forces Command, Training and Doctrine Command, USARPAC, USAREUR, the numbered armies (First Army, Third Army, etc.), and various other commands like Army intelligence, communications, health services, and so on. We spent five days going over problems brought in from the field, all the way up from company level. I required those with problems to come in ahead of time with their packages so I could farm them out to the staff, so that when we gathered around the conference table a lot of the answers were already at hand.

Those conferences were a sophisticated tool to provide input from the lowest levels of the Army right on up to the Army Staff. We dealt with things like getting permanent change of station orders to soldiers in a timely fashion, so families weren't uprooted with little notice for major overseas assignments—ninety days or even six months in advance instead of only three weeks.

There are times when people have to be moved in a hurry, but our belief was that those occasions should be the exception and not the norm.

We continually adjusted the number of participants at those conferences to keep up with the size and mission of the Army as they fluctuated and changed over time. I stopped inviting the sergeant major of the Sergeants Major Academy, as an example, because as the academy got established in the Noncommissioned Officer Education System, there was no longer a valid requirement to brief the conferences on how that was progressing.

Before I left Fort Bliss I was interviewed by the *Monitor*, the post newspaper, and by the El Paso papers. They wanted to know what my goals would be as the new SMA. I had no problem with questions like those, because I didn't see how I'd be operating any differently at the Pentagon than I had in any other assignment. I envisioned myself as the eyes and ears of the Chief of Staff for the entire Army just as I'd been the eyes and ears of the Sergeants Major Academy, the USARPAC CG, etc. Now I'd be performing the same duties but on a global scale. I was confident that with my experience at the different levels of the Army I wouldn't have any problems talking to soldiers in the field or explaining their problems at the highest level.

We went through the normal process of moving, shipping our household goods, cleaning our quarters, getting a second car—a Pinto. My good friend Sgt. Maj. Virgil McNeill gave me a small trailer hitch to go on the Buick and took me out to a place in El Paso to get it welded on. When we got there the man at the welding shop asked me what I was going to tow with it. I explained I was going to pull a Pinto back to Washington, D.C., use it as sort of a private U-Haul. He refused to put Virgil's hitch on my car. He said, "You'll be looking back down the road after about a hundred miles and the Pinto won't be there anymore and you'll come and sue me for the loss." He said he would put a hitch on if I'd let him select the proper kind. So he installed a four-inch channel-iron hitch that is still on my old '68 Buick, sitting out in the garage.

We towed that Pinto all the way to Fort Myer, Virginia, with that hitch. We dropped the driveshaft, hooked up a harness so that the brake lights on the Pinto would work, the usual.

We had our cat with us on the trip, the second to be named Kat. We'd brought her back from Hawaii. This cat had a natural crook in her tail, like the dog in the cartoon strip "Out Our Way." She'd remain quietly in the Pinto until we'd hit a town, and then she'd stand up on the front seat with her paws on the steering wheel.

You can imagine the doubletakes we got as we drove through intersections, people staring at that cat "steering" that Pinto.

We spent three days on the road. We stopped at my parents' house in Knoxville, Illinois, and took some leave. I'd already made arrangements to stay in an apartment when we got up to Washington, since our quarters at Fort Myer wouldn't be available right away. We couldn't bring Kat with us because we didn't know if we'd be allowed to have her in the apartment, and my dad, who loves cats, had agreed to keep her. That cat disappeared two days before we were to leave and didn't show up until the day after we left. I guess she understood we weren't going to take her with us and was pouting over it.

We also stopped at Hazel's mother's, in Essex, Illinois, and spent a couple of days with her.

We were to report in at Fort Myer, which is on a ridge above the west bank of the Potomac River, just west of Arlington National Cemetery. Having never driven in traffic around the District of Columbia before, I got caught in its famous traffic patterns, towing the Pinto. I spotted Key Bridge and pointed at it. "Over there's where we need to go, and I'm not sure how to get there." But we made it and parked the Pinto in front of our quarters, and then went on to our rented apartment.

This was Bragg Towers, on the left of I-395, as you head north, just off Duke Street. We stayed there about three weeks while our quarters were being made ready. This place really wasn't an apartment, it was a tunnel—a one-room apartment with a kitchen and a bathroom stuck on and two beds. But it was the best we could get at the time.

It did not take me long to discover how to work the traffic in the Washington area. I could see I-395 going north into Washington from our apartment. After about two days I noticed that fifteen or twenty minutes made all the difference in the world. I could start out at seven o'clock and it'd take me an hour to get to the Pentagon; I could start at half-past six in the morning or a quarter to seven and get there in fifteen minutes.

I did not have a reserved parking space at the Pentagon. I arrived in town on June 15, although I wasn't scheduled to take over as SMA until July 1, but I was still going in to work every day. Once SMA Van Autreve left, I got a parking pass for the Mall Parking Lot, as distinct from the Mall itself, which is right in front of the Mall Entrance to the Pentagon. They gave me a sticker to put on my car, and I was told it was my "parking pass."

Well, I found out that "parking pass" was really a "hunting license." It permitted me to hunt for a parking space in the Mall Lot, and if I found one, it would be mine. For the next four years I took care of that situation by getting to work before everybody else. I understand the SMA now has a reserved spot up on the Mall itself.

Of course, I didn't have very far to commute, living at Fort Myer and working at the Pentagon.

Fort Myer is a beautiful old post that was originally established as a bastion in the Civil War defenses of Washington. It was called Fort Whipple until 1881, when it was renamed Fort Myer, in honor of the first chief of the Army Signal Corps. Army aviation was born there in 1908, when the Wright brothers made a flight, and the first air fatality occurred there, also in 1908, when Lt. Thomas Selfridge was killed in the crash of a Wright flying machine.

The Chief of Staff of the Army, the Chairman of the Joint Chiefs of Staff, and other high-ranking generals have their quarters at Fort Myer. At one time George S. Patton, Jr., was post commander there. Today it's home to a battalion of the 3rd U.S. Infantry ("The Old Guard") and the U.S. Army Band ("Pershing's Own").

We were assigned quarters at 435A Sheridan Avenue, just across the road from the post commissary and behind the NCO club swimming pool—not a very quiet residential area. The quarters were a brick duplex that had been remodeled for SMA Wooldridge with a finished basement that included a small den. My next-door neighbor was the post sergeant major. The current SMA occupies quarters at 17 Lee Avenue.

Hazel and I had our "coming out" at the Washington Capital Center at that year's "Spirit of America" pageant. That is an annual show put on by the Military District of Washington that recapitulates the Army's—and the nation's—history through live interpretations of historical events, all done with soldier talent. It is a wonderful, spectacular event, complete with military pomp and music and magnificent period costumes.

They had a night set aside in honor of the Sergeant Major of the Army. SMA Leon Van Autreve and his wife, Rita, asked Hazel and me to sit with them that evening, and they put both of us into the spotlight. That was our first official recognition in town.

So there I was, in-processing, getting my Pentagon ID card and so on, the usual stuff you have to do to get squared away at a new duty station, and Van Autreve invited me one day to sit down behind his desk and "try it out." I said, "Van, the day you walk out the door and I'm sworn in is the day I'll sit there. Until then, it belongs to you. I don't want to mess with it."

On July 1, in the Chief of Staff of the Army's office, Gen. Fred Weyand swore me in. My older daughter and her three children and Hazel were present at the ceremony. We have a picture of us all that was taken at that time, and at Christmas 1990 we presented copies to all three of our grandchildren, who were knee-, chest-, and shoulder-high when it was taken. The oldest of those grandchildren now has three children of her own, so here we are, great-grandparents. People say, "You're a great-grandfather?" and I tell them I've always been a "great" grandfather, but now I'm a *great*-grandfather.

In that regard, Hazel was asked one time if she was really a grandmother, and she answered yes. The other person then asked if that bothered her at all, being old enough to be a grandmother, and Hazel responded, "No, it doesn't bother me at all. But the worst part about being a grandmother is that you have to sleep with a grandfather."

One policy of my predecessors that I implemented right away at my new office was that no word went out to the field that was incorrect or that would cause any discredit in any form to the office in particular or the Army in general. I told both Sam and Raylene that before we sent any answer to any inquiry we'd better make damn sure that answer was correct. I'm happy to say that in the four years we were together, only one answer went to the field that was the wrong one, and that was because we'd gotten the wrong information from the Army Staff.

I was always concerned that when we came to Washington the Army couldn't find a set of military quarters for us to stay in temporarily. I had four years to think about that, and well before that time was up I had a place for my replacement on the post, so *he* wouldn't have to commute from Bragg Towers.

Our quarters at 435A Sheridan Avenue required some modest renovation, such as new carpeting and some reupholstering, but it was in good shape overall when we moved in. The little trees in the backyard whose branches I used to have to lift up to mow under them when I cut the grass have grown to be thirty feet tall. I stayed in the Washington area long enough to see a small forest grow behind those quarters.

* * *

The Pentagon Building is a fascinating place. It was built between August 1941 and January 1942 at a cost of $87 million in
1941 dollars—I'd hate to guess how much such a project would
cost today, probably many hundreds of millions. The building is
on the Virginia side of the Potomac, just east of Arlington Cemetery. Although it uses a Washington, D.C., zip code, the telephones use the Virginia area code. The original construction site
was boggy, so the engineers had to put down almost 700,000 tons
of sand and gravel they dredged from the river. Then they poured
over 400,000 cubic yards of concrete to mold the building's form
around and over 40,000 concrete piles.

The Pentagon consists of five floors extending seventy-seven
feet above ground. The building itself spreads over nearly thirty
acres; it sits on five hundred acres of grounds. Inside there are
more than six million square feet of floor space with about seventeen miles of corridors and 100,000 miles of telephone cable. During the time I was there, the daily average work population at the
Pentagon was around 25,000 people.

The secret to finding your way around inside the Pentagon is to
remember that it's shaped like five big wheels, one inside the
other, which are called "rings." From the center of the building ra-
diate ten spokes or "corridors." The rings are lettered A (inner)
through E (outer) and the corridors 1 through 10. My office was
located in Room 3E677—third floor, E ring, corridor 6, room 77.

I met the staff and began my round of briefings. The Army Staff
is a general staff, as at division level and up, and while it functions much the same as the lower staff organizations, the principals are called deputy chiefs of staff (DCS), not G-1, G-2, etc.
The Army Staff is separate and distinct from the Office of the
Secretary of the Army, who is a civilian and whose principal
assistants are also civilians.

The immediate Office of the Chief of Staff of the Army consists of a small suite of administrative aides and executive assistants, such as speechwriters; the SMA; the vice chief of staff
(VCSA), a four-star general (Gen. Walter "Dutch" Kerwin; my
nickname for him was "sir"); the General Officer Management
Office; and the director of the Army Staff (DAS), a lieutenant
general. The DAS is responsible for running the Army Staff and
has a number of directors (one- or two-star generals) who assist
him in interfacing with deputy chiefs of staff, such as logistics
(DCSLOG), operations (DCSOPS), and personnel (DCSPER),
who are also three-star generals. For some reason, intelligence, in

those days, was run by an assistant chief of staff, the ACSI, who was a two-star general.

A special staff of three- and two-star generals runs things like the offices of the Chief of the Army Reserve and the National Guard Bureau, the Chief of Engineers, the Chief of Chaplains, the Surgeon General, and the Judge Advocate General.

I was briefed by the entire staff and got the message that they were going to support me in any way they could. As I've mentioned before, I've always tried to work with the staff, and as I was being briefed by each one—in most cases the principal staff officer himself—I let him know that I was not going to be running across the hall to the CSA with every problem I found as I traveled around. I told them they were going to be asked to give me answers to the questions I couldn't provide to the field myself and I intended to work with them. I would brief the chief on the completed action, as information only, but initially I would take each matter up with the staff and then I would take it to the chief with the recommended solution. That's how it worked for the four years I was in that position.

About the middle of July, I got a call from a retired lieutenant colonel named Leland Dillon, from Knoxville, Illinois, where my mom and dad were living. Knoxville is where the Knox County Fair is held each year. Colonel Dillon had been talking to my mother and had asked her if she realized what an accomplishment it was that I had been selected as SMA. I think he gave my mom more information about the selection process and what it meant than I had, and he went on to tell her that he was going to be sure that the county recognized me for it.

So Colonel Dillon was the catalyst in organizing "SMA Bill Bainbridge Day" at the Knox County Fair in late August 1975. The Chief of Staff was thrilled. They set aside a day during the fair, and I attended. Knoxville is a small town of 3,400 people. I got a "Distinguished Citizen" award with a medal and a scroll, and the entire day I sat in the grandstand with my family and friends. That was a humbling experience. Knox County was where I was born and raised and spent most of my formative years, and here we were at the county fair, a whole day set aside just to honor me.

I wore my dress whites that day. Most people out there had never seen that uniform and didn't realize it was an Army uniform. This was the set I'd purchased before going to Fort Shafter in 1969. I still have 'em in the closet.

* * *

General Weyand called me in one day and said he wanted me to start attending sessions of the Army Policy Council. That was a first, for the SMA to be a part of that. The council consists of all the principal Army Staff members plus the Secretary of the Army and his principals. The council met weekly to discuss the things that were going on in the Army.

I don't know why General Weyand decided to include me in the council's deliberations, except that in the three months I'd been in the job I'd learned a lot and established a good enough rapport with him that he felt confident having me there to present issues to the council.

At the first meeting, General Weyand had me at one end of the table and sitting at the head was the DAS, Lieutenant General William Fulton, a big, tall guy. We held these meetings just off the Mall Entrance, in the Garand Room, named for the famed World War II basic infantry rifle; one hangs on the wall. General Weyand said he wanted everybody's attention for a moment. "I have just appointed SMA Bainbridge as a member of the Army Policy Council. He will be attending the meetings from now on, and the reason I want him here is because when we get to flying too high, he'll get our feet back on the ground." That made me feel good; evidently I'd given him solid information up to that point, and that's what had led him to conclude I could pass on that kind of information to the staff.

Soon after that, he appointed me as a member of the Army General Staff Council, the Chief of Staff's council. That was also a first for the SMA. When he met with his principal staff assistants I was also present. It was a fairly small group, the VCSA, DCSOPS, DCSLOG, and so on. I felt good about this decision, too. Again, it reaffirmed General Weyand's confidence in me as his SMA, providing him and the staff with a formerly unexploited avenue of information about the Army.

I was also a member of the Army Uniform Board, an unwieldy creature, but it was where all the changes and modifications to the soldier's uniform began. The board was just so big it was hard to get anything approved by it. I wasn't the first SMA to sit on the board, but I was still the only enlisted representative. Decisions were made by voting, and I recall that the DCSPER, who had about four of his people with him, had a bloc of votes, so I'd always try to get them on my side on an issue.

The CSA and his major staff had a lot of input to that process, as did Natick Labs, which developed the uniform material. But it all started at the Army Uniform Board.

As the SMA I could provide practical input that affected soldiers. At one session we were struggling with trying to develop a decent fatigue cap. There was no neutral ground on the "baseball" cap, which was the authorized cap for wear with the fatigues in those days—you either hated it or loved it, and I think most soldiers hated it. We'd thrown away one of the best ever, the old Army field cap. It looked good and wore well. You could stuff it into your pocket and when you took it out it still fit properly. But we'd messed around and messed around and never could get it right after that.

Back when I was a sergeant first class we had the "Louisville Spring-Up," a hat made by the Louisville Cap and Uniform Company. Commanders required soldiers to wear this nonissue thing, but the only place it was available was in the post exchanges, so soldiers had to buy their own. It was a flat-top cap with wire reinforcing the crown, and you couldn't wash the damn thing because it would cave in and lose its shape. I promised myself then that if I ever got a chance to say something about caps I would.

One time Gen. Marvin D. Fuller, the Inspector General, and I were traveling in Europe together and I was wearing the field cap with my fatigues and he was wearing some other kind. He said, "I don't like your hat, Sergeant Major," and I replied, "Yes, sir, and I don't like yours either, but I'll tell you one thing—the soldiers like mine better." He said, "Yeah, I know it, dammit."

One day when Gen. Bernard W. Rogers was Chief of Staff he was reviewing different styles of caps modeled by a soldier from the 3rd Infantry. He asked one of the young soldiers, "By the way, what do you think of that uniform you're wearing?"

The young SP4 said, "It's terrible, sir. In garrison it's okay, but in the field it doesn't stand up, it tears easy, and if you're in a nuclear environment it melts and becomes another skin, sticks to you."

The general turned to me and said, "That's exactly what you've been telling me," and then he turned to the DCSPER and said, "We've got to fix that," and the battle dress uniform (BDU) was born. It took a while to get the BDU into the system, but that's how the concept was born. The Uniform Board couldn't fix the problem, but that SP4 did.

One of the few times I ever went to the Chief of Staff and told him we couldn't fix something without his personal intervention was over the mess dress uniform for enlisted personnel. We'd been wrestling with the concept on the Uniform Board and the members just couldn't make up their minds. I gave him my pitch. I told him we, the senior service, were the only one in our armed forces and indeed the only major army in the world that didn't have a dress mess for enlisted personnel. That surprised him. I told him that when we attended formal functions we should be able to dress as formally as we wanted to—the mess dress didn't have to be required for enlisted people, just an option. I stood out like the proverbial sore thumb in my dress blues, compared to the Air Force, the Navy, and the Marines in their formal mess attire, and I'd attended functions all over the world where those guys— and the Aussies and the Brits—were dressed to the nines and I wasn't. I said even if I were the only guy in the Army who wanted to wear a mess dress uniform I should have the privilege of buying one to wear. General Rogers said, "Tell 'em we're going to do it."

At the next meeting of the board I brought the subject up again, and again it was shot down around the table. I said, "Let me tell you something, ladies and gentlemen—I've already talked to the Chief of Staff about this, and he says we ought to do it." In this case I had the one vote that counted—the Chief of Staff's.

Right away the atmosphere changed. The Natick people said, we can design this, and why don't we come back to the next meeting with some drawings? So the Natick people, in concert with the Heraldry Institute, came up with a couple of drawings, and by the time Bill Bainbridge left the Sergeant Major of the Army's Office, he was wearing a mess dress uniform.

Now since then they've gone and screwed it all up. It used to be like the officer's version, with high-waisted trousers and a cutaway jacket with a fleur-de-lis design on the cuff, different for officers, warrant officers, and enlisted people. You could tell an officer, warrant officer, or enlisted person across the room by the design on the cuff of the uniform coat. We had it arranged so that you could affix a pin-on insignia inside the fleur-de-lis. It was an outstanding and professional-looking uniform. That was changed when Glen Morrell was Sergeant Major of the Army to full-size chevrons on the sleeves, and that ruined the uniform jacket completely. Glen thought the original design "looked too much like an officer."

Frank Wrenn, TRADOC sergeant major, wanted to call that mess dress jacket the Bainbridge jacket, because I'd gotten it approved, but I said we'd just be content that we got it.

Another project was the Army green uniform. We had two

weights in 1975. We managed to get it down to only one, and that
one an improved weight. Those were the days when we had
"summer" greens and "winter" greens, and there were fixed dates
when you would switch from one weight to the other, depending
upon the climate you were serving in. But the clothing industry
had proved it could develop cloth that you could wear 365 days
a year. Why not do the same thing for an Army dress uniform?
So we did.

General Weyand was a great guy to work for. He had a wonderful
sense of humor and a brilliant mind. I don't think he ever intended to do more than serve out the remainder of General
Abrams's tour and then retire. General Weyand took over the
CSA's job when Abrams passed away in office. He'd been vice
chief of staff before that.

Arlene Weyand, General Weyand's wife, was just a super gal,
charming, a lady who really enjoyed people. He has one of the
greatest senses of humor I think I've ever come across in a general officer.

One day we were going back to our office from an Army Policy Council meeting in the Garand Room, about four-thirty or
quarter to five in the afternoon, and we found that the escalator
from the Mall Entrance to the third floor on the E ring was running down to the second floor instead of up—they reverse the es-
calators in the afternoon, when everyone's going home. General
Weyand, Secretary of the Army Martin R. Hoffman, and I got to
the foot of the escalator, and Marty Hoffman challenged General
Weyand to a race up the down escalator. I declined and used the
stairs.

Just as I got to the top of the stairs on the third floor I heard
this *pop*, and saw General Weyand limping across the hall from
the escalator to his office muttering, "Damn! That hurt!" In running up the escalator he'd stumbled over Marty Hoffman and broken a bone in his ankle. I forget now who won the race, but when
I came back to the Pentagon ten days later after a trip, here's the
Chief of Staff of the Army in a walking cast. The *Army Times* reported only that he had broken his foot playing tennis or something like that.

Anyway, tall as General Weyand was, I told him he didn't need
the extra height they'd given him by building up the heel of that
cast. "You know, you're right," he told me. "The other night I
was at a party when suddenly I realized I wasn't *under* the chan-
delier, I was *in* it."

I remember another time he and Secretary Hoffman were at an AUSA conference and as they entered one of the hospitality rooms, General Weyand put two fingers in his mouth and gave out this ear-piercing whistle and hollered, "Awright, attention! We're comin' in to add a little class to this joint!" What other Chief of Staff of the Army would have done such a thing?

At an annual AUSA luncheon one year, when he was the guest speaker, General Weyand told us how he'd just taken his physical, which included the proctoscope exam. Afterward his doctor, a young major, asked him, "Sir, this is the first time I've ever worked with the Chief of Staff of the Army. What should I call you—'sir,' or 'general,' or 'chief'?" General Weyand told us, "I looked at him and said, 'Young man, after what you just did to me, you can call me Fred.' "

General Weyand was a soldier's general. He understood soldiers, and I think that's another reason I got on those councils, because he knew that in order for the Army to operate he had to get input from the soldier's side of things. That's not to say that officers aren't soldiers, just that NCOs and officers view things differently, and in order for the Chief to run the Army properly, he's got to have the view from the enlisted side as well as from his officers. Officers command the Army and NCOs run it. Officers don't have time to do both.

Essentially, General Weyand let me do what I'd been doing all my career, but his door was open to me all the time. I never abused that privilege, but that's the way I'd always operated, so I had no problems when I got to the Pentagon.

My main focus when I went on a trip was the soldier's side of things. If a logistical problem arose, okay, I'd be a messenger to the DCSLOG's people on such a matter, but my concentration was on the personnel side. In order to be able to handle those things before going on a trip anywhere, I went to the Military Personnel Center (MILPERCEN) to find out in detail what the problems were in the area I was scheduled to visit—personnel shortages, replacement problems, whatever. So I went to the field armed with information and was able to squelch a lot of the rumors I'd encounter during a visit. That also enabled me to separate fact from fancy.

When I brought a problem back to the MILPERCEN or the DCSPER, he knew I'd developed the facts on it from a good solid background because I'd gone out armed with the information necessary to find out what was going on. When I did this I'd go either directly to the DCSPER or his executive officer or work with the action officers whose assignments included responsibility for solving the particular problem. I dealt with these people in person but always followed up with memorandums. On big trips, such as the long ones that covered whole overseas commands, Sam Walsh went along, so we could have our stuff thoroughly organized by the time we got back.

Sam was a very astute individual, possibly one of the most intelligent people I've ever known, and very good at problem-solving. Often he'd pick up things and we'd discuss them in the evenings. Of course, we were never out of touch with the Army Staff, and often we'd have relayed problems back to the Pentagon or to the MILPERCEN while we were out in the field and they'd be working on the solution even before we came home. If we found something we thought could be solved immediately, we didn't wait until we got back to raise it with the appropriate staff office at the Pentagon. Many times I'd talk to the MILPERCEN sergeant major from a sedan driving down the highway somewhere in Europe, and often the problem discussed would be solved before we left the overseas theater.

You should always learn something every day. On our first big trip to Europe in the fall of 1975, CSM Ken Tracey, U.S. Army Europe sergeant major, prepared our itinerary. We received it the day before we left Washington. We hit the ground at Frankfurt running on a three-week tour of all of USAREUR. That first trip taught Bill Bainbridge that he should always check his itinerary three or four times *before* leaving home station. Being the new kid on the block that first time out, I discovered that everybody and his brother in Europe wanted to see me to discuss problems, voice concerns, or just have a chat with the SMA.

Well, that particular itinerary wore me to a frazzle. Every evening on that trip we were doing something at some sort of function. Not a good idea, I found; there's a limit to what you can do and do effectively. I was busy eighteen hours a day. About five or six days into the tour I was just not as effective as I should have been, because I was beat. We never repeated that mistake. On the way back, Sam and I decided that henceforth we'd have no more than one social function at each area we visited and that would be it—and it wouldn't be a long, dragged-out affair either, maybe a dinner or a stand-up reception. We also decided to plan an hour or two of free time every evening to discuss the events of the day.

I understand why people wanted to talk to me on those trips, but we had better control of our itineraries after that first one and we operated better by having that control.

We planned a trip to each major command—Eighth Army, USARPAC, USAREUR, particularly Eighth Army and USAREUR, because that's where we had the bulk of our overseas soldiers—every year. Those trips also included visits to the "two-four-sixes," because not everybody goes to the smaller detachments.

The trips to the units were what paid off. I remember one we made to an Army Security Agency outfit in Augsburg, Germany. I think I was the first SMA ever to visit that kind of unit. One SP5 came up to me and said, "Sergeant Major, I want to thank you a lot for getting my husband's pay squared away. You probably don't even remember it, but we called your office and within a week his pay had been straightened out." She didn't remember what the problem was precisely.

"Well, tell your husband that we were happy to be of help to him."

"Tell him yourself," she replied. "He's standing right over there!" So I got to talk to him also. Of course, it was the ever-efficient Sam Walsh who'd fixed the man's problem, but the office got the credit for it.

I can't give Sam and Raylene Scott enough credit for handling things like that. Sam himself built up a lot of credibility in the field, because he was very knowledgeable about how the Army worked and could answer questions and solve problems on his own initiative. However, I was always briefed by him.

I recall another trip to Vincenza, Italy, traveling with CSM Ken Tracey. We visited the airborne battalion stationed there. They'd just come back from maneuvers in Germany, and when I went through their barracks they had weapons stripped down and shelter halves hanging out the windows. They were cleaning, polishing, scrubbing all equipment, having a real GI party. My visit was at ten-thirty on a Monday morning, and these guys had been cleaning their stuff all weekend.

When I got ready to depart I hollered out, "You guys have done such a good job you're going to get the rest of the day off!"

The battalion sergeant major turned to me and asked, "How in the hell did you know that? You just let the cat out of the bag."

I was just trying to give them a little shot in the arm, and by golly, the battalion commander already had it planned.

Sgt. Maj. Don Peroddy comes to mind. He was the Eighth Army sergeant major, a colorful figure and a real soldier's soldier.

He told me once he didn't know how I did it—and I don't know how I did it either—but he'd observed me in action, walking along somewhere, and something would just tell me I needed to talk to some soldier on the other side of the parade ground. "Almost invariably," Peroddy said, "that would be a problem soldier. I always winced when you started to walk over to someone like that, because I knew damn well that guy would have a problem we hadn't heard of, and here you are, hearing it from the soldier the *first time* you've seen him!"

In those days we were having problems defining how short soldiers' hair should be. We'd taken that job away from the squad leaders and put it into a regulation, and then everybody was thoroughly confused. The problem was that the regulation was full of pictures showing hair styles, before and after, with no specific instructions on what the lengths should be, so essentially the local post exchange barber was deciding what the soldier's haircut should look like.

Anyway, soldiers weren't allowed to grow any hair under their lower lip, and Ken Tracey told me once that one advantage to my being so short was that I always found the little goatees that he missed.

I really enjoyed getting out of the Pentagon and talking to soldiers. That was the only way you found out what was going on in the Army. During the four years I was the SMA I spent better than half of my time out visiting field units.

In 1975 the Army was just beginning to get itself turned around after Vietnam, particularly in Europe, where we now had enough soldiers to man the units over there. We were beginning to get a grip on some of the racial and drug problems that had surfaced during those lean years. One of the big challenges was restoring the quality of the Army to what it had been before Vietnam. The major priorities were recruiting quality people and designing a school system to provide good training. The challenge was to establish the Noncommissioned Officer Education System (NCOES) as a solid feature of the training program so that when the Army's leadership next changed it wouldn't just be dumped to make way for someone's brilliant new ideas.

At that time Gen. Maxwell Thurman was the CSA's chief of Programs Analysis and Evaluation Directorate (PA&E). As I traveled about the Army I'd been finding lots of senior noncommissioned officers and company-grade officers who were concerned that we would lose our grasp on the NCOES. The problem was that senior commanders in the field were chipping away at

NCOES funds, using them for other purposes—not sending soldiers to the schools so the money could be used elsewhere in their commands. As the money got scarce, commanders sent fewer of their soldiers to school, and those they did send were not always their best.

After trips to the major Army commands—not just overseas either, but TRADOC and Forces Command and their units—I became convinced of the seriousness of this problem. I got an appointment with General Thurman, then a brigadier general, to lay out the problem as I saw it. I told him that as we filled fewer and fewer of our school quotas we were creating a mediocre Army—we were sending to school only those soldiers commanders felt they could afford to send, whereas we should have been sending only the very best. When you don't send your best, it isn't your best people who get promoted, because they haven't been to the schools, they haven't climbed the rungs of the promotion ladder. I hesitate to use the phrase "ticket punching," because I think good soldiers never punch tickets—they look to be better soldiers, and that's what the NCOES was designed to make them.

I spent two hours with General Thurman, going over these problems. I told him I was afraid that the situation would snowball and sooner or later we'd look around, the funds would be gone, and our good noncommissioned officers would not receive the proper training. General Thurman told me after we'd finished talking, "Sergeant Major, I don't know how I'm going to do it, but you can rest assured that the funding for your NCOES is going to be 'fenced.' "

When I look back at my whole career in the Army, the one thing I'd hang my hat on as a solid accomplishment was convincing General Thurman that funding for the NCOES had to be preserved. That wasn't something I did for myself, but for the Army. If that system had been allowed to deteriorate as I was afraid it would, we might not have fielded the Army we did for Operation Desert Storm. The NCO Educational System is the thing that put our Army back together.

The Army's senior leadership would agree with that statement. When Gen. Carl Vuono became Chief of Staff, he made a commitment to the Army's noncommissioned officers that while he was Chief of Staff, there'd be no degradation of the NCOES—people who were supposed to go to those schools would go to them, and only the best would go. He backed that up right after Desert Storm when he said there would be no "constructive credit" for wartime service. The Army is famous for giving "constructive credit" to soldiers for doing everything but going to school. General Vuono told the Army that this time soldiers would make up the seven months lost because of their time in the Persian Gulf—nobody would miss his training. That took care of the old philosophy that officers go to school and NCOs go to units.

I also talked to a lot of the Army's officers while I was SMA. By the time I got there, the Office of the SMA had been firmly established by those who preceded me, and I was carrying on from where my predecessors had left off. I was just putting the "Bainbridge stamp" on the job. Because of this, most of the officers in the Army today accept the principle that NCOs run the Army so that the officers have the time and the privilege to command it.

When I took over as SMA, Bo Callaway was the Secretary of the Army, but I didn't get to know him very well, because he left to become Gerald Ford's campaign manager in the presidential elections of 1976. Marty Hoffman, who'd been Army general counsel, became the new Secretary of the Army.

I had great rapport with Secretary Marty Hoffman. He had been a captain in the airborne and was an easy man to talk to. I recall after one Army Policy Council meeting he asked me to stay behind and talk to him a bit. He wanted me to make a trip with him to Fort Sill, Oklahoma. He told me the dates, and I said I couldn't make it because I had a White House invitation that conflicted. "Goddammit, Sergeant Major, here I'll have been Secretary of the Army almost a year and we haven't made one trip together!"

When I got back to my office I asked Sam to check out that White House appointment, and it turned out that the occasion was a Medal of Honor ceremony for an Air Force officer, so I felt I could back out of it and go with Mr. Hoffman to Fort Sill. I thought I could justify the trip because at the time we had a program that took soldiers in "overage" specialties and retrained them for jobs in specialties that were short of qualified people, and I knew the trip to Sill would get into that.

We flew down to Fort Sill in Mr. Hoffman's aircraft, and that night we attended an AUSA dinner, where he was the guest speaker. After the function was over, I went to my quarters. The next morning the post sergeant major picked me up, and we went out to check on the retraining of NCOs at Fort Sill in the artillery specialties. There were all kinds of problems, and I spent the whole day getting them straightened out. The program was brand-new, and they didn't have enough of the proper manuals. We located the manuals and made arrangements to have them shipped to the classrooms. I felt I'd accomplished something, but I hadn't seen the Secretary of the Army all day long. Meanwhile, he'd held a couple of press conferences and so on.

When it got time to leave, I got on the airplane ahead of the Secretary, and he came by with his wife, Muggy—that's the way she introduced herself, as Muggy Hoffman—and asked me where I'd been all day long.

"Sir, I thought we came down here for that dinner last night. As soon as it was over, I left, and I've been sitting here on this airplane, waiting for you."

"Bullshit!" he said. "I'll talk to you later."

Talk to me later he did. He came up and sat down beside me and said, "Now I'm serious, Sergeant Major—I want to know where you've been all day. I brought you down here to be with me on this trip."

"Sir, I appreciate your bringing me down here," I said, "but let me tell you, you're just transportation to me, because if I'd been all the places you've been today I'd have missed doing something for the Army." I explained what had happened. "If I'd been at your press conference I'd just have been listening to what you were saying, and you can tell me that or I can read it in the papers. But today I found out some things that you would never have found out, and it's important that I did. I didn't come down here to trail around with you. I came down because traveling with you was an opportunity to give you some insight on the things I found once I got here, which I wouldn't have discovered otherwise."

He slapped me on the knee and said, "You can continue to operate that way as long as I'm Secretary of the Army." I made several trips with him afterward, but only as transportation.

When my grandson, Ryan Koop, was in preschool, they taught him a little song that included the words "I'm not in the artillery or the infantry, I'm in God's army." He asked his mother afterward what were the artillery and the infantry, and she explained. "Well," he wanted to know, "does Jesus have his own jeep, or does he have to borrow God's?" I thought that was so precious I told the story to Secretary Hoffman. "Bill," he told me, "you tell Ryan I'll find out, and if He doesn't have His own jeep, I'll have one issued to Him!"

At the time I made that trip to Fort Sill with Mr. Hoffman, we had a lot of overages in certain combat-support and combat-service-support jobs. As always, there was a shortage in the combat specialties. We had drivers, dental assistants, all kinds of jobs where we just had too many people—good people, but too many of them. So rather than send some of those people home, the Army decided to give them an opportunity to volunteer to be retrained. Why not retrain a SP5 who knows something about the Army instead of discharging him because he's surplus in his specialty? Why lose the six or eight years' experience he has? We'd just have to recruit new soldiers to fill the jobs in the shortage specialties. Since the SP5 was good at what he was doing, he probably had the potential for retraining. Besides, since the SP5 had already invested considerable time in the Army, he was at the point where if we could keep him we'd have him for a full twenty years.

Walt Kruger, then sergeant major of the 1st Cavalry Division at Fort Hood, put it best. He said if he had a choice between training a new soldier or retraining a good SP4 who had been in the Army for a while, he'd take the SP4 anytime. Gen. Julius Becton was division commander then, and the division retrained a lot of its NCOs. The program worked well. Many of those soldiers, faced with getting out or retraining and aware that once retrained their opportunity for promotion would be much better, became very motivated and dedicated. A soldier who had no chance to make staff sergeant as a dental assistant could become a tanker and go to the top of the promotion list in that field because he had the time in grade and time in service and had just been through schooling.

It just so happened that I got a chance to explain all of this to a very skeptical audience. I was visiting Fort Huachuca, Arizona, when a temporary cap on one of my teeth fell off. I went to the post dental clinic, and the dentist, a full colonel, got my mouth all stuffed full of his paraphernalia. While he was waiting for the epoxy to set, he folded his arms and said, "Now, Sergeant Major, suppose you explain to me why you're taking the best dental assistant in the Army and making a tanker out of him."

I could only hold up my hand to indicate, "Wait until my mouth is free and I'll tell you!"

He grinned, and after he got all that stuff out of my mouth I explained why, and he said, "You know, nobody ever explained it to me that way before."

His dental assistant chimed in, "Me either!"

So I convinced two people that the program was viable: the

dental assistant, who could make staff sergeant as a tanker, and the colonel, who realized he *could* after all get along without this particular assistant—there were, after all, plenty of dental assistants but not enough tankers. And my tooth got fixed properly. You can't hardly beat a deal like that, can you?

We got ourselves into the retraining business because the Army did not have a sophisticated system that would prevent overages occurring in its various fields—but, because of the NCO Education System, we did have a decent system to retrain them. And the training was done right, in a formal school, not through OJT, which as I've said before is the worst training there is.

In the fall of 1976 I had a conversation with General Weyand and referred in passing to something that I said had happened "just the other day." I stopped short when I realized that what I'd said had happened "just the other day" had actually taken place *four months* before, and I commented that time was sure passing quickly in that job.

General Weyand agreed, and then he said, "You know, you're the author of several initiatives* since you came up here, and you'll be gone before any of these programs is finished. What would you think about making this a three-year tour?"

The SMA's tour started out to be the same as that of the Chief of Staff who appointed him. Bill Wooldridge stayed two years, George Dunaway stayed two, and then Sy Copeland wound up staying nearly three years, because of the delay in confirming General Abrams. Then Van Autreve and I came in for two-year tours. Well, I had no problem with General Weyand's suggestion, and he said okay, but he wanted to check with "Dutch"—General Kerwin, his vice chief of staff. About three days later a little memo came to me saying my tour would be extended a year, and the general order was amended to reflect that. Since then, SMAs have been appointed to three-year tours of duty. That took me through June 1978 in office.

I got around the Washington social scene quite a bit, for a former pig farmer from rural Illinois. Whenever I had the major-command sergeants major conference in conjunction with the Chief of Staff's commanders' conference, we'd always have a reception to which the foreign attachés' NCOs would be invited,

---

*Strengthening of the NCO Educational System, centralized selection for drill sergeants, and cancellation of MOS tests for command sergeants major.

and we'd get invitations back from them to attend their functions. We had great rapport with those folks, particularly the British Commonwealth attachés.

My first trip over to Capitol Hill was with General Weyand, at his request. He was testifying on the commissary system. The occasion was the perennial attack on the system, when somebody in the Congress gets a wild hair to do away with it. I was sitting behind General Weyand, and at one point he was making his pitch to a senator on why he thought we should keep the commissaries. The senator was from Iowa, and being from Illinois, I always considered Iowans neighbors. This elected official said, "When I talk to my constituents back home about commissaries, they think it's appalling that the services have all of them around here." Right then I realized that his "constituents" back in Iowa, when they thought about commissaries at all, thought they were places to buy sandwiches, Coca-Cola, and deli products, and *he* (and his grocers' lobby), not they, was concerned about the issue.

"You mean to tell me," this senator asked General Weyand, "that if the President of the United States thinks we ought to get rid of commissaries you won't support him?"

General Weyand responded, "I'm not saying that at all, Senator. What I'm telling you, and what I would tell the President, is that I will support any decision that he makes, but I'd also tell him if it's a bad one."

That ended his testimony, and on the way back to the Pentagon he looked over to me and said, "Sergeant Major, I could see you leaning forward in your foxhole back there behind me, ready to say something to that senator, but I figured we'd better just leave well enough alone and let me do the testifying on this one."

I was to make several appearances before congressional committees after that, testifying on military construction, particularly military housing, and "quality of life" issues of importance to enlisted people. One time I was testifying before Congressman Charles E. Bennett of Florida and I was telling him how I could get something done by calling the post sergeant major at Fort Sill or Fort Benning, and he said, "Do you mean to tell me *you*, as the Sergeant Major of the Army, don't tell the Chief of Staff? You call the sergeant major down there, not the commanding general of the post?"

I answered, "No, sir, I don't call the CG. The Chief of Staff has the confidence in me to get things done for the benefit of soldiers and the Army. He's got other things to worry about, as does the commander at Fort Benning. That sergeant major and I get problems solved between the two of us, and then we tell his commander about it as a finished product."

"You mean they don't have any problem with that?" Mr. Bennett asked.

"Of course not," I told him. "They support it."

From then on I had no problem talking to Congressman Bennett or Congressman Wofat, from Guam, who said, "Yeah, we did a lot of that stuff in the Navy."

Bennett told him, "Well, what the sergeant major is telling me is not what you guys did in the Navy—you went around your commander, and he's supporting him."

I think we did good things for the Army during those testimonies. Of course, SMAs' visits to the Hill have escalated since I was in the job. I'd estimate that SMA Bill Gates was over there ten times as much as I ever was. When I say "we," I am referring to all the senior enlisted people of the service, because generally we testified as a group. We never ran into any really hostile congressmen, and I think the reason was that we weren't trying to blow smoke into anyone's eyes, we were only trying to get the money to support our people properly, and it was obvious we were just trying to do a job right, not run around anybody.

I would normally know in advance the line the questioning was to take—not the specific questions I'd be asked, of course—but I found out very quickly that Congress doesn't operate any differently from the Army. The Army has its "action officers" and the Congress has its "staffers." Many times during testimony these staffers would come up behind the congressman and whisper something in his ear or pass him a slip of paper and he'd say, "And my question is . . ." The staffers worked up the background for the congressman just the way action officers do for their bosses.

One day I met Secretary Hoffman in the hallway. "I was just coming down to your office," he said. "Have you ever met President Ford?" I told him I hadn't. "Well, you're going to. I want you to stand right at the top of the stairs here and you'll shake hands with him."

The occasion was the dedication of the Marshall Corridor,* a section of the hallway right outside the Secretary of the Army's Office.

*A permanent exhibit of memorabilia from the career of General of the Army George C. Marshall.

As President Ford came by, Mr. Hoffman said, "Mr. President, I'd like to have you meet the senior noncommissioned officer in the United States Army." So I shook hands with Gerald Ford, the first time I ever met the President of the United States.

We always have somebody out there who is trying to beat the system. Not many, and they're getting fewer and fewer, but I recall an incident involving a senior noncommissioned officer who wrote to his congressman about a "problem." He'd received orders to go overseas, and instead of complying with them, he decided to put in for retirement, a perfectly legitimate option. He was a master sergeant. In those days, once you submitted your retirement papers, you couldn't pull them, particularly when you did it to get out of orders you didn't like.

Well, wouldn't you know it, he came out on the promotion list for sergeant major. So he wrote to his congressman, who wrote to the Secretary of the Army, asking for an exception to policy so the retirement could be revoked. The action came to me—the Secretary asked me what he should tell the congressman.

I wrote a page and a half, and about an hour later I met Mr. Hoffman again as he was walking down the hall, and he said, "By the way, Sergeant Major, I sent you a paper on a senior noncommissioned officer looking for some help."

"Yes, sir," I said, "and I sent you the answer."

He looked at me and said, "You're telling me he ought to go home?"

"That's exactly what I said in my response, sir." He went home.

Earlier I mentioned the NCO at the Sergeants Major Academy, the one with two kids in school, who found out how hard life was on the outside and wanted his retirement papers pulled. The same thing with this guy. I don't want any quitters in my Army.

About halfway through what was to prove to be a four-year tour as SMA, President Jimmy Carter appointed a new Secretary of the Army, Clifford Alexander. Hazel and I, along with a lot of other people, were invited to the White House to meet President and Mrs. Carter.

Because of parking restrictions, they took us all over to the White House by bus from a big parking lot at Tempo A,* right

*Tempo is short for "temporary." Just outside Fort McNair there was a block of office buildings erected during World War II to accommodate the government

outside Fort McNair, and we got into a long line to meet Mrs. Carter and the President. I shall never forget that. We were introduced by the protocol officer, a major.

President Carter said, "I've never met a Sergeant Major of the Army before."

I replied, "Sir, we're both in the same boat, because I've never met you before, and I'm pleased to make your acquaintance and shake your hand. This is a real honor for me."

The President said, "Well, Sergeant Major, we'll try to do a good job for the country and you."

I said, "Mr. President, the Army will continue to do a good job for you."

On the bus going back to Fort McNair, Ann Stikeleather, wife of Lee Stikeleather, the Army Intelligence Command sergeant major, asked me if I knew how she could find out when her husband was due back from a trip he had taken. They'd both been invited to the reception, but because Lee was out of town on Army business, Ann had had to go by herself.

Well, when we got back to Tempo A, I went in and made a phone call for Ann and found out that Lee wasn't back yet. I started jogging through the parking lot, trying to catch up with the gals. I was wearing a pair of dress shoes that had been issued to me by the Old Guard at Fort Myer, with metal plates on the heels, and when I tried to stop my feet flew out from under me and I landed flat on my back, dress blues and all. I hit so hard that my watch flew off my wrist. A SP4 medic appeared from somewhere and advised me to just lie still. I said, "No, no, I can get up!"

I struggled to my feet, all my wind knocked out, and put my hat back on, and the medic said, "Sergeant Major, you should have just lain there for a while."

I walked to my car and drove back to Fort Myer. By the time we got there I was really in pain. I dropped Hazel at our quarters and drove down to Rader Clinic, the Fort Myer dispensary.

Who was the first guy I ran into down there? The same SP4 who had advised me not to get up when I first fell down. I confessed that I was really hurting. "I told you, Sergeant Major, you should have taken my advice and lain there for a while before you got up."

expansion as a result of our entry into the war. They were intended to provide only temporary office space, but were continued in service well into the 1970s. There were three of them at that location, and they became known as Tempo A, B, and C.

The doctor examined me and sent me over to Walter Reed. When I got there they put me in a wheelchair. "I don't want this!" I said. The medic told me I had to get into it or she'd be in trouble, so I did.

She wheeled me into the X-ray department. I had a heck of a time climbing up on that table, let me tell you. I spent the weekend in bed with some painkillers. They told me to go on sick call Monday morning. I took one of those painkillers and within an hour I was sick to my stomach. I didn't realize it was those pills until I took the second one—then they all went down the toilet.

Monday morning the doctor at the Pentagon dispensary looked at my X-rays and told me I'd torn four or five inches of muscle where the rib cage connects with the spine. By that time I'd developed a ten-by-four-inch bruise that had turned almost black.

The doctor ordered seven days of bed rest on a hard mattress or on the floor. I told him that would be impossible, because I had a trip to Korea coming up on Wednesday of that same week.

He looked at me for a moment and said, "You've got two choices, Sergeant Major: you either go home and get in your bed or I'm gonna put you in one of mine."

"Well, what are those people going to do in Korea?" I wanted to know.

"Whatever the hell they want to. But if you get on that airplane and fly from here to Korea, you won't be able to get out of the seat when you arrive."

Well, I took his advice, and as it turned out that doctor was a hell of a lot smarter than Sergeant Major Bainbridge. If I'd gone on to Korea and toughed it out I might have had one hell of a problem with my back later on, and it wouldn't have proved a thing. Even the Sergeant Major of the Army can screw up.

But that was just an ordinary accident. I didn't fall down because of anything I had at the White House reception. All I got by way of refreshment there was one cookie and a glass of nonalcoholic punch.

≡ 12 ≡

SERGEANT MAJOR OF THE ARMY, 1977–1979

I did not have the same rapport with Secretary of the Army Alexander that I did with Secretary Hoffman. It was just a different association, maybe because Marty Hoffman knew soldiers from his own military experience, which Clifford Alexander did not have. I think he had been an enlisted man in the National Guard and that was it. I had a good personal relationship with him, but actually I didn't do that much business with Mr. Alexander, because things that would have required closer contact just didn't come up that often. Also, while he was soldier-oriented in the humanitarian sense, he didn't have the hands-on interest in personnel affairs that Secretary Hoffman did.

I made only one trip, to Europe in the spring of 1977, with Secretary Alexander. Like the ones I made with Mr. Hoffman, it was merely transportation for me. I remember his aide coming down and confirming that Hazel and I would be flying with the Secretary. He told me there were four bunks on the aircraft: There was one for Mr. Alexander, another for his wife, and a third for Hazel. "I don't know who's going to get the last one," he said, "but I know it isn't going to be you or me." I don't recall now who did get that other bunk, but it was a comfortable ride anyway, a Boeing 707 with a VIP suite, first-class airline seats, so I didn't suffer. It was a lot better than flying commercial.

On that trip we visited our counterparts in the British Army, including the Scots Guards, in Cheltenham, England. We had dinner hosted by the regimental sergeant major, and the next day we were escorted by a retired regimental sergeant major who worked for the Chancellor of the Exchequer.

Our escort said he wanted to show us "me boss's office," and when we walked in, the Chancellor was inside. He talked to us for a while, then said, "By the way, Sergeant Major, would you like to see my mace?" I hefted it and put it on my shoulder, and he told me I was the first enlisted person of the U.S. Army ever to hold the mace. The person who carries the train of his ceremonial robe when he officiates is a retired admiral in the Royal Navy.

The next day when we left the barracks they piped us off, and they said afterward that was the first time they'd ever done that for an enlisted person. We also visited Sandhurst, the West Point of England.

Mr. Alexander was very interested in the status of minorities in the Army, but I never, in thirty-one years in the Army, ever had any problem with minority soldiers at any level. I think those who did have problems just didn't know how to deal with people, and that might have been due to their upbringing. Perhaps they were just not big enough to rise above what they were taught as children. It's obvious to me that in order to be a good soldier you've got to give everybody his or her due and treat everybody based on his or her abilities. I don't think soldiers should be promoted because of gender, color, or religion, but on how they perform their duties.

We had no dealings with minorities back in Illinois when I was growing up because we didn't have any. We had one black person in the town of Elmwood, Illinois, near where we lived when I was a kid. He was called Nigger Ben, and that's a word I hate to this day. Of course, there were black folks living in Galesburg, but my family didn't live there. I went to the Army without prejudices because I didn't develop any growing up. I had no reason not to like a person because of his color or religion. And I don't today either. We just didn't have any of that in our family, thank the Lord and my parents.

During this time we not only initiated integrated basic training— men and women in the same unit—but OSUT—one-station unit training. Both were things being tried out by the great training minds of the Army, and we had some great ones. As I traveled around the Army and saw the troops in the field it became increasingly evident to me that one of the biggest problems with women in the Army was men. Some of them just did not accept women in the Army, and some of them do not accept them even today. Twenty percent of our Army today is female, and during Operation Desert Storm the women acquitted themselves, according to everything I've read and heard, as well as the men over there did. I believe the reports are true, because of my experience talking to women in the service and observing their training. They tried harder. They felt, as a group, that they were up against it, that they had to prove themselves. Prove themselves they did.

My old outfit, the 28th Infantry, is a basic training unit down at Fort Jackson, and I went to a graduation ceremony down there in 1990. The second-best rifle shot in that unit was a female. The ability is there. All you have to do is develop it. I've seen women who cry, yet I've also seen men who cry, so you can't take the tears of the woman any more than those of the man as an excuse for not being able to train.

I recall an example out at Fort Lewis, Washington. As SMA, I was visiting a signal unit on a training exercise. The sergeant major was Orie Berndt, an old friend of mine. They were loading spools of WD9 wire from a three-quarter-ton trailer onto a two-and-a-half-ton truck. Because the trailer and truck beds were about the same height, there was little actual lifting required. I saw two women soldiers standing by, watching the men unload those spools. Not one NCO in that outfit was saying anything, so I walked up to those two women and asked them if they were part of the unit and if they were, why weren't they helping with the loading of the spools. One of the women said that the spools were too heavy for her, so I told her to grab one and see. She did and came back with a grin on her face, saying, "I *can* lift it!" The two of them would have stood there and let the men unload that truck.

Orie Berndt and his NCOs got a little lesson from that. He said, "I've known you a long time, and I should have known better than to bring you out here with people standing around, not taking their share of the work detail. I accept the ass-chewing because I should have had somebody take care of that situation."

We did have some problems. Women's feet are different from men's, and they can't wear the boots as issued. But if you just go back and look at all the male soldiers who had foot injuries while they were paratroopers, Rangers, infantrymen, who ran in their combat boots when all the orthopedists in the Army were telling the commanders that the combat boot was a terrible piece of footwear for running, you can understand that the women's problem with those boots wasn't strictly a female one. We finally got around that difficulty by having soldiers do some PT in athletic shoes, until they'd had time to break in their boots. When commanders saw soldiers running around in fatigues with soft shoes, they complained about how "unmilitary" that was, so we put the soldiers into PT outfits.

Some people object to women in the military because of the problem with single parents. But we have single parents of both genders. The increased opportunity for sexual harassment is another problem often cited to support the view that women don't fit in the military service. Well, we have rules and regulations telling commanders how to handle those things. All they have to do is apply them. If a man or woman can't perform his or her duty, he or she has to be discharged. The time to find out is during training, not in war, and the solution is to get commanders and NCOs to weed out the problem soldiers.

I have absolutely no problem with women in combat units. When I came into the Army, women were just clerks—hell, I never even saw a woman anywhere near a unit when I came into the Army. We were not ready to accept women in combat roles in those days, and a lot of people in the Army and in society at large still aren't. But we had women killed in Desert Storm, and the country still goes on and the services are still operating, and that kind of thing will happen more often in the future. Congress just directed the Navy and the Air Force to let women fly combat aircraft and serve aboard warships. As I told General Rogers one day when the subject came up, we *already* had women in combat roles, flying helicopters and so on. That's a combat role. We had them flying under fire in Desert Storm.

Women will go into combat because they think it is part of their Army responsibility. Do they want to do it to get promoted? I don't think so, no more than the men. There are women who don't want to go into combat, and that's pretty smart, because combat is not fun. But there are women who say they should be able to do anything the Army asks of them, and theirs is the side I'm on. I believe that when the time comes, and it is going to come, they'll do just as well as the men. They've already proved that in Desert Storm. That was combat. We had women in combat support units who were killed and wounded by enemy fire. We had women captured. If a support unit gets overrun, as can happen, are all the women going to run back to the rear? They'll have to defend the unit just as the men will. And by "combat," I mean being close enough to the enemy that you hear something go *crack* beside your ear—that's a bullet.

There's no doubt in my mind that when large numbers of American female soldiers die in the next war, it's going to be a very traumatic thing for all of us. But it's no easier to have a young father killed in war than a young mother; somebody's parent is gone. You never get used to having casualties in war, but

I think in the next one we're going to get used to having them of both sexes.

I do not think I'll see in my time females in the infantry, as "riflepersons." But what about artillery? If an artillery outfit is seventeen kilometers behind the front lines throwing 350-pound shells out there, that's considered combat. I think we'll have women in artillery units.

Is there any innate difference between men and women when it comes to killing other people? Throughout our history, women have had to kill to protect themselves and their homes. Look at all the female police officers trained to use deadly force on the streets. I've dealt with a lot of soldiers, and if somebody's shooting at you, you're going to shoot back. I know I've had women shoot at me, in Vietnam, and I shot back. So I think women who fly helicopters in support roles could just as well be flying the armored gun platforms or firing the artillery pieces or Patriot missiles.

There's the objection that women can't handle the heavy work men can. I ran across a SP5 in a unit at Fort Riley, Kansas, who was driving a five thousand-gallon gasoline tanker in a divisional support unit. The best-looking truck in that motor park was hers. She was not big enough to reach the pedals in the cab of her vehicle without additional support behind her, but she was a qualified heavy vehicle driver. I asked her if she was really driving that thing or if it was just an act put on for me because I was visiting. She told me that in the last thirty days she'd delivered thousands of gallons of fuel to "her guys" in the field with that truck. I asked her what she'd do if she had a flat tire. She pointed to another driver, a man twice her size, and said, "I do the same thing he does. I get somebody to help me. I can't do it by myself, and neither can he." Now, she was in a combat service support unit, two echelons removed from the front lines in traditional battle formations, but she would get right up there with the mechanized infantry if they ever went to war.

The time will come when we'll have women in combat units, maybe not rifle units, but in others, and we can deal with that. The idea that women can't make good soldiers is a mindset, not an incontrovertible fact.

I mentioned earlier that during this period we instituted the one-station unit training (OSUT) program, in which the soldier didn't have to move to another post between basic and advanced individual training—like from Fort Dix, New Jersey, to Fort Sam Houston, Texas. That was primarily for the combat arms and some of the combat support jobs. For instance, military policemen could take their basic training in one place, at Fort McClellan, Alabama, and then move across the post to take their MP training. That provided continuous training and a huge savings in permanent change of station (PCS) costs.

One of the best training changes that the Army has ever seen came to pass while I was the SMA, and that was the drill sergeant program. I pointed out earlier the problems we had at Fort Benning when I was the training center sergeant major, getting enough drill sergeants to take care of our training when at the same time they were three and four deep in instructors up at the infantry school.

Our schools for training drill sergeants were mediocre at best, and our selection process was even worse. Units were selecting and sending soldiers to the school, and in some cases only those the commanders could afford to spare were the ones sent. Prior to the establishment of the NCO Education System, that problem was universal throughout the Army.

Also, as I noted earlier, when you leave people in the drill sergeant program too long, as we were doing when I was back at Benning, they lose the edge they need to be good platoon sergeants, artillerymen, and so on. Some stayed in the program because it was personally beneficial to them. Those were few in number, but just one is too many. They went from post to post to stay in the program and avoid assignment to line units.

We initiated centralized selection of drill sergeants. That isn't what they called it in the field. Those who didn't want to go said they'd been "drafted," "shanghaied," and other things. What the process really did was put the drill sergeant into the same system we were using for other school selections and promotions. Under centralized selection, when a soldier went to the drill sergeant school he had been picked based on his proven abilities. And after graduation from that school the soldier was faced with a two-year tour as a drill sergeant with the possibility of a one-year extension if the soldier applied and the application was approved by his or her commander. No more did drill sergeants remain in the program five or six years. When their two or three years were up they went back into the field to perform duty in their basic specialities.

A lot of people went into those drill sergeant schools leaving two heel marks in the sand, where they had to be dragged through the doorway, but eight weeks later, their heels were firmly planted as they walked back out that door, because they knew they'd learned a skill—the skill of passing on what they knew to the civilians they were required to transform into soldiers.

So we selected the best men and women to be drill sergeants and didn't keep them in the business too long, but they worked hard while they were in the program. They were mother, father, sister, brother, confessor, everything to their troops. That's hard work. Some of them could not stand the pressure of eighteen-hour workdays and the responsibilities that went along with the job, and they were removed from the program. But the program itself turned out to be of tremendous benefit to the Army.

Today when you look over promotion lists or talk to the students at the Sergeants Major Academy, or observe good-looking soldiers leading troops, you notice that a good percentage of them wear the Drill Sergeant Badge on the right breast pocket. In my mind that program was one of the biggest steps toward good training for soldiers that the Army's ever taken, and I'm proud of my part in it. I argued hard for that system, because I saw firsthand the problems we had at Fort Benning and I knew, from traveling around the rest of the Army, that those problems were paramount everywhere we taught basic and advanced individual training.

The noncommissioned officer academies we had were a great thing, in their time. They were excellent for teaching discipline and self-respect, because they went beyond what soldiers learned in their advanced individual training courses, but somewhere along the line they got off the track. The Seventh Army NCO Academy at Bad Toelz, Germany, is a good example of what I mean. There they had what was called the "Autobahn." That was a strip of the floor down the center of a hallway that was marked off and polished daily with shoe polish, just like spit-shining a pair of shoes, and nobody was allowed to walk on it. I don't believe that Gen. Bruce C. Clarke, who set up the Seventh Army NCO Academy, ever intended that sort of thing to develop. If it evolved while he was there, he might have tolerated it because the NCOs running the place thought it contributed to esprit.

Well, this old infantry soldier walked on the Autobahn during a visit there on one of my trips as SMA. Somebody, one of the students, hollered out, "Oh, you can't walk there!"

"Why not?" I asked as I continued to walk right down the center of that highly polished section of the corridor.

"Because we have to polish it!" the student said.

So I stopped and asked why they had to polish a section of the floor.

"That's the Autobahn—that's part of our training."

I had a long talk with the commandant of the academy, who was a sergeant major. "This may be backed by you," I told him, referring to the Autobahn, "and it may be backed by your commander, who may be backed all the way up to Seventh Army, but by God, I don't see where this teaches soldiers anything, other than disdain for having to polish a section of the floor with shoe polish."

The next time I visited the Seventh Army NCO Academy, the Autobahn was gone. That thing really upset me, and I had walked on it on purpose. I apologized to the soldiers, because they were going to have to repolish the damn thing to get my footprints out of it, but I think the results were well worth the trek. In my mind the Autobahn typified what the NCO academies became, before the NCOES—tight-bed-making, shoe-shining, and brass-shining academies.

I found a similar problem at the NCO academy located at Camp Jackson, Republic of Korea. That's located at Uijongbu, just north of Seoul, where I Corps Headquarters is located. An old friend of mine, Sgt. Maj. George Otis, was commandant at the time I visited there when I was the SMA. George now works for Arlington National Cemetery. In his younger days he was the "father" of the U.S. Army Drill Team of the Old Guard, the 3rd Infantry.

The Eighth Army NCO Academy at Camp Jackson was part of the NCOES at the time this incident occurred. It occupied the best damn cantonment area in all of South Korea, bless old George Otis's heart—spit-and-polish, but they were getting the right kind of training; George was turning out good soldiers and noncommissioned officers.

But George had put a plate of polished brass into the floor in front of his desk, and I walked on it too. He said, "Yike! God, you're stepping on my inspection plate!" I was standing on it and asked him what it was for.

"When somebody comes in here to get their butt reamed they've got to stand behind that plate and they end up polishing it."

I asked, "Who's going to polish it now, George?"

He said, "I suppose we'll have to paint the son of a bitch now!"

Guess what? That brass plate disappeared too.

I think such things are degrading to a soldier. I think you can make a soldier *want* to do anything as long as you let him retain his dignity. Once you take away his dignity, you've destroyed him. He might still do what you ask of him, but it won't be done as a soldier should do it. I was in a position to change those things, and I think the change was for the better.

We still have the NCO academies, but they are part and parcel of the Noncommissioned Officer Education System today, and they're all MOS-oriented—combat, combat support, combat service and support, etc.—until you get to the Sergeants Major Academy.

Incidentally, George Otis, along with the Eighth Army sergeant major, CSM Don Peroddy, instigated naming all the streets at Camp Jackson after former Sergeants Major of the Army. There's a Bainbridge Boulevard there.

George was a hell of a soldier. I mentioned that he's working at Arlington these days. When CSM Frank Bennett, formerly CONARC sergeant major, died, Hazel and I went to the interment of his ashes at Arlington. As we drove through the cemetery I noticed that the sprinklers were going, and there was George Otis, standing alongside the road. As the remains went by, George saluted, and we waved at him and he waved back at us.

About twenty minutes after the interment ceremony, we were coming back, and there was George, still standing in the same spot. I asked the sergeant major who was escorting us back to our car, "What in the world is George standing there for? He was there when we came down and he's still there."

He told us that where George was standing, one of the sprinkler heads was off, and it had been spraying a column of water across the road, and George didn't want CSM Bennett's cortege to have to pass through it. "So George is standing on that broken head. As soon as we get by—look now in the rearview mirror."

I turned around, and George had stepped off the sprinkler head and the water was spraying all over the road back there. That's the kind of soldier George was. He wouldn't permit any interruption in Bennett's funeral ceremony.

That incident reminds me of something else I got started while I was SMA, although it fell to SMA William A. Connelly, my successor, to finish it, and that was arranging for more elaborate honors at the funerals of senior noncommissioned officers, in this case sergeants major, command sergeants major, and Sergeants Major of the Army. At Arlington interments, that means a caisson, music, and a troop escort. What enlisted people had been receiving up to then was an honor guard to fire the last salute and a bugler to render Taps. I was reading the regulations one day and found there was nothing in there that said senior NCOs couldn't receive honors, but it did specify that lieutenant colonels and above would receive honors.

I called General Robert G. Yerkes, who was commanding the Military District of Washington at the time, and asked him why we didn't render more elaborate honors to deceased senior NCOs. He explained that the regulation had been written with the capabilities of the supporting unit in mind, and most units could not sustain anything very elaborate for burials.

"We've got the Old Guard here, sir," I said. "They take care of all the funerals at Arlington, and it would appear to me that for no more than what this would add to their burden we could change the regulation so that it would also include senior noncommissioned officers." I asked what that would take away from the officers. General Yerkes agreed it would not deny honors to those already receiving them.

That was still thrashing around when I retired and Bill Connelly became SMA. I'd told Bill this action was in the mill, and he added it to his agenda. During his tenure it did get written into the regulation. Where it can be done, and at Arlington it can be, senior NCOs get those last honors, and the Old Guard is proud it can do it for them.

Near the end of my tour, the CSA approved a distinctive chevron for wear by the Sergeant Major of the Army. The idea had been kicking around the Army Uniform Board for some time. We were the only service that did not have a distinctive insignia of rank for its senior enlisted person. We'd had distinctive collar brass insignia incorporating the design of the flag of the Chief of Staff of the Army. But we had no special insignia of rank.

I brought the subject up at a board meeting because it had been referred to me from the field. It went around the board, then back out to the field, and three or four dozen designs came back. The board narrowed it to two. While all this was going on, I'd made a visit to the Army's Heraldry Institute and talked to the deputy director, Dr. Opal Landrum, and asked her to have her unit come up with a chevron design. I asked that she incorporate stars into it. Stars have been part of the sergeant major's chevron since the supergrades were created—three up and three down with a star; then we had a star with a wreath, when the command sergeant major chevron was designed.*

*Between 1920 and 1958, the U.S. Army did not have a sergeant major grade in-

It took Dr. Landrum about two days to come up with a distinctive design—two stars centered between the arcs and bars. She said there was no question that was the correct progression of symbols. It would be easily recognized by everyone, and it followed what the other services had done, because they also incorporated stars into the design for their senior enlisted position.

The design finally picked by the Army Uniform Board looked like what a SP4 wears, a shield with a circle and bars and slashes and an eagle. It evolved from the West Point system, and I didn't know what the hell that had to do with enlisted people. I told the board I wanted a design that had evolved from the enlisted system.

"How about this?" I asked, and I unveiled Dr. Landrum's design. Around the table went my chevron with the two stars, and after the comments I said, "Incidentally, this was designed by the Institute of Heraldry. Has yours been there?" It hadn't, and I suggested they submit it.

Those two designs went up to the CSA. The day he made the decision, he had copies of both in his office, and he and I were discussing which should prevail. General Rogers asked how it had all evolved, and I told him. He sat there thinking and finally said, "I kinda like this one, based on what the captain of cadets up at West Point wears." Then he smiled and asked who was going to wear the winning design.

"I am, sir, if you approve it, but I'd sure like to have you approve the other one."

He replied, "So be it."

The first set of the new chevrons were pinned on me by Gen. Bernard W. Rogers on December 12, 1978, at approximately 3:15 P.M.

I was able to wear those new chevrons for only about seven months, but at last we had a distinctive chevron for the SMA. I received sundry remarks from the field on the new design. One was from a staff sergeant at the Pentagon health clinic. I went down there to get an inoculation for some trip I was about to make and he said, "That's the new chevron, eh, Sergeant Major? I don't like it."

signia. Instead, master sergeants serving in sergeant major positions were so designated, but the chevrons they wore were those of a master sergeant, three arcs (stripes) over three bars (rockers). Before the 1920 revision of the enlisted grade structure, sergeants major were designated by a chevron that looked much like the modern master sergeant's but upside down.

I said, "Guess what? It doesn't make any difference whether you like it or not, because you aren't the one who's wearing it. I'll tell you why you don't like it. It's something new. You're not used to it. Give it a little while."

About four months later, I was back down there again and the same sergeant said, "Sergeant Major, you're right. By golly, they look pretty good."

A little while later I was attending the Forces Command sergeants major conference hosted by Bill Connelly in San Francisco and told him he would have some people who didn't like the new chevron.

After Bill had been sworn in as SMA, he was at a conference somewhere and somebody came up to him and said, "Sergeant Major, there's been a lot of controversy over the chevrons you have, and we'd just like to know what you think of them."

He put that to rest forever by saying, "I haven't heard any controversy, but it doesn't make any difference anyway, because since I'm the only son of a bitch who's going to wear 'em—and I like 'em!—I don't think we're gonna change them."

Shortly after General Rogers came up from Forces Command to be Chief of Staff of the Army, I had a luncheon appointment with him in his office. We spent about two hours discussing what he wanted me to do, what he considered my role as the SMA would be and the kind of support I could expect from him. There was no change from the way I worked under General Weyand. The door was still open to me.

If a personnel issue having any impact on soldiers came across General Rogers's desk, it came right back out if it didn't have my commentary on it. After that luncheon, as I was leaving, General Rogers shook my hand and said, "Sergeant Major, I'm glad you are the SMA." Our relationship was never "Bill and Bernie," but we had the greatest respect for each other. His wife, Ann, is a beautiful person, both in appearance and in her personality. Hazel and I have been to their house on numerous occasions, not just because I was his SMA but because we are their friends.

One day in 1979 I was in the office with General Rogers. The assistant deputy chief of staff for personnel, Gen. Joe Kingston, was also present. General Rogers said that for the past four years—as DCSPER, Forces Command commander, and Chief of Staff—he'd been making the leadership speech to the graduating class of the U.S. Military Academy, and that year he wanted me to make it. He turned to Joe Kingston and told him, "Make sure the SMA gets up there, okay?"

As I left the office, General Rogers told me, "And don't come to me to get any ideas for your speech."

So I made that speech to the graduating class of the U.S. Military Academy in 1979. I prepared for it by jotting down thoughts and notes, and then I visited Col. Harry G. Summers, Jr.,* who was a speechwriter for the CSA at that time, and together we worked up an outline. Harry's a great writer and an intellectual. I delivered my address on April 17, 1979. My theme was "Trust the NCO and use the experience that's there." I couched it in terms of friendly advice. It began like this:

"Walking down the road one day at Fort Benning, I saw a group of airborne trainees in the front-leaning-rest position. Their arms were shaking and quivering, and I heard one call out in a weak and plaintive voice, 'Sergeant . . .' This massive airborne NCO leaned over him and yelled in his ear, 'You don't need to call me sergeant, soldier, 'cause I'm your friend. I'm your friend.' "

I sat up on the "poop deck"** with the captain of cadets for a meal and then addressed the graduating class. I told them what they could expect to find in the field when they got out there as second lieutenants. I advised them that they could speak to their noncommissioned officers and it wouldn't hurt them a bit. I told them they could have their platoon sergeants over for dinner and it wouldn't hurt their stature as officers one bit. I told them that the old saying "Familiarity breeds contempt" was a load of hogwash, because talking to their enlisted leaders establishes rapport.

I gave them an example of what I meant. I told them I'd been to the Chief of Staff's home on several occasions, for dinner. "I enjoyed it, had a good time, but that doesn't mean the next morning I went into his office and said, 'Hey, Bernie . . .' And your platoon sergeant won't do that either. He may even have *you* over

---

*Now retired, Colonel Summers is a syndicated newspaper columnist, editor of *Vietnam* magazine, author of *On Strategy: The Vietnam War in Context*, and other books.

**A small balcony in the cadet mess hall that resembles the afterdeck of an eighteenth-century sailing ship. From his position there the brigade adjutant issues orders to the cadets at mealtimes. At least as early as 1910 the cadets were referring to material for memorization as "poop." The meaning spread from there to the entire Army and eventually entered the American slang lexicon as "information," particularly official and inside.

for dinner." I told them what they had to remember was that their platoon sergeant had been leading soldiers since before they ever went to West Point, because he'd have twelve to fifteen years of service, and they shouldn't walk in and say, "Okay, I'm taking over this platoon." I told them to talk to the sergeant, find out what the platoon needed, what the two of them could do to fix things. "When the platoon's ready to be turned over to you," I told them, "the first guy to walk up and say, 'It's all yours, sir,' will be that platoon sergeant."

I also told them that the Chief of Staff could tell them who his first platoon sergeant was, but probably didn't remember one goddamn thing about his first company commander.

They do not get enough of this at West Point. They need more noncommissioned officer involvement. They need to find out what the Army's really all about. It isn't West Point. I think West Point is the greatest military institution in the world, but you have to be practical, and having noncommissioned officers on the faculty would introduce that practicality.

General Rogers wanted to put a command sergeant major into each of the cadet brigades at West Point. The commandant up there already had a CSM on his staff, but we were going to put one in all the brigades. We had outstanding men nominated for those positions, the action had been directed by the Chief of Staff, and the assistant deputy chief of staff for personnel, General Kingston, was the action officer on the project. The men were assigned. The program continued for a year or eighteen months. Then it finally met its demise, and that was because it was not supported at West Point the way it was supposed to have been.

Those sergeants major were assigned there to provide the cadets some realistic input to their training from the noncommissioned officer's viewpoint. An "old grad," a retired colonel living in California, wrote to the commandant and wanted to know what "this sergeant" was doing in his son's quarters at West Point. He was of the opinion that no noncommissioned officer should be permitted to go into a cadet's quarters. That was typical of the attitude toward senior noncommissioned officers in the tactical department at the Military Academy.

Some of the commissioned officers serving as cadet brigade commanders did support the idea, but others did not, and when I visited there and talked to the sergeants major, that became apparent to me. When I took the matter up with the commandant, he assured me that the program was being fully supported by the brigade commanders. I asked how that could be the case when in at least one of the brigades the CSM assigned there was not permitted to enter the cadets' rooms. I told him the program had to be implemented all the way across the board or it would fail. And it did.

I don't recall that particular commandant's name, but the fact is, he did not support the idea. He never grasped the importance of noncommissioned affiliation in the training program at West Point. He later retired from the Army because he was displeased with the assignment offered to him after his tenure at the Military Academy. In my opinion, that tells it all.

I think each SMA should go to West Point—as well as other places where officers congregate—to speak to the cadets. These days, the SMA gives his viewpoint to the four-star commanders' conference. I think that's great. When I was SMA, I talked to the "Charm Course," when the colonels selected for promotion to brigadier general are brought to town to find out how to act as generals.

There's an amusing story I once heard about the Charm Course. It was told to Gen. William Rosson when we were on the plane returning from Korea by Gen. Edward L. Rowney, I Corps commander. He told us that the distinction between how a colonel acts and how a brigadier acts is that when you're a colonel and a subordinate tells you something you don't agree with, you tell him, "Horseshit!" But when you're a general officer, you say, "Incredible!"

General Rosson turned to me and winked. "Well, I didn't get that part of the course." General Rowney was the kind of person who wouldn't say "garbage" if he had a mouthful of it. "I really believe if you want to get your point across," General Rosson continued, "saying *'Horseshit!'* is one way to do it."

General Rowney replied, "Yes, sir, yes, sir, you may be right!"

In the fall of 1977 I made a trip to the West Coast to visit the Army Reserve Commands (ARCOMS), everything west of the Mississippi. In the spring of 1978, my tour as SMA was due to expire. In November 1977, before leaving on that trip to the ARCOMS, I briefed General Rogers on the process to select my replacement. I anticipated that by the time I returned in mid-December, we'd actually be into the screening process and he'd have the names from which to select the next SMA by the following April.

It happened at this time that my mother had taken a fall while shopping and broken her arm badly. I was scheduled to pass through Chicago on this trip, so I decided to go out on a Friday evening and spend that weekend with her. I could take a little commuter line out of Chicago that served Galesburg.

That Monday morning I was coming back through O'Hare with an hour-and-a-half delay before my flight to San Antonio, so I called the office. Sam answered the phone and said, "You got my message, Top?" No, I said, and asked what message. "I've called every doggone airline that services O'Hare to page you, because General Rogers wants to talk with you."

He transferred me over to the Chief's executive officer, who told me, yes, General Rogers wanted to talk to me, but at the moment he was "indisposed"—could he call me back in fifteen or twenty minutes?

I gave him the number of the telephone at the airport, and in about ten minutes it rang.

General Rogers came on the telephone and asked, "Sergeant Major, where are you?" I told him I was at O'Hare. "Listen," he went on, "I've decided who your replacement is going to be."

I replied, "Damn, that's quick, sir! You're not going to have a board or anything?"

"No, no, what I've decided to do is to ask you if *you* would like to spend another year as SMA. Before you answer, though, tell me—do you know anybody out there who'll get all hacked off if I extend your tour like this?"

I told him I didn't, although that didn't mean there weren't a lot of people in the Army who'd like the job. General Rogers said he'd talked to some of the Army commanders since I'd left and hadn't found anyone who objected to the suggestion, so he wanted me to stay on for another year. I agreed. He asked me not to say anything until he made the official announcement.

I spent the next two weeks traveling, and everywhere I went, all the sergeants major and their commanders wanted to know who I thought the next SMA was going to be. I had to say I didn't know, and that wasn't actually a fib, because I didn't know who'd replace me after the year's extension was up.

Up to that time, I'd only told Sam and Hazel, and while I was at Dugway Proving Ground, Utah, I had a premonition that I should call back to the office because I'd suddenly made up my mind I had to tell Raylene Scott too. She needed to know. I asked for a secure telephone line so nobody could eavesdrop on my conversation and got her on the line.

"Raylene, are you in the outer office?"

"Yes, I am."

"Put me on hold, go into my office, and shut the door," I told her. I wanted her to do that because I anticipated a slight reaction over the news of my extension, and while I knew Ray was fully capable of keeping it a secret, I just didn't want to take the chance anybody would see her react to the news and start to speculate.

I told her what General Rogers and I had agreed to, and she started laughing and crying at the same time.

"Are you okay, Ray?" I asked after a moment.

"Yes, Sergeant Major, but you must be psychic! I was going down to personnel today to submit my resignation. I just don't want to break in another Sergeant Major of the Army. I want to leave when you do."

"You aren't going to put it in now, Raylene?"

"No, of course I'm not!" she replied.

That was to be the first time anybody had served a four-year tour as SMA, and I considered that another highlight of my career. I'd been selected by General Weyand to serve a two-year tour, and he'd changed the regulation to make the SMA's tour three years. When General Rogers became Chief of Staff, he could have selected anybody he wanted to fill the job, but he asked me to stay on, which made me very proud.

As I've noted, General Rogers and I had a very good relationship, and his door was always open to me. Only once did I have a problem getting in to see him about something, and that was when Carl Vuono, then a full colonel, and later Chief of Staff of the Army himself, was General Rogers's executive officer. One day I asked to see the Chief about a matter that was really pressing, and Colonel Vuono told me there was really no way he could get me in there at the moment.

"Wait a minute, sir," I said. "You know I'm supposed to be able to go in there anytime I want, and I don't come over here unless it's really necessary to see him. I've *got* to see him now."

He said, well, he just couldn't get me in there now.

I looked at my watch and asked when General Rogers would be going home that evening.

"About six o'clock," he answered.

"Okay, would you get a message into him that I'm going to ride home with him? I'll talk to him on the way home, since I can't get in to see him this afternoon."

Colonel Vuono looked at me for a second, then said, "Goddammit, I'll get you in there! Just a minute!"

The matter I wanted to see General Rogers about involved a sergeant major assigned to Fort Devens, Massachusetts, who'd asked for Devens and then decided he wanted an airborne unit instead. This guy had decided to pull an end run on the assignment system and he'd worked up a deal to have his original orders revoked. I'd already talked to Ray Martin, Forces Command sergeant major, and he'd talked to his boss, Gen. Fritz Kroesen, who'd agreed to stop the man's maneuver. I needed to brief General Rogers in case the matter escalated and he got into it through some other channel.

Another executive officer was Col. Victor Hugo, a great friend of the soldier, as I've noted before. I never had any problem getting in to see the Chief when he was around. I never had any problem with Colonel Vuono after that one time either.

One day somebody was having a birthday and they were having cake and coffee in the Chief's outer office. I walked across to see what was going on, and Colonel Hugo offered me a piece of the cake. It was the typical military cake, with butter-cream icing, as much icing as cake. Having been associated with the food service school, I knew how butter-cream icing was made, so I didn't eat too much of it. Anyway, as I was standing there talking to Colonel Hugo and eating my cake, some of the frosting fell to the floor. I didn't notice it, and when I moved my foot I stepped in it. Colonel Hugo said, "Lookee there, Sergeant Major, not only do you drop your frosting on the floor, you step in it!"

"My God, how'd I do that?"

"*That's* why we don't let you guys into the officers' club!"

Well, some time after that incident, somebody got promoted and we had another little reception over in the Chief's office, and as Providence would have it, Colonel Hugo dropped a piece of his cake on the floor—and stepped on it. "Well," I told him, "that's the reason we don't let some folks into the NCO club."

"*Touché,* Sergeant Major!" he replied.

We had some good people up there. The fixture in the Chief's office was Margaret Norris, his confidential secretary, who has since retired. Margaret wasn't any bigger than a minute, but she was a great lady, and I always enjoyed talking to her whenever I went into that office.

There were a couple of notable exceptions, who will remain nameless. One was a guy who worked for General Rogers and who was the "Fort Polk of the Human Race"—if the good Lord wanted to give the human race an enema, he'd put the tube in at Fort Polk. Apropos of nothing, this guy had once been an enlisted man.

One of the things we started at this time was replacing commissioned action officers on the staff with noncommissioned officers. A notable example of this was SFC Gary Rice, who is now living at the Soldiers' and Airmen's Home. He was one of the first action NCOs in the Chief of Staff's office. He was one of the first NCOs in history to be awarded the Army General Staff Identification Badge, or the "Liver Patch," as it was called, because it's worn on the right breast pocket, just above the liver. It's quite a prestigious award for an officer, because it recognizes service as an action officer on the Army General Staff and it's awarded based on successful performance of duty of not less than one year on the staff. It's also quite a nice-looking device, a spread eagle mounted on a five-pointed star superimposed on laurel leaves. Once awarded, it can be worn as a permanent part of a soldier's uniform.

There was a great battle over awarding that badge to enlisted folks. Since it had first been created in 1920, it had been given to officers exclusively, and there were a few people who didn't want to see that changed, but bigger minds prevailed, and Gary Rice was one of the first NCOs to get one. That kind of recognition for enlisted people who'd served on the Army Staff was a great morale-builder and took nothing away from the officers. I got one too, but after I had retired. Gen. John McGiffert, the director of the Army Staff at the time, presented it to me in his office at a ceremony attended by Hazel, my bride of some fifty years.

We also got enlisted action NCOs in the Secretary of the Army's Office. M/Sgt., later Sgt. Maj., Jim Hughes was the first one assigned there. He went from the DCSPER to the assistant secretary of the Army for manpower and Reserve Affairs (Robert Nelson at that time). Later another notable who was assigned there was my esteemed buddy Sam Walsh. He went down there as a master sergeant, and his boss was Mr. Harry Walters.

Sam was promoted to sergeant major while in that job, and I recall what Mr. Walters said on that occasion: "There are a lot of folks in the Army who get promoted and we get a chance to pin on bars and stars and all that, but today we get to promote a master sergeant to sergeant major. I want to tell you, Sam Walsh is a Category I sergeant major. What that means is, he's as smart as hell."

Mr. Walters was not just making an idle compliment when he said that. He later became administrator of the Veterans Administration, and he saw fit to take Sam with him as his special assistant for veterans' services organizations. He was still on active duty, on "loan" to the VA, and he filled a job that previously had been held by a GS-15. Sam retired from that position. Soon after he was hired at a very lucrative salary to be an officer in a credit union based in San Antonio, Texas. Today he works for the VA in Pittsburgh, PA, back helping soldiers, the thing he's always been best at.

As Sergeant Major of the Army I sat on the board of commissioners for the U.S. Soldiers' and Airmen's Home (USSAH), as did the Chief Master Sergeant of the Air Force, and some time before my retirement a story in the *Army Times* claimed that general Ferdinand Unger, commissioner of the Soldiers' and Airmen's Home, had said that a Chief Master Sergeant of the Air Force could never be governor of the Home because he didn't have the training and experience for the job. Whether he actually said that or not, he did send a letter of apology to me and Bob Gaylor, who was the Chief Master Sergeant of the Air Force at the time. When this subject came up at a meeting of the Home's board of commissioners, Bob said, "The least you could have done, General Unger, was to pick on your own service."

The upshot of all this was that the Judge Advocate General of the Air Force looked into whether or not the law required that only officers be appointed to positions at the Home. I sat on the ad hoc committee, and the decision was that there was nothing in the statutes that specified only retired officers could be appointed to those positions. That may be one of the reasons I got a chance to apply for the job of secretary to the board of commissioners that was to become vacant before my retirement.

While I was on the board of commissioners, the subject of bequests to the Home came up. From time to time, residents out there would leave their entire estate to the Home in their wills. These were people with no immediate families, and the Home accepted that money and deposited it in the trust fund.

One day an out-of-session paper came through proposing that everyone living at the Home who was eligible for burial at Arlington National Cemetery should be interred there, to save the spaces in the Home's National Cemetery. The place was running out of gravesites, and as many as could be were encouraged to have their families put them into Arlington, but some of them insisted on burial at the Home.

I called General Unger and told him I took exception to this proposal. "You just told us a couple of months ago about all these people who give their money to the Home, and now you want to tell them that when they die they can't be buried at the last and just maybe the only real home they ever had?"

He replied that the Home was running out of space in the cemetery. Who cares? I wanted to know. Sooner or later we'd run out of space anyway. I suggested plowing up the roads to get more gravesites, plow up the golf course if necessary, before taking that privilege away from those members who wanted to be buried in the USSAH cemetery.

I talked to Tom Barnes, who was Chief Master Sergeant of the Air Force at the time, and he agreed with me. At the next meeting, Tom and I were the only two who voted against that proposal. The board of commissioners then consisted of representatives from the DCSPER of the Air Force, the Air Force Judge Advocate General, the Chief of the Army Engineers, the Army Surgeon General, the Army Adjutant General, the chairman, and us two enlisted people. They all voted for the proposal except Tom and me.

General Unger said after the vote, "Well, why are you against this?"

I said, "I've already told you that, and I am prepared to take this to the Chief of Staff of the Army, if necessary. I just don't think it's right."

General Unger said, "We've always managed to have unanimous votes on this board."

I replied, "You ain't gonna get it on this one."

Tom Barnes spoke up and said, "That's right."

So they went back to the drawing board, and that proposal was never approved.

Incidentally, we now have a retired sergeant major, Bob Brown, who runs that cemetery, so it isn't too hard to get things done right out there.

I was selected to be secretary to the board of commissioners about three months before I retired from the Army. Although that's a Civil Service job, it's an "excepted" position in that it is not filled through Civil Service competition but by appointment. It was a GS-12 position when I was appointed.*

*At that time the Civil Service grade of GS-12 was paid at the rate of $11.10 per hour or $23,087 per annum, approximately equivalent then to the base pay of a lieutenant colonel with over eighteen years of service. The basic pay for the Sergeant Major of the Army then was $1,652.10 per month. When I retired from the Civil Service twelve years later as a GS-15, step 6, I was earning $71,918 a year, equivalent to the base pay of a brigadier general with over sixteen years of ser-

* * *

Two accomplishments as Sergeant Major of the Army I was particularly proud of had to do with the training and preparation of soldiers as NCOs.

I had been against having the MOS test—proficiency test—for command sergeants major for some time. By the time I got to be SMA, there was a well-established progression all the way up to CSM, and how long could the Army continue to have the person who'd made it that far continue to go to school or take tests to prove his worth? How long could you make a schoolboy out of these people? By the time a soldier makes CSM, he or she is only about six years from retirement anyway, and the formal training process should be complete.

TRADOC definitely wanted to continue the CSM testing. At my first command sergeants major conference I told John LaVoie, TRADOC CSM, that we were going to get rid of it. John was dead set against that. "No," he told me, "that's our business down at TRADOC, and we need to continue testing these guys to keep them sharp, and we as CSMs can't require other NCOs to be tested if we're not tested ourselves."

"John," I told him, "that goes right back to the quarters business. There're no staff sergeants hollering because you've got a good set of quarters. What he's saying is, 'When I get to be a command sergeant major, *I'll* get a set of quarters like that.' The same thing with MOS tests. He's going to say, 'Okay, when I get to be a CSM, I'll have proved myself and I'm not gonna have to take that test anymore.' "

Well, this was one of those few matters I had to take to the Chief of Staff, General Weyand at that time. He proposed that we not tell TRADOC we were going to do away with the testing. "What we will tell them," he said, "is to justify to us why we still have to do it."

I worked with the DCSPER and we asked TRADOC to justify that testing program. They didn't do that to General Weyand's satisfaction, and he approved discontinuing the testing for CSMs.

vice. In 1984, I opted for inclusion in the Civil Service Retirement System. To be eligible as a military retiree, I was required to pay into the CSRS 7 percent of all the pay ($204,237) I had earned as a soldier after January 1, 1957—$14,269.53. This entitles me today to a Civil Service annuity of approximately $4,100 a month, $1,000 a month more than an active duty sergeant major with over twenty-six years of service was paid in 1992.

In November 1975, the Military Personnel Center sent to the CSA an efficiency report to be filled out on me. Sam Walsh held the thing about a week and then sent it to the Chief. It sat there about two days, then came back with a note on it to the MILPERCEN commander, copy to us. General Weyand reminded him we'd already taken steps to eliminate the CSM MOS testing. He continued, "And it appears to me that since Sergeant Major Bainbridge has been selected to be the Sergeant Major of the Army, now might be a good time to discontinue his efficiency reports. I think he's passed the test up to this point. From this day forward there will be no more efficiency reports written on the Sergeant Major of the Army."

Little things like efficiency reports seem to have a life of their own simply because they've always been there, even when there isn't any reason for them to continue to exist.

My contribution as SMA, I believe, is that I was responsible in part for the strengthening of the Noncommissioned Officer Education System and for the programs associated with that system. That was because of my commitment to soldiers and their training. I believe I made a difference.

An example of that commitment is that one day an action officer out of the DCSPER came to my office with a sheaf of papers about an inch and a half thick proposing that the requirement for a high school diploma or GED be temporarily waived in order to have more sergeants "eligible" for promotion to staff sergeant. We'd fought like hell to get education and Army schooling as a major consideration for promotion, and here was an action officer from the DCSPER preparing an action to *remove* that requirement for a year or eighteen months.

"Wait a minute," I said. "Do you mean to tell me that after all the trouble we've had getting that education requirement in place, now you're going to regress? What's gonna happen when you get ready to promote that staff sergeant to sergeant first class? Are you going to give him *another* waiver on the requirement to have a high school diploma?" I told him that guy would go all the way to sergeant major without a high school equivalency, because once he got by staff sergeant he'd go right on up to the top—waiver, waiver, waiver.

"Well," he responded, "we'll give him constructive credit." Whatever the hell that is! I told him he wanted to promote mediocrity, and he wouldn't get my approval on his paper. Without it, that paper would be dead in the water.

I asked him if he'd ever heard of ACB-3. Right after the Korean War, we had a mandatory reduction in the size of the Army and if a soldier didn't have three scores over 90 on the Army Classification Battery tests (thus the name ACB-3), plus fifteen or more years of service, he was gone. The result of that was that we had a lot of mess sergeants, motor sergeants, and platoon sergeants, people who had been doing one hell of a job since they came in the Army in World War II, now being arbitrarily put out of the Army because of low test scores, even though the Army had done nothing to help them improve them through school, training, or re-testing.

. I told him how I and thousands of others during World War II rode the train to Camp Grant, Illinois, or some other processing station, got four or five shots in the morning, and then took tests up until three in the afternoon. I was fortunate enough to score well, since I was just three weeks out of high school. Many never made the grade. If there had been better planning, those soldiers would have done much better. Now this lieutenant colonel wanted to pull an old ACB-3 by waiving a high school education for pro-motion to staff sergeant. My philosophy, I told him, was that if that guy couldn't get at least a high school GED by the time he was up for promotion to staff sergeant, then I didn't want him to get promoted. There's no soldier who doesn't have the time to take that high school GED and pass it.

He folded up his papers and said, "Sergeant Major, don't worry about this proposal going across the hall."

I mentioned Sgt. Maj. Rodney Southpaw, at the Sergeants Major Academy. I was to run into him again when I was the SMA. I'd advised him at Fort Bliss not to return to Special Forces from the academy, but to serve in a line unit for the experience and then re-turn to Special Forces. I told him that would enhance his chances of getting picked for CSM. Rodney chose to ignore my advice at the time.

Rodney was not selected for CSM the first two times he was eligible. The second time, he was stationed down in Panama. I happened to be there on a visit, and he asked if he could talk to me about it. "I cannot, for the life of me, figure why I wasn't se-lected," he said.

"Remember our conversation back at the academy?" I asked him. "That's the first reason you weren't picked. The second time around it was the same reason. You're not gonna make it, Rod-ney."

He asked if there was anything I could do to help him.

"There *was*," I told him, "at Fort Bliss. But you chose not to take my advice seriously, so there's nothing I can do to help you now. You've put your record before the rest of 'em, and you didn't stack up."

Rodney came to see me just before my retirement. He was in an ROTC assignment someplace up in Maryland. He came by the office with the same problem—he wanted to talk about CSM again. This time he brought with him his former Special Forces A-Team commander, a lieutenant colonel, who was assigned to the Pentagon at that time. I gave them the same answer: "You screwed up, Rodney, when you left the Sergeants Major Academy. You've been in Special Forces all your career," I told him, "and you just don't stack up against your contemporaries. In SF, when you get somebody who doesn't work out, you fire him and he goes to some line unit where some first sergeant's got to deal with him. They're in the real world."

I told him I didn't have anything against Special Forces, but I pointed out that they got the best the Army had to offer, so how could he stack up against the sergeant major who's out in the Army, dealing with the everyday problems of soldiers?

The colonel came into the conversation and said, "Wait a minute. I've been associated with Special Forces for a long time now. Are you telling me I'm not going to make full colonel or get a brigade command?"

"You're the one who said that, Colonel," I replied, "but that's right. You don't stack up either." He never did make full colonel.

Talk about stacking up, I mentioned previously that Sgt. Maj. Bill Connelly hosted a conference in San Francisco, which I was invited to attend. I was on my way back from a trip to the Western Pacific at the time. We went to dinner one night with the Connellys, and goddamn, it was cold! We had on clothes fit for Hawaii, not for that San Francisco wind. We almost froze our fannies off.

Anyway, a sergeant major from Fort Bragg, North Carolina, who had not been selected for retention beyond thirty years of service, was also at the conference, and he said he wanted to talk to me about his problem. As a sergeant major, while he was stationed at Bragg, he'd swung a deal to attend Bootstrap,* even though CSMs weren't authorized to enroll. After completing his

---

*A program that allowed selected officers and noncommissioned officers to attend various civilian colleges and complete work on an academic degree.

degree, he returned to Bragg. But he wasn't selected to be retained on active duty for thirty-five years.

I explained to him that since the selection board had already met and announced its decision, there was nothing he could do about it. I pointed out that inasmuch as those boards were picking only five people at a time, it was a very select group, and obviously he hadn't managed to measure up.

He said, "Sergeant Major, I'll put my record up against anybody in the Army!"

I told him, "You just did, and you didn't make it." End of conversation.

This guy had been a hell-raiser in his early career and then finally got religion, and what he'd forgotten was that *all* his service record, not just the last few years, counted. That program was intended to pick a few very outstanding soldiers who could do something for the Army if kept on beyond thirty years. It has expanded since then. Neither that program nor the CSM program was intended to be an ego trip.

But if soldiers don't want to serve in the position of CSM, then they should withdraw their names from consideration. And once a person's selected, there should be no withdrawal. The argument against that was, well, he or she won't do a good job. That's bull. Of course anyone selected will do a good job, because if you don't do your job the Army's got all kinds of ways to adjust that attitude.

When my time came to retire, I was ready. I went out on July 1, 1979, four days shy of thirty-one years in the Army. General Rogers had commented that as SMA I wasn't eligible for consideration for retention in the Army beyond thirty years, as was the case with other CSMs. However, I was already beyond thirty at that time, because General Rogers had chosen to keep me on that extra year. But I told him that my getting permission to stay thirty-five years wouldn't help the Army or me. I believed that the only course for me was retirement.

Anyway, where would they have sent me, after I'd been the SMA for four years? That would not have been fair to me or to the commander who got me. Somebody out in the field was bound to ask what I was doing out there after being the Sergeant Major of the Army. Even though I would never have done it, people would have thought I'd be second-guessing them all the time.

But in July 1979, I thought it was time for me to go, and go I did.

I left the Army with mixed emotions. I like to tell the story that one day I was walking down the stairs into the basement at my quarters and I heard something going "bump, bump, bump" behind me as I descended and when I turned around I saw that it was my rear end dragging. Here I'd been in the job four years, more than half the time traveling all over the world, and it had sneaked up on me. I was worn out.

About that time I was making my final trip to Europe and was visiting the 21st Support Command. Sgt. Maj. Ted Spellacy was the CSM of that unit. Because we were traveling to another unit that day, we were having breakfast early in the mess hall, before the troops came in, and as we went through the serving line a young specialist who was serving asked me what I wanted for breakfast. I asked for SOS,* one egg over easy on top, and a dollop of peanut butter.

He looked at me for a moment and then said, "Will creamed beef on toast do?"

I told him that would be fine, then turned to Ted and said, "It's time for me to get out of the Army when a SP5 cook in the mess hall doesn't know what SOS is!"

I was ready to go. I had already been selected to be the secretary to the board of commissioners at the Soldiers' and Airmen's Home. We'd already moved into quarters on the grounds out at the Home, so I was more than ready for new challenges.

At my retirement review on Summerall Field at Fort Myer, Monday, June 18, 1979, General Rogers made some remarks, one of which was that in more than seventeen of my thirty-one years in the Army, I'd been the senior noncommissioned officer in every unit to which I'd been assigned.

I told those soldiers assembled there that for the first time the Chief of Staff of the Army and the Sergeant Major of the Army who would succeed General Rogers and me were coming into those positions without any World War II experience. That meant the beginning of a new era, a divide between what had been going on in the Army since 1945. I wound my speech up like this: .

As Americans we don't usually pay much attention to history, but my charge to you today is to remember the lessons that my generation learned the hard way on the battlefields of World War II. Although we may be leaving active duty, our ex-

*Shit on a shingle, i.e., creamed beef on toast.

perience remains in the military textbooks and the military histories. Take advantage of it. God forbid, you may need it.

In closing, I want to give my heartfelt thanks to all who gave this Illinois farm boy—a farm boy, I must admit, some thirty years removed—a chance to serve our great nation. Thank you to the officers under whom I've been privileged to serve. Thank you to the corps of noncommissioned officers for welcoming me into your ranks and showing me what professionalism is all about. Thank you to our soldiers—America's sons and daughters—who make this Army what it is. Thank you to the dedicated professional civilians for your support and assistance. I salute you!

Hazel and I departed the reviewing stands through a cordon composed of all the major command sergeants major and stepped into the "marriage carriage," a horse-drawn two-passenger carriage like a brougham or a coupé that took us for a ritual last spin around the post and back to the service club, where my retirement reception was held.

So ended my thirty-one years of service to this country as a soldier.

≡ 13 ≡

SIXTY-FIVE-YEAR-OLD SQUAD LEADERS

Until the United States Soldiers' Home was established, disabled men of the Regular Army were "cast adrift with a tiny pension, or none at all, dependent on uncertain charity."* In 1851, Jefferson Davis, then a United States senator, introduced legislation to establish an "asylum" for "every discharged soldier, whether regular or volunteer, who shall have suffered by reason of disease or wounds incurred in the service and in the line of his duty, rendering him incapable of further military service." The legislation was approved on March 3, 1851.

The original funding for the Home's operation came from a draft for $118,000, part of the tribute levied on Mexico City in lieu of pillage by Gen. Winfield Scott after his army captured the city in 1847, during the Mexican War. To this was added $54,000, the unexpended portion of a fund set up to return wounded and disabled veterans of the war to their homes. Aside from this $54,000 sum, no taxpayer money has ever been used to support the Home.

The Home is supported today by deductions from the monthly pay of enlisted men and women and warrant officers of the Armed Forces; by fines and forfeitures deducted from the pay of military personnel; by the collection of a monthly user fee from the members of the Home; by gifts and bequests; and by the interest on a trust fund administered by the Secretary of the Treasury. The trust fund contains approximately $200 million, and because expenditures have been running somewhat behind the money coming in recently, the value of the fund has remained fairly constant these last few years.

*Paul R. Goode, *The United States Soldiers' Home: A History of Its First Hundred Years* (Richmond, Va.: Privately published, 1957).

The name of the institution was originally the Military Asylum, then the U.S. Soldiers' Home, then until recently the United States Soldiers' and Airmen's Home. The Armed Forces Retirement Home Act of 1991 incorporated the U.S. Soldiers' and Airmen's Home and the Naval Home into one institution, the Armed Forces Retirement Home, with a Navy Branch at Gulfport, Mississippi, and a Soldiers' and Airmen's Branch in the District of Columbia.

The legislation also changed the eligibility requirements for membership in the Home. The following persons who served as members of the armed forces, at least half of whose service was "not active commissioned service," are eligible: (1) persons who are sixty years of age or over and were discharged or released from service under honorable conditions after twenty or more years; (2) persons incapable of earning a livelihood because of a service-connected disability incurred in the line of duty; (3) those who served in a war theater during a time of declared war or who were eligible for hostile fire special pay, were discharged under honorable conditions, and are determined to be incapable of earning a livelihood because of injuries, disease, or disability; and (4) persons who served in a women's component of the armed forces before 1948 and whom the Home Board determines to be eligible "because of compelling personal circumstances."

Originally consisting of about two hundred acres of land that was once part of the George W. Riggs estate, and expanded in later years to over five hundred acres, today the Home occupies three hundred acres across North Capitol Street from Catholic University in the northwestern suburbs of the District of Columbia. Over the years, some two hundred acres of Home property were given to the District of Columbia to widen or extend roads and to build the Veterans Medical Center and the Washington Hospital Center/Children's Hospital, which lie just to the south of the main grounds on the west side of North Capitol Street.

When I left there in July 1991 there were 1,950 residents at the Home, but there were eighty-odd individuals in the process of being admitted, so the total population for which the Home was required to have beds through August 1991 was over two thousand. The oldest member at that time was ninety-nine, a World War II WAAC.* On average, the women who served during World War II were older than the men. The average age of the male residents was sixty-nine, which put the average member in the Army four

---

*A member of the Women's Army Auxiliary Corps. Established in May 1942, the WAAC was redesignated the Women's Army Corps (WAC) in July 1943.

years before me. When I came in the Army I was eighteen, so these guys would have been twenty-two and the gals twenty-six. The average age for the ninety-odd female members at that time was seventy-three.

In October 1990 we lost our then oldest member, a World War II engineer by the name of Horatio Stoner. He missed his 104th birthday by about a week. He didn't come into the Home until he was one hundred. He had been living in Alexandria, Virginia, in his own apartment, but his daughter got a little concerned about him, although he was still driving his own car and doing his own cooking. He was a remarkable man. He worked in the woodworking shop, making little pencil boxes, until his 103rd birthday. That's what kept him going.

The grounds at the Home are one of the quietest and most beautiful places in the District of Columbia, certainly one of the most beautiful places Hazel and I have ever lived. It is also the place where we have lived longest. When we moved there in 1979 to assume my new civilian job as secretary to the board of commissioners, hardly did we realize it would be our home for the next dozen years.

It was my job as the secretary to the board of commissioners to support the board in and out of sessions and also the governor of the Home, Lt. Gen. George McKee (USAF, Retired). I was an officer of the Home, and was the first former enlisted person ever to hold such a position. As I mentioned earlier, when I was Sergeant Major of the Army, we'd determined that the law merely stipulated that the officers of the Home be retired from the Army or the Air Force; nothing barred former enlisted people from holding such positions.

I arranged the quarterly meetings for the board of commissioners, made sure there was a conference room at the Pentagon to hold each session, notified all the principals when the meetings would be held, kept the minutes, and so on. One of the problems was scheduling the meetings so everybody could attend, and I had to make sure they were all notified as much in advance as possible, so they could get the dates on their calendars.

Once the board was in session, I kept the minutes, circulating them later as a record of the proceedings. As happens with all such bodies, I always had to send everyone a copy of the last session's minutes before the next meeting, because invariably somebody would misplace them or forget to bring them to the sessions. I reported to the board the events that had happened at the Home during the preceding quarter, told them the status of the Trust Fund, including the interest rates, which changed from quarter to quarter, reported on our budget, and summarized the status of admissions and discharges and dismissals. I had to report twice a year on "temporary members," or those admitted to the Home who did not have twenty years or more of service or were under fifty years of age (at that time there was no mandatory age for eligibility). Each April and November they had to be "reboarded" to determine if they were still eligible to stay at the Home or were again able to earn a livelihood, in which case they had to be discharged.

Determining eligibility for membership was also one of my tasks. I had an office staff assisting me in this, and all of them were members of the Home. My applications examiner was a retired Air Force master sergeant by the name of Lucien Bilodeau. In the twelve years I was the secretary of the board and later director of member services and responsible for admissions, Mr. Bilodeau never made a single mistake in reviewing anyone's record to determine eligibility.

The only time he missed one, it wasn't his fault. That case involved a veteran of the Philippine Scouts, who are specifically forbidden membership in the Home by federal statute. The veteran himself was unaware of this restriction when he applied, and when we verified his service with the National Personnel Records Center they neglected to inform us that he had a PS—Philippine Scouts—prefix to his Army Serial Number. It was the Veterans Administration that confirmed his PS status, but we took that man anyway, because he had traveled all the way from the West Coast to report, and we felt the mistake was an honest one on the part of the record-keeping folks at St. Louis. Since he was already there, it wouldn't have been fair to make him go all the way back to the West Coast. So I recommended to General McKee that we keep him, and the general agreed. He was still there when I retired in the summer of 1991.

During my years at the Home, we averaged one person a day coming in and going out, so we stayed pretty even. Members went out by taking a discharge, dying, or being dismissed. Most of the losses were from deaths and discharges, very few because of dismissals.

I was secretary for the first two and a half years of my employment at the Home, and that job included all the specific duties I've described as well as anything else the governor directed.

I mentioned my duties in connection with determining admission eligibility. In my office we had admissions files that dated back over a century. When I took over the job I asked why we were keeping them that long and was told they were "permanent" records. My opinion was that the official personnel records of those folks were in St. Louis, so I checked into it. I found out that at one time we had been retiring individual members' records to the National Archives, which had finally refused to take them anymore because it had also concluded that the permanent records on those soldiers and airmen were at the National Personnel Records Center. What we had were records that belonged to the Home, not in the individual's military personnel file.

I convinced the governor there was no need to keep all those records back that far—those people weren't going to show up and request readmission. So we wrote a new regulation stipulating that admissions records would be kept up to the eighty-fifth birthday of the individual concerned and then destroyed. We kept the Statement of Service, which is required to reconstitute a record of that type, up to the individual's hundredth birthday. That proved to be a wise decision, because afterward we did have one individual who, in his late nineties, reapplied for admission about forty-five years after he was discharged from the Home. So far nobody over one hundred has ever reapplied, and if anyone ever does, well, they can start *him* all over again.

This may all seem like the most mundane office paperwork routine, but there's a point to the story. All my life I've run into this situation time and time again. Otherwise very good people just fall into a rut and commit themselves to doing the dumbest things simply because no one has ever asked, "Why do we have to do it this way?"

We had a lot of history in that office. There was at one time a gentleman named Holmgren, the senior member by age, and I was looking at his record one day when I noticed that he had come into the Army in April 1897, the year of my father's birth. Mr. Holmgren didn't apply for admission to the Home until he was eighty. He'd served in the Army for over twenty years, and then when he got out he'd run a chain of health spas. After he retired from that line he spent the last ten or fifteen years of his life at the Home. He passed away at the age of 102. We always used to have him on the reviewing stand for the Founder's Day celebrations, sleeping through it all but still up there, collecting his due.

In 1982 the Home staff was reorganized. The last reorganization had been sixty years before, when the Home had begun operating,

much like the Army of the day, under the departmental concept—
Quartermaster Department, Health Care Department, and so on. In
1982 we reorganized under the directorate concept. We then had
a Director of Health Care Services, Director of Logistics, Director
of Administration, and so on. The secretary to the board of commissioners job became a "second hat" worn by the Director of
Adminstration, and a new directorate was formed, Member Services, and I became its first director. The secretary job was taken
over by Col. Robert Hampton, who was also Director of Administration. The deputy governor became deputy governor/chief of
staff, and where before we'd all reported straight to the governor,
we now went through the DG/CofS. This turned out to be a very
efficient arrangement.

The DG/CofS transferred his responsibility for the dining room/
mess hall to the Director of Logistics. I kept the admissions function and took over security, special services, housing, and
housekeeping. We took 'em in, housed 'em, entertained 'em, kept
the common areas clean, and provided their security under Member Services. The chaplaincy also fell under my jurisdiction.

The admissions process worked this way. When an individual
applied for admission to the Home, the applications examiner determined the applicant's eligibility. I signed the verification and
sent it to the Director of Health Care Services, who determined
whether or not we had the capability of taking care of that person.
Sometimes we just couldn't provide the service required, and we
knew it was unfair to accept an individual whom we could not
properly care for. The regulations required that one other director
review the application and concur. Approving admissions was
under the direct authority of the board of commissioners, but it
had been delegated to the governor and further delegated to Director of Member Services.

If there was a divergence of opinion during this process, the application was sent to the rest of the officers before a determination
was made. If necessary, final action could be referred to the
governor, but I only went to him if we needed a deciding vote. I
can remember maybe five cases that had to go that far during the
dozen years I had that job.

I sent the letters of notification to report to the Home out of my
office, and approved applicants were given ninety days to report.
In cases where applications were turned down for some reason, I
informed the applicants of the reasons why, and normally they
took it well, because by the time we completed a review, there
was just no question that we could not admit the applicant.

For instance, we simply could not handle certain types of psychiatric disabilities, because our medical staff didn't have the proper facilities. Incidentally, the new legislation specifically prohibits the Home from accepting applicants with alcohol, drug, or psychiatric problems. There are other facilities for people with those conditions, and when we considered such people, we had to think about how their presence would affect the other members.

When I came to the Home, 125 people were on a "medical waiting list." In the two years before I got there the Home had gone out twice each year to those folks, asking if they were still interested in coming in. Most of them were. I began reviewing that list, and I could see that based upon the number of people we were admitting and the number of beds we had in the hospital, there was no way we would be able to take them. I didn't think it was fair to ask twice a year if they were still interested when in all probability we couldn't take them anyway.

I suggested to the governor that we reevaluate everyone on the list one more time and then go back to them, take the ones we could, and let the rest know they'd have to look for some other place to stay. The board approved that, and surprisingly we received several letters from people who thanked us for telling them the facts of life and saving them the wait for an opening that would never come.

Our security department took care of everything from automobile registration to identity cards and grounds patrols; we issued our own speeding and parking tickets. We weren't able to fine anyone, but we assessed points for different violations, and once a person accumulated eight points in a one-year period he was walking for the next six months. We had to have a system like that, because we had two thousand people living at the Home most of the time I was there. A lot of those people couldn't see or hear too well and weren't agile enough to jump out of the way of a speeding car. The speed limits at the Home were pretty low, but even so, you could drive from one end of the grounds to the other in about six minutes.

Our security was run by Mr. Israel Tew, a retired inspector of police for the District of Columbia. His deputy was a retired D.C. deputy police captain, Maurice MacDonald. They were the only people on the security force who were not also members of the Home. The beauty of that was that members understood other members and could take care of little things without making big things out of them.

There was a big turnover on the security force, and each week the chief conducted a training class for new employees. Each year we sent a selected few to a one-week course conducted by the FBI at the VA hospital. But the force was primarily gate guards and observation patrols. The chief and his deputy had great rapport with the District of Columbia police. You saw their cars out in front of the security office all the time, because the D.C. police officers came out for coffee or sandwiches with the Home security patrolmen whenever they could, and they exercised their dogs down in the southwest corner of the grounds. Officer D. B. Williams, a D.C. police officer who came out there all the time, even kept his insulin in the security office refrigerator so he could take his medication. When the D.C. police parked their patrol cars on the Home grounds, they knew they wouldn't come out to find their windshields smashed, so it was also a safe haven of sorts for them. And their presence was good for the Home because of the security their visibility brought.

In the spring of 1986, two intruders went into the west end of the Scott Building and accosted a resident in the latrine. He was hard of hearing, and when they demanded his wallet and he didn't respond right away, they worked him over, until his yelling attracted attention and they fled.

It so happened that one of our security officers, Mr. Kenneth Leonard, who has since passed on, was meanwhile outside writing them a ticket for illegal parking. They hadn't been in the building fifteen minutes and Ken was writing them up. They burst out of the building, jumped into their car, and roared out Eagle Gate onto Rock Creek Church Road, leaving Ken standing there with their license number and a description of the car. The Fourth District had those guys under arrest within forty minutes.

We had two bank robberies while I was at the Home. In one, the robbers got away clean, but during the other a member jumped the culprits and got shot. It was a bad round, however, barely penetrating his clothing and leaving just a little bruise on his rear end. About three months after the incident, he got a citation for bravery from the undersecretary of the Army, and during the ceremony, while the undersecretary was telling everyone how brave this guy was, he interrupted and said, "Wait a minute! I was a supply sergeant in the Army, and if I'd known that guy had a gun, I'd have been runnin', not jumpin'!"

The undersecretary said, "Well, I guess I can't add anything to that," and gave him the citation.

* * *

The Home was a highly organized institution.

Domiciliary services took care of cleaning the common areas in the living quarters, although members were responsible for cleaning their own rooms. A retired Air Force Chief Master Sergeant ran that service then. There was also a supply section that took care of issuing cleaning supplies to the members.

Special services operated a nine-hole golf course on the grounds and scheduled trips to everywhere—Disney World, the Grand Ole Opry, the Kennedy Center, plays in New York City, shopping expeditions, etc. It scheduled four big dances every year, and band concerts. It maintained a 45,000-volume library and a gym with the latest Nautilus equipment. Every year it hosted a pro/member golf tournament; local pros came out and put on a clinic, played nine holes with our guys, and attended a cookout afterward. Special services tried to have something always going on for the members, so they wouldn't just sit around contemplating their shoelaces.

There was an Army Air Force Exchange Service outlet at the Home, a lounge run by the AAFES where members could get a drink before dinner, and several places around the grounds where beer was served all day long. Areas were provided where members could practice their gardening techniques. There were pool rooms and card rooms, and the management was always coming up with something new for the members to pass the time with. The Home had its own post office. Every resident had his or her own box, and those who couldn't get to the post office box had their mail delivered to them by their floor manager. There was a branch bank at the Home, and also a branch of the Andrews Air Force Base Credit Union.

Members had their daily newspapers delivered to them and could have a telephone installed in their rooms, although they had to pay for the service; the Home just provided the line. Members could also have cable TV at their own expense in their rooms if they wanted it. There was an administrative channel on the cable system so that messages could be broadcast to the members; there was even a voice override that could be used in case of emergency.

I mentioned floor managers a bit earlier. The Floor Managers Division at the Home in my time was headed by Mr. Dick Boyd. That position used to be filled by a member, but we changed it to a Civil Service position. Dick himself used to be a member, so he was tuned in to the membership's needs.

Each floor in every building had a floor manager, who was

himself a member. The floor manager operated like a charge of quarters in a military unit, but his basic job was to take care of the needs of the members on his floor. If a member needed work done in his room, the floor manager took care of it; he delivered messages; he signed for packages in a member's absence and delivered them.

Every morning at six o'clock, the floor manager would go to every room on the floor and knock on each member's door. That was our morning "health check." The reason for that was to discover who might be in need. The Home didn't care if the members got up for breakfast or not, but it wanted a response out of each room, and if there was none, the floor manager went in and checked on the occupant. From time to time he would find somebody who needed help, who required medical attention, or who had died in the night. Even if the member was signed out on a pass or leave, the floor manager checked that room, in case the member came back in the night without telling anybody. If something happened that required a doctor, the floor manager would telephone down to the King Health Center* and an ambulance would be dispatched immediately.

Living accommodations for the members ranged from four-man squad rooms to single rooms. The squad rooms were in the old Grant Building, which was built in 1910, and in the Sherman Building, which was built in 1854. These are the two oldest dormitories at the Home. The latter had some singles and doubles as well as squad rooms. When I retired, everybody who wanted a single room could have one. The Sherman Building, since it had few residents—less than a hundred then—got by with a floor manager and an assistant for three floors. The Grant Building had a floor manager and an assistant for two floors.

The Sheridan Building, which was constructed in 1885, had two wings added in 1962, and those wings were air-conditioned. All the rooms in the Sheridan were singles. The reason for this was that in the early 1980s, General McKee took $195,000 I had earmarked in the budget to buy a tour bus and sank it into renovations at the Scott and Sheridan buildings, to convert all the double rooms into singles. I used to kid him that that was the biggest "bus" I ever saw. But it was a good move, because later on we got two buses for free from the U.S. Air Force Academy.

Privacy was the single greatest desire of the members, and a

---

*Named for Dr. Benjamin King, first surgeon and secretary-treasurer of the Home in 1851.

single room was a way to provide that. Each room in the Sheridan Building had about two hundred square feet in area. Each had a sink but no bath. In 1989 we remodeled the Scott Building, which was built in 1954. We lost 140-odd beds with those renovations, but we provided a private bath and a walk-in closet for everybody assigned a room in that building.

Change *always* bothers people to varying degrees, and that was the case when we renovated the Scott Building. "Why in the hell are we spending all that money to convert to single rooms?" some members complained. "I don't want a single room!" others said. "I don't want to clean my own bathroom—I'd rather use the one down the hall!" And on and on. But when I left there was a two-to-three-year waiting list for rooms in the Scott Building. The rest of the membership then wanted into the Scott Building, to get the private bathrooms some of them pooh-poohed when we were building them.

The Home had a continuing program to make the same kinds of renovations in the Sheridan, Sherman, and Grant buildings. A private bath for every member was the goal.

Prior to the 1988–1989 renovation projects, only 20 percent of the living quarters were air-conditioned. Once, when the governor was testifying before Congress, the congressmen couldn't understand why all the rooms weren't air-conditioned, and General McKee said, "Because you haven't provided us the money out of the trust fund to install air conditioning." He was asked how much was needed, and it was appropriated, and when I retired every bedroom in the Home, including the King Health Center, was air-conditioned, either centrally or by a window unit. The ultimate goal was central air for every building.

About 70 percent of the members then lived in the Sheridan and Scott buildings, which are connected by a tunnel that General McKee had constructed back in 1980. The majority of the members didn't even have to go outside to go to the dining hall—or to the library, the post exchange, or the theater.

In 1987 we remodeled the theater in the Scott Building. It used to be like the theaters or auditoriums found in the old Army cantonments—seats narrow and close together, no aisles. We put in the biggest seats we could find—there were some pretty wide bodies at the Home—and placed them farther apart, and we installed aisles down the center of the theater so people didn't have to go across fifteen seats to get to an aisle.

* * *

Oddly enough, the members who were living in the older buildings, like the Grant Building, really liked it. Once, when we were conducting a Friday-morning visit to the Grant Building, General McKee asked one of the members what he thought about closing the Grant Building and moving its occupants into the Sheridan, which was the newest one. This member replied, "Governor, I don't want to go to the Sheridan, because the Sheridan people come over here for R&R."

The Grant Building had big, spacious rooms and hallways twenty feet wide, built in a turn-of-the-century style that provided the air conditioning of that day. The rooms all had transoms above the doors, for instance, so the air could circulate more freely. Of course, in my day the fire department had had them all blocked off, because they would work like chimneys if there was ever a fire.

All the rooms in the Sheridan were the same, with window air conditioners in the center core, central air in the two wings, a sink in each room, and communal bathrooms. In one wing of the Sheridan is the Ladies' Wing. There were ninety-one ladies there when I retired. This wing had a female floor manager. We sometimes had male floor managers over there, when we couldn't find a woman who wanted the job, and it worked out fine.

When I retired, we were in the process of developing an "assisted living" program on one wing of the ground floor of Sheridan for those who needed a walker or wheelchair to get around, and we were modifying the shower rooms and toilets so they could get in without any trouble. There would also be twenty-four-hour health-care coverage there.

The domiciliary chief assigned members to all the floors except Sheridan 1 and Scott 1 and 2, which my chief floor manager and I and the King Health Center coordinated, because of the special needs of disabled members. Whenever possible, those people had to be assigned rooms on the ground floor so that in a fire or an emergency they could be evacuated more easily. The ambulatory residents got assigned to the rooms on the higher floors.

Although members were kept in the dormitories as long as possible, folks did get to the point where they no longer remembered to take their medicine, became incontinent, and so on. When a member could no longer live in one of the dormitories, he was transferred to the King Health Center, where there was skilled care. It is amazing how this was accepted by the other members. They were just like soldiers and airmen everywhere. So long as you explained to them what you're going to do and why you have to do it, there wasn't any problem. But woe unto you if you didn't tell them up front of any changes about to be made.

Down at the King Health Center they were constructing a two-hundred-bed unit to take care of those on the first floor of the Scott and Sheridan buildings that was completed in 1992. People at the Home were like most folks in that they don't want to go into the hospital. Well, the King Health Center was not really a hospital, it was a long-term-care facility. But another reason they didn't want to go down there was that in years past, once a member went there, he never seemed to come back. In my time we made it a strict policy to bring members back into the dormitories just as soon as they were capable of taking care of themselves again. When there was no admission waiting list, we let members keep their rooms in the dormitories for ninety days before reassigning them to the Health Center. That helped them psychologically because they knew they had a "home" to come back to.

And when that new two-hundred-bed facility opened in April 1992, every room had a private bath. There are some double rooms, but private baths are a big improvement. One reason members didn't want to go to the Health Center or to a civilian hospital was that they feared they'd lose their valuable privacy.

The members of the Armed Forces Retirement Home were not just ordinary old folks, they're extraordinary old folks. With their military background, the war stories they could tell were great, and they just would get better every year. They were from all parts of the country. Most of them there in my day were born in the Northeast—Pennsylvania, New York, New Jersey. We would make a careful note of two things about people when they reported to the Home: where they were born and where they had been living when they came in. In the last few years I was there the places of last residence moved steadily down into the Sun Belt.

The Home is not for everyone, but it is a godsend for those who need support. You might say there were two thousand reasons why people came to the Home, a different one for each person, but there were four main reasons—money, medicine, marriage, and management.

Money because many members—say, a master sergeant who retired in 1950—didn't get enough in their pensions to live on, so they needed the Home. Medicine because many of the members had chronic medical problems, and a good part of the cost was covered at the Home, though members were encouraged to have supplemental medical insurance. If the King Health Center couldn't handle a medical emergency and Walter Reed didn't have a bed, the member had to be taken to the Washington Hospital Center, and the Home didn't have the money to pay for civilian hospitalization.

Marriage because when members lost their spouses and didn't want to live with their families, they could come to the Home to live out their last days in dignity. They didn't go there to die, they went there to keep on living. The place is a retirement home, and we always stressed that fact. And management because some folks just got into situations they couldn't handle by themselves, and it wasn't always their fault.

I was closely associated with the Home from 1975 on, first as Sergeant Major of the Army and then as an officer on the governor's staff. The law required that a member of the board of commissioners visit the Home each month. Sometimes when I made those visits as the SMA, people wouldn't even speak to me; they didn't even speak much to each other. That attitude turned around in the time I was out there, because the membership was told that the only reason all the rest of the staff was there was to serve them. We told them it was their Home; they deserved it; they had paid for it; they were not on the "dole." We assured them the place was theirs and we were there to support them.

And we initiated actions to prove what we said, to make the members' lives better. I've mentioned the single rooms, air conditioning, telephones, and cable TV. Just after General McKee took over as governor he opened up the mess hall to cafeteria-style dining. Before that it had been family-style—the members called it "prison-style"; everybody had an assigned place to sit and the food was brought out to the tables and served from containers.

After a while people would holler at you across the quadrangle and there was no more looking down at the feet. In my day the members *enjoyed* being at the Home, 98 percent of them anyway. I'm sure there were a few who didn't, but they were free to go. We had people who'd been in and out of the Home twenty or twenty-five times, because there was no restriction on anyone's movement.

There was a leave and pass policy, but not like in the Army. Leaves were formal absences of more than seven days' duration that affected a member's admission status. When I first went to work at the Home, the leave policy was that every member could take ninety days per year. I recommended it be increased to 120 days. These people were retired, I reasoned, so why shouldn't they be able to take a long absence without risking losing their home? So in my day, members could be away from the Home for up to 120 days in any calendar year without being discharged and having to go through the readmission process. One day I was talking to a man who traveled all the time. In August 1991 he was going to hop a freighter bound for South America, and he wasn't planning to come back until October. That guy was *doing* something.

We encouraged the members to work, either for us or somewhere else. We had 'em working from the State Department to bagging groceries in the commissaries. They might be retired, but they were good people and dependable people.

The regulation said members must live in their rooms 50 percent of the time if the Home was full to its capacity, so somebody who wanted to come in was not denied a place while a resident was off gallivanting. What if a person took 120 days and then needed sixty more? We gave it to him. We didn't care, as long as he'd paid his user fee. We had maybe five cases a year of people calling in for extensions. Other people might use only ten or fifteen days of their leave time a year. We had a member pass away who'd been at the Home fifty-one years, and I don't think he'd ever been off the grounds all that time.

Under the new regulations effective in November 1991, members were authorized only forty-five days of leave, because the new law established a more stringent leave policy. I know how I'd take care of that. I'd charge the members leave just as I was charged—weekends and holidays wouldn't count, so a person could get about ninety days out of the forty-five authorized, and if a member wanted an extension he'd get it.

From time to time we had little disciplinary problems at the Home, and I mean "little." We didn't have courts-martial and all that business, but we did have a "hearing officer" who adjudicated problems. As the Director of Member Services I was the hearing officer.

Suppose two members got into a fight that couldn't be settled amicably at the time and it was reported to the chief floor manager or to the security office. A report would be written on what happened, and statements would be taken from the individuals. In my role as hearing officer, I would try to figure out what really happened and then I'd make a recommendation for appropriate action to the governor for his approval. Most of the time these incidents consisted of somebody referring in a disparaging manner to somebody else's ancestors. Or maybe a long-standing feud would flare up over dinner. When an incident occurred and it was decided that a hearing was required, the individuals had seven days to prepare for the hearing.

Because of the mostly inconsequential nature of these events, my recommendation was generally very lenient, a slap on the wrist—restriction or a reprimand. The more serious incidents could result in dismissal. One such case concerned a big fellow who worked as a guard at Lorton Reformatory.* He threw a chair at one member and placed a knife at the neck of another. He was dismissed. When a member was dismissed he had thirty days to appeal to the board of commissioners through the secretary in writing, and while the appeal was working he could stay on at the Home, unless the governor considered him a danger to other residents, as in the case of the Lorton guard. He still had the right to appeal, but he had to do it from the outside. The Lorton guard was not let back in, and I suspect he never will be.

The most common reason for dismissal while I was at the Home was for nonpayment of the user fee. The user fee consisted of 25 percent of a member's retired pay or VA pension. Payment was required by law and there was no waiver to this obligation. Once in a while a person would get into a financial bind or just refuse to pay the fee. Of course, we were willing to work with those who were strapped and were making a sincere effort to get their finances squared away, but when members didn't try hard enough, we had to dismiss them.

I always tried to give those people every break I could—get them loans from the Army Emergency Relief, arrange for them to pay the fees in affordable increments, and so on. I remember one man for whom we bent every rule. He had no money for payment of a user fee when he came in, which we didn't know when he arrived, but he promised to get it straight. He went on for six or seven months, borrowing money to pay the fee while getting deeper and deeper into debt each month. He began writing bad checks, too. We had three separate administrative hearings for this member, to try to help him with his problems. Well, he never got out of them, and in my view he never will. He was dismissed. Under the new law, if you're not disabled you've got to be sixty years old to get into the Home, and he wasn't. I didn't think he'd

*A long-term confinement facility located in Virginia where the District of Columbia's convicted criminals are incarcerated.

ever make it, either, because someone would shoot him for welshing on his debts before he ever got to be sixty.

Some of the disciplinary incidents were absolutely hilarious. We had one individual who worked as a security officer downtown. He came back onto the grounds early one morning. He lived in the Scott Building. Since every room there had its own bathroom, there was a special visitation policy for guests of the opposite gender. In the other dormitories, members couldn't have female guests in their rooms (or in the case of the Ladies' Wing of Sheridan, male guests) because the bathrooms were communal. But in the Scott Building, between 8:00 A.M. and 9:00 P.M., they could have female visitors, provided they were properly signed in and out with the floor manager. After 9:00 P.M. was "quiet hours," when no loud noise was permitted in the dormitories, because many members went to bed early and got up early.

Well, this gentleman came in at five o'clock in the morning with a lady in his car and stated he was only going to the dorm to get his Visa card, so he could take her to the hospital. When he did not come back through the gate after a few minutes, the security guard called the floor manager, who checked and found the lady in the member's room.

We had an administrative hearing over the matter. He said, "Sergeant Major, I should have just turned around and headed out the gate when the guard told me to and it would have been all over." The member thought I was going to recommend dismissal, but I just told him not to repeat the mistake. "You can bet I won't!" he promised. He breathed a sigh of relief and told me he'd really thought he was out.

I recall another big fellow who caused all kinds of problems at the main gate on two or three occasions. We had a hearing, and he was counseled not to hassle the security guards. About three months later, he got into another altercation with the guards. Even though I had all the statements taken from the various witnesses, I asked him to explain to me in his own words what had happened. He started out telling me all the reasons why this incident happened and why the security guards were "down" on him, and I suppose he went on for ten minutes in this vein. Finally he sat back in his chair and said, "Sergeant Major, I don't know why I'm telling you all this. You've been in the Army a long time, and you've been here a while, and you've heard every story in the book, and there's no sense adding mine to it. I did exactly what they charged me with." I told him he should have said that out at the gate and none of this would have happened. I also told him, as I told all the others who came before me, that I could think of many things I would rather be doing than holding those hearings.

During my time at the Home, the number of disciplinary cases was reduced considerably, because we permitted only the chief of police, the chief floor manager, the directors, and their administrative officers to prefer charges. It used to be that all floor managers could prefer charges. We changed that so they had to make a complaint to the chief floor manager, who might not have been willing to prefer charges, so this cut down on the number of hearings.

You might suppose that with such a large number of retired military people in one place, everyone would be very conscious of everyone else's former rank and service, but we purposely deemphasized that aspect. Everybody out there was "mister" or "miss." When I left we had four former commissioned officers and seventeen former warrant officers living at the Home. Resident commissioned officers were men who were retired from the service in an enlisted grade and were later advanced on the retired list. Among the members there was no such thing as a "pecking order" based on former military rank. In my time, 88 percent of the people at the Home were retired from the Army or the Air Force and Category I and the other 12 percent were Category II or III, under the rules that obtained in my time.* Everybody knew what category everybody else belonged to, and every now and then you'd hear someone asking "Why do we have all those Category IIIs around here?"—but it was a friendly rivalry.

You'd hear members chiding each other because one was older than another or had more service, but that also was a friendly rivalry. The average member had more than twenty but fewer than twenty-five years of service. A little over fifteen hundred of them fell into that category. They were retired between the pay grades E-5, or sergeant/tech sergeant, and E-7, SFC/master sergeant. When I went there, there weren't any retired E-9s at all, but when

*Before the new law was passed, the categories were: Category I—enlisted or warrant officers and Navy limited-duty officers (LDO) with twenty or more years' active honorable service; II—any regular enlisted or warrant officer and LDOs with a service-connected disability and unable to earn a livelihood, as determined by the USSAH medical board; III—any regular enlisted or warrant officer and LDOs with a non-service-connected disability and unable to earn a living, but with some wartime service. With LDOs, at least half their service had to be in the enlisted ranks.

I left there were thirty-eight of them and approximately seventy-five E-8s.

I used to say that eligibility for membership for retired personnel was based on three little words—not "I love you," as in the old song, but "some regular service." Under the new regulations, of course, that has changed to "active service," and for Category III it is now persons who served in a war theater during a time of declared war or were eligible for hostile fire pay. That will take care of those who were stationed in Korea north of the Imjin River after 1954 and who participated in the post-Vietnam expeditions, including the Persian Gulf. That will open up membership to a lot of people, because "active service" includes a lot more people than "regular service." Under certain conditions, former draftees will be eligible.

Up until the Armed Forces Integration Act of 1948, women in the armed forces did not serve in a regular component, and I've always considered that a great injustice. But under the new legislation they are now eligible. I think that could bring in up to one hundred more female members. In my time we already had a few female members in the Scott Building, because each room there had an individual bath, and since they got the rest of the rooms converted they're just like apartments or hotel suites, so men and women can be assigned rooms based on where there are vacancies. That means that the Ladies' Wing of Sheridan will cease to exist as a separate entity.

Another big change was that people who were once only eligible for one place or the other—Navy for the Gulfport Home, Army and Air Force for the D.C. facility—are now eligible for either place. Gulfport was undergoing renovations when I left; its capacity was six hundred but it had only three hundred in residence then with well over two hundred more on the waiting list. Under the new regulations a person can now apply for transfer to the Navy Branch, but I think there are more people going up to the D.C. branch than to Mississippi.

Just as a matter of historical record, the Naval Home predates the Soldiers' Home by almost ten years. For most of its life it was based in Philadelphia. Incidentally, it was founded by Commodore William Bainbridge. He commanded the USS *Constitution*, 1802–1803, although he was born a British subject. As I noted earlier, I can't be directly related, because he was childless.

Another thing that changed with the integration of the homes in 1991 was that 25 percent of *all* federal annuities paid to the members, including Social Security, now comes to the Home in user fees. But when you actually put pencil to paper, 25 percent of all of a member's annuities is still a pretty damn good deal. Those who were under the old system only paid 12.5 percent of the new assessments the first year. It goes up 2.5 percent each succeeding year until it reaches 25 percent of all annuities, the same system as when the Home first started charging user fees back in 1976.

We always talk about how the Army "takes care of its own," and the Home is truly one example of how that is done. The Army can't really take care of everyone, but those who are at the Home are being looked after in a very good fashion.

The trust fund was in pretty good shape when I left, up around $200 million. It was costing us about $48 million a year to operate the Home, and we were taking in around $50 million. We put most of the remaining $2 million into capital improvements. The Treasury paid interest on the balance of the fund plus the going interest rate for the operating budget, so as long as the Home could avoid spending that money it could collect interest. The money in the trust fund was invested in government securities. But as the armed forces have been reduced in size, and the courts-martial and nonjudicial punishment fines have become less, fewer dollars will have been coming in, and the interest and user fee will have become the major sources of income. In the past the big source was from courts-martial and Article 15 fines.

When we moved to the Home we were assigned Quarters No. 4, a fourteen-room duplex with a full basement, five bathrooms, and twelve-foot ceilings, built in 1870. It took us several weekends after we moved to get the house cleaned up, because it had been empty for a while and hadn't been kept too clean by its former occupants.

The Army didn't have to spend too much to move me from my last assignment—from Fort Myer to the Home, about fifteen miles. Quarters No. 4 was a block and a half from my new office. If I came out of my house and turned right, it was a five-minute walk to my office; if I turned left, it was a five-minute walk to the golf course. However, Monday through Friday I always turned right.

That old building required constant maintenance. For instance, the brick exterior had accumulated many coats of paint over the years, and it had to be removed, because the pointing, the mortar between the bricks, was getting bad. Once the paint was taken off with chemicals and sandblasting, the pointing receded even deeper, half an inch in some places. After the outside of the house was repointed and sealed, it looked so good that we talked the governor into not repainting it. I think one of the things that sold him on leaving it unpainted was that everyone who walked by the place would comment on how much better it looked with all that peeling paint removed from the bricks.

The Home had a lot of period furniture stored in a warehouse, and when General McKee became governor he started putting some of it back into use so that it could be properly cared for. Hazel got a chance to go to the warehouse and look at some of the items, and she found an old armoire that looked as if it would fit very nicely in the hallway off the entrance.

I noticed a tag affixed to the armoire. On the back of it was written, "Do not remove from warehouse without the approval of the governor." It was dated 1925, the year I was born. We also had a dining-room table that seated twelve people very comfortably. Not bad for two folks who had started out their Army career in a little old house trailer.

There were originally only two closets in that house, one on the third floor and one on the second. Others had been installed since the place was built, of course. In the 1870s, people apparently only had two suits, the one they had on and the one hanging in the closet.

While we were living in Quarters No. 4, I had what I hope was my last combat experience.

Hazel and I used to take walks down around the golf course at day's end, and one evening in 1985, we decided to go out for a stroll. We'd been sitting in the living room listening to the stereo, and I left it on when we went out, since we were going to be gone only a few minutes. On the way out, I closed and locked the front door. Normally I didn't even do that, our walks were of such a short duration.

We walked down around Scott Circle that evening, where Gen. Winfield Scott's statue stands—just a very short distance from our quarters—and on the way back we stopped and talked to the chief surgeon and his wife at Quarters No. 6. We were gone twenty-five minutes at the most. As we came back to our place, I remarked to Hazel that evidently she'd left our bedroom lights on. Hazel said no, she hadn't been up there. Neither had I. Just then the light went out. We realized that either the light had come alive by itself or somebody was up there.

When we got back to the house, we noticed that the glass in a floor-to-ceiling window off the front porch had been kicked in. I told Hazel to go next door and call security. About that time, one of the members, John Gibson, who'd been down at the golf course, drove by, and when he slowed down to say hello, I asked him to notify security that there was someone in my house.

I went up on the porch, and as I did a foot appeared through the broken window. I challenged the guy, and the foot disappeared at once. After maybe a minute, when the foot didn't reappear, I heard Hazel holler, "Bill, back here!" I ran to the back of the house, and Hazel said, "He went that way," pointing toward Rock Creek Church Road.

That guy had come from the bedroom to the front of the house and then had run all the way through the house and down into the basement and out the back basement door. That was very strange. When the police arrived, Chuck Walker, who was my admin officer and was on the scene by then, said he didn't understand how the guy had gotten out of the house. He asked one of the detectives how he'd have gotten out if he'd been the burglar, and it took the detective three or four minutes to find his way from the front to the back of the place. I'm convinced that the intruder knew he could get out through the basement.

We never found the guy, but he was a young black man about five feet ten to six feet tall, probably 175 to 180 pounds. We knew that much because I took him on. When Hazel pointed the way, I went after him at a dead run, across the service road behind the quarters and into the woods next to the western boundary wall of the grounds. This guy, holding a bag, was crouched on all fours, and when he saw me coming he stood up. I never even broke my stride. I collided with that son of a bitch full force, and into fist city we went.

We were really getting it on when my right thumb ended up in his mouth. He bit all the way through the nail from the top and into the bone from down below. He was hollering between clenched teeth, "Turn me loose!" I was trying to figure out how in the hell I was to do that, since he had ahold of *me*. As it turned out, I was twenty years too old and forty pounds too light to hang on to him.

The guy got away with about $2,000 worth of things out of our bedroom. The insurance company reimbursed us, but some of the things we lost were irreplaceable—an opal ring Hazel's aunt had left her, for instance.

Evidently the guy had been watching when we left the house and knew just where to go. He couldn't have looked anywhere in the house except the bedroom during the time he was in there, because nothing was missing from the other rooms. One thing he didn't get was an opal mounted in white gold I'd given Hazel for our twenty-fifth anniversary. She'd worn it just before the burglary and hadn't put it back into her jewelry case.

One week before that, someone had cleaned out Quarters No. 2, which was occupied by Gen. Joe Kingston at the time. That happened during the day, and a whole lot more was stolen, because Mrs. Kingston had gone out for a couple of hours. The security chief was of the opinion that both jobs were pulled off by the same man, someone who knew the insides of both houses. The same prints were found in both houses, but evidently the thief had no record, because the police couldn't identify them.

I don't know what I was thinking that night. Evidently I wasn't thinking too clearly or I would never have gone after him. I believe what really set me off was Hazel. When she hollered out, I thought she was in trouble. In retrospect, it was a stupid thing to do. I got a cracked rib, my face got all scratched up, and of course he bit the hell out of my thumb. But I do feel good that I got in a few licks. If I'd have had a goddamn club it would have turned out differently.

In more recent years, there were random shootings in the neighborhood, drive-by shootings that in one case shattered the glass in the security gatehouse. The security guys on duty said they had a real race to see who could reach the floor first that night. The 9mm slug that hit the window was spent after it penetrated the glass, but what if it had come through the open door instead? We replaced all the glass in the gatehouse with bulletproof glass.

Sometimes at night, when the windows were open, we could hear automatic fire from places outside the grounds. That kind of thing became so common it was not even reported in the papers the next day.

We lived in Quarters No. 4 until 1988, when the deputy governor departed and General McKee asked Hazel and me if we'd move into Quarters No. 2.

Quarters No. 2 is a large old detached home, with twelve-foot ceilings and floor-to-ceiling windows. The house was built in 1854 and is on the National Register of Historical Landmarks. It does not have central air, only window units here and there, but we found it very comfortable in the summer because it's constructed out of quarried Maryland sandstone twelve to fifteen inches thick in places, so it took half the summer to get the place warmed up.

When General McKee left, Maj. Gen. Don Hilbert became

governor, and he decided to appoint a deputy, Col. John Wesley Gheen, the former executive director, who moved into Quarters No. 2 when we left. He'd been living in Quarters No. 4 before that.

My replacement, SMA Julius W. "Bill" Gates, moved his family into Quarters No. 4.

As if working full-time as an officer on the staff at the Soldiers' and Airmen's Home wasn't enough to keep me occupied, I also performed some extracurricular responsibilities.

Shortly before I retired from the Army, a life insurance company, United Services General, approached me with a job offer. I decided that selling insurance wasn't what I wanted to do, and then the position at the Home came up. I'd been in that job about two months when an executive from USG came out and asked me to sit on his company's board of directors. I sat on that board for about three years until the company was sold, and then I was asked to sit on the board of the parent company, United Services Life Insurance Company, which I have since resigned. We met quarterly. By law, insurance companies have to have boards of directors in order to ensure outside involvement.

I started out as a member of the Association of the U.S. Army, almost from the organization's inception, and then after I retired I was asked to serve on the Retiree Affairs Committee of its Council of Trustees. I sat on that committee about a year, and then I was appointed to fill the unexpired Council of Trustees term of Maj. Gen. Thomas K. Turnage when he was appointed to be head of Selective Service. I served on the council until July 1994.

The AUSA Council of Trustees is a governing body that approves the operations of the association's executive board. It is composed of retired Army people and civilians. The chairman is Norm Augustine, former undersecretary of the Army. We also have people like Marty Hoffman, former Secretary of the Army, and Gen. Bernard Rogers, former Chief of Staff of the Army and SHAPE commander. The council meets quarterly also.

In 1990, because the AUSA membership was declining and also because SMA Bill Gates conveyed to Gen. Jack N. Merritt, the association president, that the enlisted members of the Army considered AUSA for officers only—which it never has been, because it lobbies for the benefit of everybody in the Army—the council decided to appoint a vice president for NCO and enlisted affairs. I was asked to serve in that position. Later my title was changed to vice chairman. I advised the council on methods to get the word out to the Army's enlisted people that the association supports the *entire* Army. I still work with AUSA as a member of its Organization Awards Committee.

My place on the Council of Trustees, by the way, was filled by CSM Tom Chesshire, formerly the sergeant major of the CID command and now provost marshal at Walter Reed Army Medical Center.

Several times I traveled to various places in my capacity as vice chairman for NCO and enlisted affairs to talk to soldiers during membership drives. I talked to active Army people and National Guardsmen. Perceptions, I've found, are tougher to deal with than facts, but I think we've been able to overcome some of the misconceptions about AUSA out there in the field.

Recruiting members is going to be tougher as the Army's strength is reduced and fewer defense contracts are awarded. A large amount of the association's support is derived from the industrial complex.

I was also the co-chairman of the Chief of Staff's Retiree Council and served on that through 1993. That body meets annually, and for those meetings the Army will recall me to active duty for a week.

I'm also the honorary sergeant major of the 28th Infantry Regiment, which I fought with in Vietnam. My honorary colonel is Lt. Gen. Robert Haldane, who was my battalion commander in Vietnam. I also have a standing invitation to the annual dinner of the 1st Division Officers' Association, a real honor. I intend to make those dinners for as long as I can. The dinner has been held every year since 1918.

And every year there's the Former Sergeant Major of the Army Conference hosted by the incumbent SMA at the Pentagon, something I started back in 1977. That keeps us up to speed on what's happening in the Army. Of course, all the time I was at the Home I kept in pretty close touch with the SMA, and just after Desert Storm concluded, Gen. Carl Vuono had all the ex-SMAs up for a briefing on the operation. Part of the briefing was conducted at the National Training Center at Fort Irwin, California, where today's combat units are trained in the tactics of the United States' possible foes.

I also sat on the Department of Defense board for the Armed Forces Retirement Home.

I am very proud to have been the first former enlisted man appointed as an officer at the Home, and I am elated that the job allowed me to continue doing the same thing I'd done for thirty-one years in the Army—taking care of soldiers. The only difference out at the Soldiers' and Airmen's Home was that my squad leaders were sixty-five years old.

I did that for twelve years, and with the thirty-one years I'd had in the Army, that gave me a total of forty-three years of government service. One day I felt it was time, while we still had good health, for Hazel and me to enjoy the home we built down in Florida back in 1977. That home is located in Palm Bay, Florida, just south of Patrick Air Force Base.

We just decided at last that new blood should come in and it was time for us to relax a little bit. You can't just up and quit, after working all your life, but I had enough small irons in the fire to keep myself occupied, yet I wouldn't be punching a clock either.

My appointment at the Home ran three years at a time, and I had to let the governor know six months in advance when I was going to quit. He asked me on New Year's Eve 1990 what my intentions were, and I told him then that we were leaving when my term was up in July 1991.

He said, "Well, you know you can stay as long as you want to, Sergeant Major."

I said, "Sir, I have."

EPILOGUE

Now I am looking back on forty-three years of continuous service to the Army and to its soldiers.

I have no secrets to explain how I led my life and accomplished my work, but I did have some simple advantages. I had a good childhood with a lot of tender, loving care—not much money, yet I was always clothed and fed. I lost my father at a very early age, it is true, but then, in the way the good Lord often operates, I got a stepfather who in all ways has been my father.

I've had only one sweetheart in my life, Hazel, whom I first met when she was in the fourth grade and I was in the fifth, and we've been together ever since. I have no mother-in-law stories, because I always got along well with Hazel's parents and they liked me, and that is partly why I was so attracted to Hazel in the first place. I suppose that's a story in itself.

I've worked hard all my life. I was born and raised on a farm, and from an early age I learned how to carry my load. That taught me responsibility and gave me confidence in my ability as well as a sense of pride in what I could do. Self-confidence and pride in my work have infused everything I've done since, and I sincerely hope I never went too far and strayed into vanity or arrogance.

I never put anyone down. Even the lowliest person in an army has something to contribute, and any leader who forgets that is robbing himself of one of his most precious resources. We all had a say in what went on around our house when I was a kid, and when I became a noncommissioned officer I felt I should get input from my people to make the right decisions.

Similarly, I always thought my commanders should get from me not only the fruits of my best judgment but the honest truth as I saw it, so they could have it when they made the decisions that affected my soldiers. I always talked straight to my officers, just as

I'd talk to anyone else I respected. I never used weasel words and I was never a mealy-mouth, and God willing I never will be.

On the other hand, I never could abide horses' asses, and I discovered early in my career that the higher-ranking they are, the harder it is to tolerate them. Our system weeds the worst of those people out, but some still manage to slip by, and they can do a lot of harm before they're identified and dealt with. I always did my best to help with that. I have not used this memoir as a vehicle to get even with any of those people.

I was never disloyal to my superiors. I learned early on that no noncommissioned officer worth his salt wants to see his commander go down the drain, because that means the unit goes with him—and that means everybody.

When World War II broke out, I could not wait to get into the service. I had no intention of becoming a soldier. I just wanted to do my part for America, to help win that war. When it was finally over, all I wanted to do was go home.

When I was called back into the Army for the Korean War, which ruined my prospects as a farmer, I decided to stay, but at first no longer than twenty years, just what I had to do to earn retirement. But about my fifteenth or sixteenth year of service, that peculiar chemistry made up of training, experience, and promotion began to have its effect, and I realized that I didn't *want* to be anywhere else but the Army.

I have been in two wars, two too many, and I have killed other men. Although I wish it had never happened, I feel no guilt—those other men were armed and trying to kill me and my men. A soldier does what he has to in war. My only regret is that the world believes we lost the Vietnam War. I do not doubt for an instant that had the military been permitted to do what it was capable of doing, the final outcome would have been different.

I was adamant about improving the Army's training. Whenever I had a chance to holler about training soldiers, I did. I argued for the Noncommissioned Officer Education System at every opportunity. I stayed around the Army long enough to learn all the mistakes that could be made, and I tried my best to warn my commanders about them. If I left any mark upon the Army, it is in this area, and I am most proud of what I did to improve the effectiveness of its training. I believe the squad leader of today's Army is better prepared to do his job than was my company commander to do his in World War II.

Training and the welfare of soldiers, the two major responsibilities of the noncommissioned officer, cannot be attended to properly in the headquarters building. Back at headquarters is where you solve the biggest problems and prepare yourself to tackle still others, but the best study of soldiering is soldiers themselves, and you cannot do that sitting behind a desk.

I learned early in military life that nobody has all the answers, but the good noncommissioned officer knows where to find them. I also learned that soldiers can solve 98 percent of their problems by just talking to someone about them. All you have to do is *listen*. Nobody ever learns anything with his mouth open. Gen. Ralph Haines said it best: The good Lord endowed mankind with two ears and one mouth, and people ought to use them in that proportion.

People did not work "for" me as much as they worked "with" me all those years. The way I saw it, we all had the same mission, and either we all succeeded or we all failed. While I saw nothing wrong in covering for other people, I never did anything just to cover my own posterior.

I learned that soldiers, just like people everywhere, will do anything you ask provided you prepare them with good training and treat them with dignity.

I carried these lessons with me to the Soldiers' and Airmen's Home, and if I wasn't good at the art of listening when I first went there, I sure was at the end of those twelve years.

I have no mixed emotions about my "second" retirement. I was ready to quit punching the clock. Hazel and I have a lot of things we want to do with the rest of our years. One is to see this country of ours. We've been all over the world and I've been in every state in the Union, but we haven't really seen America. We plan to drive to the end of each month's retirement check, wait for the next one, and move on.

We're going to spend more time with our family. We have a daughter and son-in-law, Mary and Paul Moore, who live about seventy miles from our retirement home in Florida. Our other daughter and son-in-law, Kathy and Steve Koop, and our three grandchildren and our three great-grandchildren are living in Salina, Kansas, and we'll spend some time with them.

I've always looked back on the time I spent with my mother before she passed away in 1985 as prime time, because we knew our presence with her in those last days made a difference to her. She was a great lady and she left a great legacy. There is no question in my mind that where she is now she is without pain. She had enough of that in this life.

I have lived through the Great Depression and three wars (four if you count the cold one), and I have seen the United States become a world power. I don't believe for an instant that that will change, but we do have some problems. We no longer have the family ties in this society that we had when I was growing up. Families once took care of their own. When mothers and fathers got too old to work, they were taken in by one of their children, not consigned to some sterile retirement home until they died.

We are today one of the most mobile people in the world, and I think that was caused by World War II and the postwar technology explosion. In a way that was a very positive thing, because it helped integrate us more than anything else in our history. But that very mobility has contributed to the breaking up of family and other interpersonal bonds and the sense of belonging to some special place.

I think education can do much to overcome that, but there is another great problem. Our public school system often seems only to be warehousing many of our children and then dumping them into society inadequately prepared for adulthood. We've got to start paying our teachers salaries commensurate with their value to our society in order to get the right ones into the nation's classrooms. Maybe in lieu of new superhighways our governments should spend our money on fixing the potholes in the existing ones and paying our teachers more money, and that goes for all the other pork barrels our legislators love so much.

We also have got to do something with our elected officials. We have got to be careful about leaving them in the seat of government for a whole lifetime. A resident once said of an officer at the Soldiers' and Airmen's Home, "He's been here so long he thinks he owns the place!" I think the same thing happens in government. Some officials stay in office so long they think they own it and forget they're sent there to service us, not the other way around.

That is not to say anything against the civil servant. These last twenty-five years I have worked with civilians very closely, and without that dedicated work force this government of ours would be dead in the water.

I am proud of my forty-three years with the government—the Army is part of government—and I do not have to back up to the pay table, because this government's gotten its money's worth from me.

So ends my story. I do not know how much time I have left to me, but I am going to enjoy what there is of it. And when at last the good Lord says, "Sergeant Major, I'm ready for you now," I will not be insubordinate, but I will likely say, "Hold on just a minute, sir . . . !"

Appendix

AUTHORIZED CHEVRONS, 1920–1948*

Design	Dates of Authorization	Rank
	1920–1948	Master Sergeant
	1920–1948	Technical Sergeant
	1920–1942	1st Sergeant
	1920–1948	Staff Sergeant
	1920–1948	Sergeant
	1920–1948	Corporal
	1920–1948	Private First Class
	1942–1948	1st Sergeant
	1942–1948	Technician 3rd Grade
	1942–1948	Technician 4th Grade
	1942–1948	Technician 5th Grade

*After William K. Emerson, *Chevrons: Illustrated Catalog and History of U.S. Army Insignia* (Smithsonian Institution Press, 1983), Table 7-3, as modified in Fisher, *Guardians of the Republic: A History of the Noncommissioned Officer Corps of the U.S. Army* (New York: Fawcett Columbine, 1994).

CHEVRONS FOR MALE PERSONNEL OTHER THAN SPECIALISTS, 1951–1994

Design	Dates of Authorization	Rank
	1951–present	Master Sergeant
	1951–present 1958–present	Sergeant First Class Platoon Sergeant
	1951–1958 1958–present	Sergeant Staff Sergeant
	1958–present	Sergeant
	1951–present	Corporal
	1951–1968 1968–present	Private First Class Private (E-2)
	1951–present	1st Sergeant
	1951–1968 1971–present 1968–1971	Sergeant Major Staff Sergeant Major
	1968–present	Command Sergeant Major
	1968–present	Private First Class
	1979–1994	Sergeant Major of the Army

SPECIALIST CHEVRONS, 1955–PRESENT

Design	*Dates of Authorization*	*Rank*
	1955–1959†	Specialist Third Class
	1959–1961†	Specialist Four
	1960–present‡	
	1955–1959†	Specialist Second Class
	1959–1961†	Specialist Five
	1960–present‡	
	1955–1959†	Specialist First Class
	1959–1961†	Specialist Six
	1960–present‡	
	1955–1959†	Master Specialist
	1959–1961†	Specialist Seven
	1960–1978‡	
	1959–1965‡	Specialist Eight
	1959–1965‡	Specialist Nine
	1959–present§	Specialist Four
	1959–present§	Specialist Five
	1959–present§	Specialist Six
	1959–1978§	Specialist Seven
	1959–1965§	Specialist Eight
	1959–1965§	Specialist Nine

†All personnel.
‡Women personnel only.
§Men only.

≡ INDEX ≡